Common Sense and Common Law for the Environment

The Political Economy Forum

Sponsored by the Political Economy Research Center (PERC)
Series Editor: Terry L. Anderson

Common Sense and Common Law for the Environment
Creating Wealth in Hummingbird Economies

The Political Economy Forum

Bruce Yandle

ROWMAN & LITTLEFIELD PUBLISHERS, INC.
Lanham • Boulder • New York • Oxford

ROWMAN & LITTLEFIELD PUBLISHERS, INC.

Published in the United States of America
by Rowman & Littlefield Publishers, Inc.
4720 Boston Way, Lanham, Maryland 20706

12 Hid's Copse Road
Cummor Hill, Oxford OX2 9JJ, England

British Library Cataloguing in Publication Information Available

Library of Congress Cataloging-in-Publication Data

Yandle, Bruce.
 Common sense and common law for the environment : creating wealth in
hummingbird economies / Bruce Yandle.
  p. cm. — (Political economy forum)
 Includes bibliographical references and index.
 ISBN 0-8476-8672-8 (cloth : alk. paper). — ISBN 0-8476-8673-6 (pbk. : alk.
paper)
  1. Environmental law—Economic aspects. 2. Right of property. 3. Natural
resources, Communal. I. Title. II. Series.
 K3585.4.T34 1997
 333.7—dc21   97-15021

ISBN 0-8476-8672-8 (cloth : alk. paper)
ISBN 0-8476-8673-6 (pbk. : alk. paper)

Printed in the United States of America

♾™ The paper used in this publication meets the minimum requirements of American
National Standard for Information Sciences—Permanence of Paper for Printed Library
Materials, ANSI Z39.48–1984.

Dedicated to the memory and in honor of
Russell Delbert Shannon
1938-1996
Professor of Economics
Clemson University

Contents

Figures

Charts

Preface

People throughout the industrialized world are searching for better ways to protect environmental assets. But people are always looking for lower cost ways to protect assets, increase wealth, and extend life expectancies. How is the search for better environmental institutions different? It is much more focused and visible. The range and scope of national and international discussions, in print or at conferences, that address the issue are broad. More often than not, the mood of these debates is adversarial.

Why is the search for improved environmental protection so controversial and seemingly unending? Compared with the much more sophisticated and highly evolved ways that other important resources are managed, the methods applied to managing the environment are crude and rudimentary; we see mandates, detailed rules, and command-and-control regulation. In most other instances, as the provision of food, shelter, transportation, and some important features of medical care, we find ordinary people quietly making private decisions with little guidance from central authorities.

Saying that modern institutions for managing the environment are less evolved than other resource management processes implies that change is underway. And without a doubt this is the case. Change is coming for several reasons. First, the United States can no longer rely on antiquated 1970s models for regulating environmental use. Rules and regulations born in a time of smoke-stack economies, when energy was cheap and information dear, are being applied to an economy dominated by high technology, cheaper information, and more expensive energy. The old ways are simply out of kilter with the new century's emerging economies. Of equal importance, the command-and-control systems currently applied to the environment are known to be far more costly and less effective than available alternatives. Finally, we now seem to be changing our focus to outcomes instead of inputs. People are beginning to take the environment seriously.

The changes that emerge will surely reflect considerable experience with environmental concerns. Since around 1970, the United States and most of the industrialized world have been engaged in a massive effort led by central governments to improve and guard environmental quality. In many cases, the pre-1970 improvements in the environment were either overlooked or denigrated. Motivated by a general concern for environmental quality and special interest lobbying, national governments pushed aside the less formal and more evolved institutions that had managed environmental rights in the past. The decentralized system was largely replaced with uniform rules devised by the national government.

The struggles along the way are well documented. Indeed, anyone who has attempted to stay abreast of the topic has built a library of hearings, books, journals, and special reports. We in the Western world should be the most environmentally informed and aware of any people on the face of the globe. But to appreciate where we are now and to speculate on where we are headed, we must consider some basics. We should first focus on the origin of the environmental problem and consider it in the simplest possible way.

Common Sense, Common Law, and the Environment

Inevitably, environmental and natural resource management problems begin with common-access resources, the world of the commons. Put another way, we begin with a world like that inhabited by hummingbirds and other creatures. Whether the topic is water quality, the ozone layer, acid rain, or access to groundwater contained in aquifers, the issue is always the same. Resources are there for the taking. The challenge: How to ration? How to conserve? Common sense dictates that we should find the simplest, most cost-effective ways to address the problem. Our common-law tradition suggests that we should enforce and protect environmental and other property rights that provide security and give incentives for good stewardship. Thus the book's main title. But since all environmental problems begin in a common-access world where there are no property rights, we are challenged to find ways to create wealth by building appropriate institutions. Hence the book's subtitle: Creating Wealth in Hummingbird Economies.

If we are to manage nature's bounty, we must have rules. And no matter what we call the rules, they always embody a system of property rights. Some person or some group has the power to exclude others from certain uses of property, including the commons. Rights to environmental use and protection emerge in a number of ways. In many places and times, these rights reflect customs, traditions, and voluntary agreements among members of a community. Others recognizing these rights assume a duty to respect them. Expectations of future dealings and knowledge of the long-term benefits of respect for property rights encourage recognition of rights and duties. In other instances, rights are defined by public authorities and political bodies. Again, these groups shoulder a duty to honor rights once established.

America's environmental protection history is filled with rules that emerged from different sources. An examination of them reveals an evolutionary process that provides a new and changing legal environment. Common-law rules historically formed the bedrock of this legal environment. Later, statute law and regulation supplemented and in many cases overrode the simpler common-law rules.

Common law is itself an evolutionary process. Decisions made by community judges in settling specific controversies yield rules that reflect and become standards of social behavior. As times and circumstances change, the rules change, but the basis for rules does not. Common law reflects the norms of a people, is rooted in rules of just conduct, and contains a realism that has been refined over many centuries. Common law provides an approach for creating wealth in hummingbird economies that is consistent with private rights and evolving markets. By contrast, command-and-control is more consistent with common access and public property rights. One is referred to as a rule of law; the other is rule by politics. There is much more to be considered when exploring evolving environmental institutions, but the themes of institutional competition and the role of common law are major elements of this book.

The Origin of the Book

This book is an attempt to record material and stories I have used in preparing lectures and presentations over the last twenty years. My audiences have included almost a generation of university students, more than a score of classes for government executives, members of trade associations, academics assembled for seminars, and a collection of highly motivated students who have participated in summer seminars at the Political Economy Research Center (PERC) in Bozeman, Montana. In this sense, much of the material is well seasoned. But while some of the stories, theories, and explanations have been offered many times, the framework that now organizes them is quite new.

In the last few years, I have found the arguments of evolutionary biologists and psychologists to be compelling. By applying the logic of selection, adaptation, and reproduction, we can gain insights to evolving patterns of environmental control. My interest in and study of common law is also relatively new. Thus, two major themes of the book are relatively fresh. Weaving the stories into the new framework has been challenging and rewarding.

How the Book Is Organized

The book begins with the origin of the environmental problem—the world of common access, a hummingbird economy. After explaining elements and tendencies of that world, chapter 1 uses some simple economic models that I have found to be helpful in explaining the dynamics of life on the commons. It is here that we encounter the first basic problem: How to limit access and increase environmental wealth? Historically, communities of people have taken two approaches to the problem: the *systems approach*, with detailed rules and centralized authority, and the *process approach*, which is decentralized and relies ultimately on incentives and transferable property rights.

Chapter 2 brings us face to face with the rationing problem. How do people establish institutions for limiting environmental use? What mechanisms do they employ? Two institutions are described and two accompanying theories are presented, one being compatible with the systems approach and the other fitting the process approach. Illustrations of these mechanisms and approaches that relate to natural resource management and pollution control are provided toward the end of the chapter.

Having seen how some apparently more effective and lower-cost process-based institutions have evolved in one environmental setting, we are left with a puzzle. If these new species are truly better adapted for the modern world, why have they not become dominant? Chapter 3 offers some explanations. Some theories of regulation are presented and related economic models are explored along the way. Chapter 3 ends with the suggestion that the logic of common-law thinking could once again become the foundation for managing important parts of the environmental problem.

The common-law theme, present throughout the book, is the focus of chapter 4. It is here that common-law rules for managing environmental quality are fully explored and then illustrated with summaries of cases that involve air pollution, water pollution, and hazardous waste. The common-law stories cut across a number of decades and move into the era when statute law became dominant. The workings of the transition are explained using case law.

When it is suggested that common-law rules might adequately, or even helpfully, protect environmental rights, a storm of criticism often ensues. The more common complaints are described near the end of chapter 4, and suggestions are made about the places where common law might work well. In some cases, it might not work so well; one of the more troublesome problems is controlling urban air pollution.

Chapter 5 explores urban air quality, the smog problem, and how it is currently addressed. While chapter 4 is heavy on common law, this chapter is loaded with command-and-control. With far more regulatory detail than presented earlier, the chapter explains the statutory framework that has evolved and how alternative fuel vehicles and other new technologies seem to be emerging. An alternate framework is presented near the end of the chapter, which features elements of other newly evolved pollution control strategies.

The book explores the evolution of institutions based on property rights and common law, the social institutions that help to avoid living in a hummingbird economy. If indeed, institutions are evolving, where is the evidence of change? And how might we characterize the competitive struggle that ensues when existing institutions begin to adapt to a changed environment? Chapter 6 addresses these questions. The chapter reports on research involving the decline of common-law remedies in the face of competition from statute law. It then summarizes survey findings that reflect the choices made by members of the environmental bar when considering the facts of an environmental controversy. After reviewing the incentives at play in the legal community, the chapter then turns to examine a resurgence of common law that is just now emerging. The places where this is happening and the logic for its newfound effectiveness are then identified. The chapter ends with a picture of evolving law.

The book's conclusion looks back at the stories contained in the earlier chapters and then looks ahead to see how communities of people may address the challenges faced when living in a world of common access. Creating wealth in hummingbird economies is the challenge that ends the book.

Acknowledgements and Appreciation

In a real sense, this book has many coauthors. Some are named in the various chapters. At the risk of omitting some vital partners, I wish to acknowledge a large intellectual debt to the late Robert Staaf, a close colleague and friend who inspired and directed me toward the common law. Without Bob's guidance, I doubt that I would have discovered the logic of the law. Roger Meiners, my coauthor of many articles, chapters, and papers and coeditor of two books, has been a mainstay and teacher as I traveled the long road this book represents. As noted in some of the footnotes, key materials included in the book are based on coauthored work with Roger. Roger accepted the task of reviewing the entire manuscript. His hand and influence are reflected at almost every juncture. To these, I must add my seasoned and able colleague, Hugh H. Macaulay, who taught me much about environmental use and the market.[1] My intellectual debt to Hugh is the largest of all.

My Clemson colleague Don Boudreaux introduced me to the world of sociobiology and evolutionary thinking. The results of countless conversations with Don exploring these and other issues are reflected throughout the book. His knowledge of law and economics provides wide shoulders to the road on which I have traveled, and I surely needed them at times.

I cannot name the host of students who have taught me more about environmental policy than I perhaps taught them. In addition to those who enrolled in my economics and policy courses, I must acknowledge a smaller band of students that form what we call our Environmental Policy Workshop. Meeting informally on a weekly basis for three years, this group of graduate students in engineering, agriculture, social sciences, economics, and other fields has explored many policy issues, written research papers, and traveled into the real world to learn more about institutions and how they actually work. Again, the students have been my teachers.

Financial support is essential in most book-writing projects. I am indeed grateful to the Earhart Foundation, the Claude Lambe Charitable Foundation, and the Political Economy Research Center (PERC) for their generous support of this effort. I also express heartfelt appreciation to Clemson University for providing a place conducive to my work.

As this book was nearing completion, a close and inspiring colleague, Russell D. Shannon, was taken from us. A dedicated teacher, friend of liberty, and gentle spirit, Russell nudged me and many others to think deeply about the social consequences of markets, property rights, and the world about us. I am pleased to dedicate this book to his memory.

Notes

1. There is an obvious play on words here that goes back twenty years. See Hugh H. Macaulay and Bruce Yandle, *Environmental Use and the Market,* Lexington: Lexington Books (1977).

Chapter 1

Everything Begins with a Commons

In the summer, I watch hummingbirds fly and hover near a feeder that Dot carefully fills with nectar and hangs in view of our kitchen window. The store-bought nectar is colored red, since people think that humming birds find that color attractive. Business around the feeder picks up following rains that wash away the birds' naturally provided food. It is then that the feeder becomes crowded and a hummingbird struggle ensues. Almost always, there is at least one bird that attempts to control access to the feeder—what naturalists sometimes call a dominant male.

The dominant male seeking to maintain control will fly rapidly to the feeder, place its beak into the small openings for a quick draft of nectar, and then fly to a nearby perch where it vigilantly monitors the feeder. When other birds attempt to feed, the monitor quickly tries to intercept and force them away from the stock of sweet food. But, while the monitor engages in dogfights with one bird, another often swoops in and takes its fill.

The feeder is a common-access resource, but not just for hummingbirds. Bees are attracted to it as well, and oddly enough, bees are able to drive off the larger hummingbirds. So even if the dominant bird is able to deflect competition from other members of its species, that is not enough to protect the nectar, and the defense itself is costly in energy burned. The feeder contents are never secure.

Hummingbirds have no way to stake a claim to the feeder. So far as we can tell, hummingbird communities have no constitution that reflects socially evolved rules for establishing a social order. Most likely, a long process of adaption and selection has generated hummingbirds capable of living in a world where nourishment is a common-access resource, a commons. The genes of dominant males and capable females perpetuate a species that can exist in a world without property rights. Hummingbirds live a life of flight, engaging in a constant search for nourishment to feed their high-energy lives and, at times, fighting for temporary control over valuable resources.

People are like hummingbirds in their attempts to use environmental resources. But unlike hummingbirds, people are able to build institutions that take the edge off the frantic commons behavior. They have unwritten and written constitutions that help to establish social order. Even for people, all environmental problems, indeed all problems of resource use, begin with a commons and end with institutions that affect environmental use.[1]

This chapter explores the problem of the commons, a hummingbird economy in which a valuable resource lacks a rationing mechanism such as property rights. The chapter begins with a discussion of the nature of the common-access problem and describes (1) two broad approaches that have been devised for dealing with the problem and (2) how people have formed rules that help to conserve environmental resources. The next section calls on some economic theory to examine how production takes place on a common-access resource. The section proceeds by telling a story about a community of shepherds. The simple economic model helps to identify specific features of the common-access problem. Any solution to problems that come with unrationed use of a scarce resource includes some form of property rights, which is the topic of section four, explaining how property rights are formed and how they evolve. To show how the commons analysis can be applied, the last section discusses water quality institutions that have been formed to conserve water quality and other forms of wealth.

The Commons Problem

The reach of history is too short to tell us about man's original struggle to tame nature, which is another way of saying to convert some of the natural endowment to resources that can be controlled and managed. In the absence of a deep historical record, we must rely on common sense, logic, and current history, which tell us that the environmental problem is about a *commons* and *common-access resources* (Hanna, et al. 1996). A commons is a free-access area where people are unrestricted in access and use. A resource is something that people value. A common-access resource is something that is valuable but is freely accessible to one and all.

What is the distinguishing feature of a common-access resource? In the simplest possible terms, common access or the commons problem relates to the absence of exclusive rights. Nature's bounty is there for anyone whose presence on the commons provides temporary control.

Calling on theories from evolutionary biology, we can imagine early tribes of people struggling to control access to important sources of food, water, and shelter. With the means for establishing social order based on recognized and enforced property rights, certain physical characteristics and skills were vitally important. Size, brute strength, and accuracy when throwing rocks and swinging clubs would be survival traits to be passed on through the gene pool. But the ability to form cooperative groups based on rules of property and resource management can substitute at the margin for brute strength.

As families formed and close-knit groups were established, some brute strength was still necessary for guarding a tribal circle. However, the emergence of rules and leadership became a way to escape the law of the jungle. As John Locke put it: "To avoid this state of war . . . is one great reason of men's putting themselves into society and quitting the state of nature" (Locke 1961, 131). Property rights and cooperation in managing a commons increase wealth and make it possible for people to spend less time struggling over access to the commons and more time producing food, shelter, and clothing. Wealth increases. Locke observed, "he that encloses land, and has a greater plenty of the conveniences of life from ten acres than he could have from a hundred left to nature, may truly be said to give ninety acres to mankind" (1961, 139). The invention and recognition of property rights, a prelude to plenty, takes the pressure off scarce natural resources. Individual action in a community context is the key.

Specialization and self-discovery of skills and abilities follow control of the commons. With more wealth and greater security, primitive groups with informal or formal constitutions tend to dominate other savages who only understand the law of the jungle. Innovations that reduce the cost of property protection accelerate wealth creation and inspire even more property specialization.

When we apply this theoretical model of survival to more modern times, we find the world populated by well-defined communities of people who in one way or another have established rules for managing the commons. We also observe times when order breaks down, or outsiders invade, and starvation follows. In the recorded portion of human history, we rarely find wealth accumulation in societies that live like hummingbirds.

Two Approaches to the Commons Problem

The social institutions developed by people for managing common-access resources can be placed into two constitutional categories. I refer to one as a *process approach* and the other, a *systems approach*. Process relies more on evolved constitutional constraints, accepted by the community, that establish binding rules for activities in the postconstitutional period. The related constitutional constraints are like the rules to be followed in baseball games. These rules apply when games are played after the rules were formed; hence, the postconstitutional period. Constitutional rules may be formal, written on parchment, or informal habits of the heart. In any case, the rules should be easily understood and applied but not easily changed.

The term *process approach* gets its name from the market process that continues in a postconstitutional period. As the name implies, the market process operates at the scale of markets where buyers and sellers engage in mutually beneficial transactions. The process itself forms functional property rights, contracts; it then relies on firm rules of law derived from individuals and accepted by the community. To be accepted, the rules must be based on a sense of fairness and common sense. The rules protect individual rights, which evolve with the rules. That which is owned legitimately by a person or family is protected by the community. Payment or recompense is required when these rights are violated or damaged. At some point in the evolutionary process, the rules must be securely anchored in a written or unwritten constitution. With rights secure in law, freedom to bargain and contract inevitably yields market transactions where prices and costs provide information-filled signals that allocate effort and resources.

Consider baseball as an analogy. The game involves innovation, skills, teambuilding, and management. Playing out the game is a rule-bound process. However, the rules do not specify how a pitcher will throw the ball or when a batter will bunt or sacrifice a hit. Winning or losing is the result of spontaneous decisions and abilities revealed in the heat of competition.

The market process yields a *spontaneous order* that is based on agreement between contracting or cooperating parties and is supported by evolved customs, traditions, social norms, and rules of law. But the spontaneous order cannot emerge unless property rights are defined, enforced, and are subject to voluntary exchange, which means that agreements will be enforced. Once property rights are defined and secure, individuals have understandable incentives to devise lower-cost approaches for managing resources. In truth, this is the only logical choice if progress is to be made. When information is scarce and valuable, some individuals will specialize in providing information and other services that reduce the cost of transacting in the market place. Constitutional constraints that prevent interference with and support of contracting and property rights provide market process bedrock.

The process approach for dealing with commons and other environmental problems is decentralized in a political and every other sense of the word. It relies on and uses dispersed knowledge, and in the Anglo-American tradition relies on law discovered and announced by judges in community settings following the common-law tradition (Leoni 1991; Hogue 1966). The process determines the appropriate scale for managing resources. Specialized knowledge is applied to situations that generate community benefits and costs.

Driven by a search for lower-cost information and economies in management, resource management that begins with the scale of the individual decision maker may move to the level of family and community and then be carried to the level of regions and states, all in an effort to provide more for less, which means that information and other valuable resources are conserved. Expansion of scale carries tradeoffs. The knowledge of those closest to the problem becomes diluted as more remote individuals become involved in determining management rules and solutions. But expansion of scale provides the opportunity to include more relevant information on the common-access resource. As the cost of gathering distant information falls, the scale of the control can expand while the scale for environmental decision making becomes more localized. Ultimately, if information were free, every individual would transact with every other individual in environmental property rights.

Process outcomes are unpredictable in the sense that no outside observer can provide precise forecasts of who will do what and how things will be done. However, while an outside observer cannot predict process outcomes under a rule of law, the observer can predict principles, standards, and rules of just conduct. Paradoxically, a rather smoothly operating social system evolves from this unplanned process.

Process and Spontaneous Order

The fundamental notion of order that lies behind the process approach was put forward by F. A. Hayek. Early in his treatise, *Law, Legislation and Liberty,* Hayek introduces his seminal notions of spontaneous and extended order. His spontaneous order maps to the idea of process. Commenting on informal mechanisms, Hayek tells us that

> Man is as much a rule-following animal as a purpose-seeking one. And he is successful not because he knows why he ought to observe the rules which he does observe, or is even capable of stating all these rules in words, but because his thinking and acting are governed by rules which by a process of selection have evolved in the society in which he lives, and which are thus the product of the experience of generations. (1973, 11)

Hayek speaks of a selection process that enables communities to survive and flourish in the absence of strong law makers.[2] Minimizing the cost of transacting within the community and accumulating wealth is central to the argument. Historian, and former Librarian of Congress, Daniel Boorstin's review of American law draws conclusions that parallel those of Hayek, but adds additional insight regarding group struggles (1970, 71-96). Boorstin sees two competing systems of law, one *immanent*, or based on an indwelling necessity (values or norms), the other *instrumental* or legislative law. Both systems are seen as order generators. Like Hayek, Boorstin speaks fondly of informal law, because to him it reflects the power of commonly held values. However, Boorstin is troubled by the tug and pull that arises when a homogeneous group, which finds order informally, confronts a heterogeneous one, which relies on formal rules that emerge in a political process. In his view, political decision making is a poor substitute for decentralized decision making that involves those closest to the problem being addressed.

The Systems Approach

In contrast to process, the *systems approach* is centralized and relies on dictators or elected politicians to write statutes and rules for managing natural and environmental resources. The presence of limited specialized knowledge is often offered as justification for taking a centralized systems approach. The scale of the decision-making unit tends to be much larger than for the process approach. Statute writers are seldom close to the problem being addressed, and the zone of control generally has little to do with the ecological limits of the problem to be solved. Constitutional constraints that favor markets, contracts, and property rights can be relaxed by statute. The subtle linkages that connect individual action to outcomes can be severed. Whereas the process approach depends on cooperation, markets, and contracting in a common-law setting, the systems approach concentrates information and then relies on politicians to write statutes that are applied to one and all by political agents. Voting, politics, statutes, and regulations are dominant themes found in the systems approach. Markets, property rights, and the rule of law are dominant characteristics for the process approach.

The systems approach gets its name from a much-repeated quotation taken from Adam Smith's *Theory of Moral Sentiments,* published in 1759. Speaking of the man of system, Smith says

> He seems to imagine that he can arrange the different members of a great society with as much ease as the hand arranges the different pieces upon a chess-board. He does not consider that the pieces upon the chess-board have no other principle of motion besides that which the hand impresses on them; but that in the great chess-board of human society, every single piece has a principle of motion of its own, altogether different from that which the legislature might chose to impress upon it. (1982, 233-34)

Smith offers the man of system explanation as counterpoint to his *invisible hand theory* that explains how a spontaneous order develops through an unplanned market process. Using the analogy of a watchmaker, zoologist Richard Dawkins gives a Darwinian description of the biological order that parallels Smith's explanation of the social order:

> A true watchmaker has foresight: he designs his cogs and springs, and plans their interconnections, with a future purpose in his mind's eye. Natural selection, the blind, unconscious, automatic process which Darwin discovered, and we now know is the explanation for the existence and apparently purposeful form of all life, has no purpose in mind. It has no mind and no mind's eye. It does not plan for the future. In has no vision, no foresight, no sight at all. If it can be said to play the role of a watchmaker in nature, it is the *blind* watchmaker. (1987, 5)

The Constitutional Fence

The two approaches—process and systems—reflect two sides of the constitutional fence that establishes two decision-making zones, one private, the other public. Representative government and majoritarian rule are found on the public side of the fence where duties of government are performed. In an idealized sense, markets and private action are on the other side. However, there are no iron-clad rules that determine where topics or problems will settle when controversies arise. Will the issue be settled in the marketplace or in the halls of the legislature? If the issue is pulled to the public side of the fence, previously settled property rights can be disrupted, and incentives for individuals to protect environmental assets can be blunted. For example, decisions regarding many aspects of land use are made by private parties who are close to the resources being traded and managed. Markets, long-established property rights, and contracts affect outcomes. But many features of land use are regulated by more remote governments that write statutes and regulations affecting the use of land. In short, we have a blending of systems and process in the management of land and other resources.

The blending of rules of law and politics is not confined to the overlay of statutes and common-law procedures that affect the use of natural resources. In its history, the American version of common law has gone through periods when common-law judges made policy decisions. For example, on hearing a complaint from a farmer about damaging water pollution from a factory, instead of enforcing traditional environmental rights of the farmer against uninvited pollution, an activist court might weigh what it called the heavy social importance of the factory and the many jobs it creates against what it might deem the lesser importance of a single farm and decide in favor of the factory. We will see more about this in a later chapter.

The systems approach has gone through cycles as well. Through a good part of U.S. history, politicians were constrained in passing laws that affected freedom to contract and the security of property rights. Indeed, federal regulation did not emerge in any meaningful way until the late nineteenth century. The eighteenth and most of the nineteenth century were dominated by the market process and property rights protection. Some would say it was not until the 1930s that pervasive regulation took hold. In any event, at some point in the twentieth century the systems approach began to dominate the process approach.

Prior to the 1970s, management of environmental resources had evolved primarily through markets, taking a process approach. There were few national statutes and hardly any federal regulations affecting the use of the environment. Environmental use was controlled by a mixture of common law rules, city and county ordinances, and state statutes. The blending of systems and process across diverse regions created an environmental protection laboratory that reflected the traditions, rules, and customs of diverse people and regions. Mobility across regions made it possible for people to vote with their feet. Competition that could arise from differences that happen to exist across groups and communities introduced a realism to law and custom that tended to reflect preferences and costs.

The Evolution of Environmental Rules

Taking an Evolutionary Biology Viewpoint

This sketch of legal history relates to a long saga that is similar to the story relied on by evolutionary biologists when they explain species evolution. When examining many generations of a species, evolutionary biologists observe mutations that occur and give rise to life forms different from those of predecessor species. If mutants have superior survival characteristics, evolutionary theory explains how adaptation, reproduction, and natural selection allow for survival of stronger mutant traits. Eventually, the mutated form becomes the prevailing traits or species and the process continues.

However, unlike the biologist's story, the saga of environmental law and regulation is driven by purposeful rule-following and rule-forming people who work strategically to alter rules in ways that concentrate benefits on one particular group or another. Constitutional rules written by community members can constrain strategic behavior and force those seeking rule changes to recognize the anchored property rights of other members of the community. Constrained or not, newly invented rules for managing environmental quality that emerge in one group can be copied or altered and used by another. With constrained competition across groups, the risks of having one flawed system imposed on all is reduced. With unconstrained behavior, it is possible for one dominant system to emerge and become the preferred rule that others adopt to improve the lives of other community members. Legal rule mutation is slowed by statute; the risk of survival of a flawed system rises. Strategic behavior is still a driving force in the process.

To gain a better understanding of how the process played out in the evolution of water quality law, Karol Ceplo and I reviewed the water quality management history from the nineteenth century forward for eight western states.[3] We found that each state's somewhat unique set of common-law rules played an important role in that history, but long before the arrival of uniform federal statutes, some states had taken a river basin management approach to pollution control. They set up water quality councils that established different goals for different rivers, depending on the intended use of the water and the problems faced by communities. The resulting state administrative law worked in parallel with common law and local government rules for managing water quality. A close examination shows some similarities and differences, with some states having such distinct water quality management approaches that one would be hard-pressed to identify them as members of the same political species.

In the study of water pollution control among western states, we encountered multistate compacts organized with permission of Congress for the purpose of resolving problems that involved more than one state. In effect, new political units were invented that fit the ecological scale of water pollution problems. In some cases, the unit was a river basin. In others, it was the state itself. In still others, the unit was a group of states.

Studying the evolving process carried us to the passage of major federal water pollution control statutes in 1972. We then observed how state law began to conform to the new federal rules and how common-law rules played a diminishing role in the protection of environmental rights. The federal regulatory approach markedly displaced process and institutions for managing water quality in the eight states as they quickly began to resemble one another. By federal statute, a period of innovation, adaptation, and reproduction ended. The arrival of federal statutes telescoped the scale of control from the local, state, and regional to the national scale.

Elinor Ostrom and Edalla Schlager have focused on the appropriate scale for environmental management in their study of centralized versus local control. They note that "locally devised systems of property rights and rules are anchored in detailed time and place information, cultural norms, and the self interest of resources users" (Ostrom and Schlager 1996, 146). They warn: "External authorities would be hard-pressed to devise such institutions, because they lack the commitment to ensuring their viability and longevity" (Ostrom and Schlager 1996, 127-56). The shift in water pollution control from state and local to federal took on these risks. A period of process-dominant management with local political decision making was largely replaced by an era dominated by national politics and systems. Local initiatives and management by people closer to the problem were replaced by a federal bureaucracy assembled in Washington for the purpose of designing and implementing rules mandated by Congress. The civil servants shouldering this responsibility were the agents of Congress, which was in turn the agent of the people.

Congress and the government agents did not lack inspiration in the pursuit of lofty environmental goals. Running with a full head of steam, the environmental movement of the 1970s saw catastrophies looming at every margin. Damaging pollution and unmanaged hazardous waste were seen as unfortunate outcomes of the market system that exploited unwitting or complacent local authorities; these had to come under the heel of centralized control. With ecologists warning that everything is connected to everything else, ancient notions of property rights and economic liberties were seen as standing in the way of necessary and crucial environmental protection. If anything that one might do on his or her land somehow imposes costs on everyone else, anchors that formerly secured the rights of ordinary people are severed from their chains (Greve 1996, 5-9). Expanded centralized control follows.

Agency Cost: Another Distinct Human Problem

So far as we know, other species do not have well-structured polities with authority delegated from the group to elected members and then to their agents for taking specific actions. This approach to governing the commons and other features of life seems to be a distinctly human trait.

Governing mechanisms solve many community problems; they are beneficial. But like all beneficial activities, governing mechanisms carry costs. One of these is called agency cost, a notion that a person delegated to act in one's behalf will seldom perform precisely the way the delegating party would behave (Klein et al. 1978, 297-326). More than just innocent slippage enters the problem. The agent may, consciously or unconsciously, impose his or her own will on the problem being managed. Using a simple illustration, a child sent to the grocery store to purchase ice cream for use on the apple pie planned for dinner may decide to buy rainbow sherbet, that being the child's favorite, instead of the specified vanilla. If no time is left to secure the specified flavor, plans for dessert may be changed at the last minute and features of the evening meal altered.

A more complex aspect of agency cost is illustrated by an enforcement activity that grew out of the 1972 Federal Water Pollution Control Act (Marzulla 1995, 39-76). Out of a statute and later amendments that never mention the word "wetlands," or recognizing the possible application of the statute to this area of ecological concern, came a program for protecting ecological areas that can provide species habitat and other social benefits. Today, a permitting program run by the U.S. Corps of Engineers involves 100 to 200 million acres of U.S. land and the processing of 95,000 permits each year (Marzulla 1995, 39). The bureaucratic-intensive program is an extreme reflection of a systems approach for protecting environmental resources and more. The use of land designated as a wetland by federal agents can be taken from its current use, such as farming or as a site for a home, without compensation.

Under authority never clearly delegated by Congress, but certainly with its awareness after the fact, regulatory officials have now pressed criminal charges against farmers, ranchers, and homebuilders for wetlands violations, meaning that a guilty party can spend more than one year in a federal penitentiary. According to Roger Marzulla, between the years 1983 and 1993, the U.S. Justice Department indicted 751 individuals and 329 corporations for criminal violations. Some 804 cases have resulted in convictions and "more than 417 years of jail time have been imposed" (Marzulla 1995, 41).

The cases here span situations where persons willfully violated orders issued by federal agents to those where persons sought and obtained permits but then unwittingly violated the terms of the permits (Ceplo 1995, 103-49). In other words, the case history is rich with facts that might cause one to be pleased or deeply troubled with the outcomes, just on the basis of facts alone. But assessing the merits of these enforcement actions does not address the basic agency cost question. The agency cost problem arises because Congress never addressed the specific matter of wetlands or defined wetland violations to be criminal. The definition of the problem and its enforcement arose from regulatory agencies that are delegated by Congress to carry out legislative mandates.

This systems approach to managing environmental quality has run head-on into the process approach that is based on property rights nominally protected by and that preexisted the U.S. Constitution. As Missouri farmer Rick McGown puts it: "If my country needs my land for a public purpose, let them have it. But if they are going to take it for a public purpose, let them do it in a legal way and let the public pay for it, not send individual farmers into bankruptcy by taking away what they have spent much of their lives working for" (Marzulla 1995, 39). McGown's statement came after a severe flooding of the Mississippi inundated his farm and the retreating waters left a significant portion as wetland and subject to federal control. He lost the agricultural use of his land without compensation, and was forced to declare bankruptcy.

The troubled farmer was referring to double-edged common-law property rights when he spoke about compensation. The double edge comes from the fact that holders of rights are prohibited from imposing unwanted costs on others, whether it be pollution or any other form of cost. At the same time, the other edge requires those who desire the owner's rights to negotiate with the owner and to pay for rights that are transferred.

As the story about the ice cream implies, agency cost is not just associated with political delegation of authority. Agency cost enters every contract and arrangement where one party carries out the instructions or acts for another party. Industrial firms encounter agency costs in operating plants that may be prone to pollute. The directors of the firm may have adopted antipollution policies but the employees and managers of the firm may have other ideas. When environmental accidents occur, liabilities are imposed, the owners are held accountable, and ineffective managers and employees may be fired. The resulting costs and threats of such costs cause directors to adopt more effective management and auditing practices and to write performance contracts that limit the freedom of agents. But while agency costs may be recognized in the political sphere, it is more difficult for the people of America to monitor, audit, and punish agents who fail to carry out "the people's" bidding. Of course, most people will not even be aware of the agency costs that emerge when countless rules and regulations are developed and enforced by almost as many agents.

Rational Ignorance Is an Excuse

Failures to limit agency cost in the private sphere can be disastrous. Firms can incur huge liabilities when pollution damages people and property. Bankruptcy and prison sentences can follow. Penalties imposed by the market process involve replacement of managers and takeovers by more efficient operators, which generally lead to replacement of senior officers. The enforcement of property rights provides powerful incentives to be informed and to minimize agency cost.

The political sphere has its incentives also. Opportunities to replace elected officials arrive every two, four, or six years, and memories of abuses can be long-lived. But the looser or longer leash that tethers politicians to the electorate causes individual voters to focus on two kinds of issues—those that have immediate impact on them as individuals and those that have a large impact on the economies of which they are a part. Individual voters tend to be *rationally ignorant* about the other issues.

Farmers are keenly aware of the wetlands issue. Petroleum companies know a lot about policies involving the Middle East, and voters employed in industries threatened by foreign competition know a great deal about tariffs and quotas. But few people in the apparel industry know about wetlands, and few farmers know about quotas and tariffs on imported sleepware. Rational ignorance contributes to the agency cost problem. It is far too costly for anyone, regardless of how well intended, to understand many issues deeply.

The combination of rational ignorance and agency costs leads to an inevitable tradeoff when we consider the appropriate scale and process versus systems for dealing with the common-access resource problem. Confining solutions to the smallest number of people concentrates knowledge and ties payoff to performance. Fishers who earn their living from oyster beds in the Puget Sound are not likely to discharge waste near the beds they fish. But a paper mill may discharge effluent that invades and deteriorates the oyster beds.[4] While a mixture of common-law rights combined with state and local ordinance might bring together information on oystering and papermaking in the same region and serve to mitigate harmful pollution activities, centralizing at the federal level can make gathering local information more costly and less likely.

Expanding the zone of control and management also dilutes the interest of less vocal and politically weaker groups. What might be most effective for one group may be less than effective for the other. And when the same official who deals with off-shore pollution has to manage other issues, like social security, health care, and national defense, the problems of fishers and papermakers may get lost in the shuffle. The more centralized the approach for dealing with environmental issues, the higher will be agency costs and more detrimental will be the rational ignorance of the typical voter.

Special Interests Enter the Problem

When the national government assumes control of problems that affect people and resources across the nation and in small communities, those groups that are better organized will have more influence than those that are widely dispersed and ill informed about highly specialized issues. Centralized control means that better organized groups have a superior chance to influence political outcomes. Rational ignorance suggests most people will not even know about specialized problems, and high agency cost suggests that even if many people are informed, trying to deflect the special interest forces will be costly. If papermakers are better organized than fishers, then rules that manage the Puget Sound will likely allow some damaging effluent to be emitted, and the rules that apply to paper mills in one location are apt to be similar to the rules to be followed by paper mills in very different ecological settings. Uniform legislation is generally the result when a national government assumes control of problems formerly managed by smaller units of government or by private parties.

Under the U.S. Constitution, politics can displace the rule of law. That is, unless stated otherwise, federal statutes and their subsequent regulations preempt the common-law rules that secure a farmer's property rights as well as local ordinances and state statutes. Even when federal statutes leave room for state and local control, the more active (and for some concerned parties, cheaper) machinery of federal control tends to dominate. In other words, a federal water pollution control statute can override in some cases, and in other cases replace, rules that may have been determined through markets and the political process of smaller governmental units. At the same time, some parts of the legal environment, both formal and informal, can survive as long as the resulting strictures do not violate federal rules.

Statutes inspired by special interest groups can alter property rights that provide incentives for stewardship. When private property rights are honored, landowners look far into the future when making decisions about land use. Important expectations of future costs and benefits enter the decision-making process, and these are anchored by property rules. Regulations that alter those plans disturb the system of rights and force landowners to struggle over a political redefinition of rights. With incentives lacking at the margin for protecting the commons, efforts to produce and conserve environmental wealth tend to be diverted to efforts to redistribute wealth through the political process.

In effect, the previously privatized commons becomes a political commons where special interest groups struggle to define new property rules. Statute writers have the power to redefine property rights in ways that reward particular groups at the expense of others. Vote trading becomes a substitute for resource trading, and securing political favors can be falsely perceived as a route to creating new wealth as opposed to engaging in a costly effort to reshuffle existing resources. Unless the favor-giving process is constrained, the political pasture will become overgrazed and collective wealth will fall. The constitutional wall must be stout indeed to avoid a political tragedy after having avoided an ecological tragedy of the commons by defining property rights.

The interaction of statutes, common-law rules, and informal customs determines the institutional environment within which environmental and all other resources are managed. But to understand how the various institutional components evolve, we must begin with a clean slate, a world of common-access where people attempt to produce a living by using parts of the natural endowment. We must return to the commons.

Production on a Commons

Lucid and insightful stories about commons usually tell about pastures and shepherds (Hardin 1968, 1244; Ostrom 1990; Libecap 1989). The story, like most theories, begins with important assumptions. There is an open pasture with free access and a group of unorganized shepherds who individually make decisions regarding the number of sheep they will move to the pasture. The pasture is valuable, but its use is unrestricted. Each shepherd has the same goal: Maximizing the average weight gained for his herd. With open access, each shepherd has an incentive to expand his use of the pasture, moving sheep from an inferior grazing place to the pasture that provides improved production. The act of moving from the inferior pasture is then a foregone opportunity, which generates opportunity cost. The thoughtful shepherd seeks to gain more than enough by moving to another pasture to cover this opportunity cost.

As individual flocks expand on the new pasture and eat it clean, the average weight gained falls. That is, the pasture becomes crowded, and what were greener, more lush locations become deteriorated. But expansion will continue as long as more is gained on the now busier pasture than what was gained on the previous pasture. Expanded grazing will cease when the average gain is just equal to that of the next best grazing place. And if the next best pasture is itself deteriorated, the shepherd community may face a survival challenge.

If the shepherds become organized and share information, they may learn that each additional sheep reduces the weight gained for the collective flock. This marginal product, which is the change in total weight gained by the flock with the addition of one more sheep, declines faster than the average weight gained per sheep. By seeking to maximize personal gain, and without being penalized for the cost imposed on others, each shepherd's actions cause the pasture to deteriorate to the point that it is no better than the overgrazed pasture from which they moved. As Garrett Hardin put it:

> Therein is the tragedy. Each man is locked into a system that compels him to
> increase his herd without limit—in a world that is limited. Ruin is the destination

toward which all men rush, each pursuing his own best interest in a society that believes in the freedom of the commons. (1968, 1244)

The relationship is exactly that of an early morning expressway where drivers are waiting on a down-ramp to enter the flow of traffic. Each car that enters has the right to gain access to the city. But, as the expressway slows from crowding, each entering car reduces the average speed for every car rolling along behind the new entrant. The small reduction in speed for a large number of cars summed together can be larger than the amount of speed gained by the new entrant. Indeed, by the time the average gain for the added car yields a speed equal to that of the next best route to town, the marginal gain is negative.

In the shepherds' case, flock production would improve if fewer sheep were placed on the pasture. Pastures are depletable resources, but they are also sustainable. With appropriate safeguards in place, a shepherd community can engage in pasture rotation and maintain an economically efficient level of sustained use. However, no shepherd will independently reduce flock size in the hope that things will improve. Like the driver of a car entering a congested expressway, each shepherd is concerned about his own situation. Without cooperation, a new sheep will enter for each one removed by a kindly shepherd. Since the pasture's capacity to support sheep relates to grazing intensity, unrationed grazing can ultimately destroy the pasture. When that happens, there is a tragedy of the commons.

Analyzing the Commons

The elements of this story are described in Figure 1.1, which shows the relationship between the number of grazing units on a pasture in a day and the resulting average and marginal weight gained. Each shepherd has another resulting grazing opportunity where sheep may be moved to gain weight. A decision to enter the pasture described in the figure carries an opportunity cost, which is shown by the horizontal line. As indicated in the story, sheep will enter the pasture as long as the average gain is at least equal to the next best grazing opportunity. Herd expansion will finally stop when the marginal gain is negative. A reduction in grazing will increase average and marginal product.

The figure shows where a grazing club would set its limits, if somehow the shepherds were organized. The club would allow sheep in the pasture until opportunity cost was equal to the marginal product of the pasture, read at OA on the horizonal axis of the figure. Operating at that point, the shepherd club would produce the largest amount of weight gain possible; each member could conceivably be wealthier than before, depending on the rule for output sharing.

It is easy to find and fix this location in the diagram, but it is difficult to bring about similar changes in the real world. Shepherd clubs don't emerge out of thin air. Indeed, some of the world's most tragic struggles have been associated with

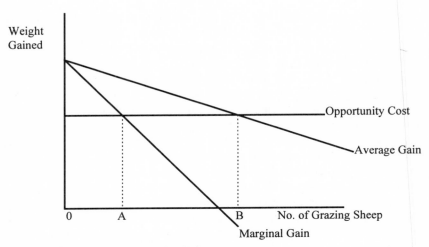

Figure 1.1 Commons Analysis

fights to gain control of the use of natural resources. Still, more often than not, people find ways to avoid the tragedy of the commons.

Each way for avoiding the tragedy trap, the point at which the pasture turns into a baseball field, carries cost, and once an unrelated group finds itself approaching the tragedy point, each member has an incentive to stay with the tragedy. Calling for change carries risk. If others fail to heed the call for cooperation, the valuable time and energy of the failed organizer is lost. Better to graze thin sheep and dream of fat ones than to waste time calling for change.

But people learn, experiments take place, adaptation occurs, and others notice the improvements. There is reproduction of ideas, in this case by learning, across groups. The first group that learns about rationing and actually applies it will become a dominant group. These shepherds will be wealthier than others, and they will be able either to push other shepherds out of business or find ways to attract them to their employment. The efficient user of resources, natural and otherwise, tends to overcome the inefficient user.

Property Rights: A Peaceful Solution to the Tragedy

Discussion of clubs and group management of the commons implies a definition of property rights, communal, public, or private. If the club is to be successful, it must be able to limit use and exclude nonmembers. Otherwise, club activities will be a waste of time. Exclusion means property rights. Club members must monitor the pasture and exclude poachers. Here we have another cost to be borne by the shepherd club. The first cost was that of organizing and maintaining the club. The next comes with devoting scarce time and resources to monitoring and protecting the pasture property.

The invention of low-cost monitoring and exclusion techniques is a necessary part of solving the tragedy problem (Anderson and Leal 1991). When low organizing costs are joined with low-cost monitoring, we can predict that some form of crude property rights will emerge sooner. Our story suggests that the pasture could first become common property, an asset owned jointly by members of the shepherd club. Only club members have access. Rules enforced by the club limit the collective use of the common property. Rules for sharing the gain provide an incentive for membership. But the overall gains from rationing use must be large enough to cover all the costs of organizing and running the club and monitoring and protecting the common property.

Common property can work well in relatively homogeneous static communities. Consider the shepherds. If each shepherd expects to live out his days as a shepherd and then to see his sons, daughters, and grandchildren follow in his footsteps, common property with rules of inheritance will be adequate. In some cases, restrictions on inheritance may be desirable for maintaining appropriate size and use of common pastures and farmland (Ensminger 1996, 179-203). But if individual shepherds wish to respond to the beck and call of other opportunities, they will value a process for transferring their shares in the pasture to someone who will pay for the wealth received. Of course, there can be rules for transferring club memberships to new members, which preserve the common-property status of the pasture. But even weak transferability enhances the value of the pasture to each member, giving an additional incentive to protect and enhance the scarce asset. An expansion of transferability can further enhance the value of the pasture. In more dynamic settings, club members have an incentive to push for full transferability.

Suppose an outsider observes the pasture and sees it as an ideal place for building a home. Joining the club by purchasing a membership will not accomplish the goal. The prospective homebuilder needs exclusive rights to a specified part of the pasture; the rights will be more valuable for the prospective buyer if they are fully transferable. With fully private rights, the owner can use the rights in any fashion accepted by the larger community, which is to say any legitimate use. The larger the range of uses, the greater the potential value of the rights. But transferability requires measurement, monitoring and enforcement, and these activities are costly. In other words, transitions across the property rights spectrum will occur when the expected gains of expanded ownership are larger than the costs of transferability.

All along our story has focused on a natural resource, a pasture, that was first common-access, then limited-access or common property, and now private property. Each move implies an increase in value for the parcel of land, and each move implies a different use of the land. The value of the land rises with opportunity cost. That is, if someone sees a better land-use opportunity than raising sheep, that person will bid more for rights to the land, which makes sheep raising more costly. Higher opportunity cost implies more effective use of the land. The land is more valuable because it produces more value when privately held.

This story of property rights, transferability, and rising land values suggests that each person in the shepherd community would gain if land rights were transformed and community property was made private. But while everyone collectively might gain, it is possible that some community members would suffer with the advent of a fully developed land market. Think of people who rent land instead of owning it. If land values rise, rising land rents will follow. And if the price of mutton and wool is fixed, then rising rents will diminish the wealth of people who rent land. Renters will understandably oppose efforts to open the market for land, something landowners would likely favor. If collective choice favors renters, then transferability may not evolve as quickly. The lesson here is clear. Changes in the status of property rights can generate changes in the distribution of wealth. How the gains in wealth are distributed determines the success of efforts to expand the market process.

Returning to the Commons Analysis

We can modify Figure 1.1 just slightly and capture some additional elements of the shepherd story. Figure 1.2 looks like Figure 1.1 with one important modification—the addition of a line showing marginal monitoring cost added to opportunity cost. Monitoring cost represents the cost added when members of the shepherd community devote part of their time to monitoring and guarding the pasture. The cost rises with more intensive use, since each user has to be monitored, which is more costly when there are more entrants to the pasture at a given time.

The addition of monitoring cost to the line representing opportunity cost yields a new total opportunity cost, which in turn yields a new ideal point for operating the pasture, shown at opportunity cost in the figure. The intersection of opportunity cost plus monitoring with the marginal gain curve also implies that a fee could be charged to club members or a price to be charged when members sell their rights. This is read off the figure's vertical axis. The area included below the marginal gain curve and above the summed cost curves represents the gain from ownership and exclusive use. How the gain is shared depends on whether membership rights are fully transferable and on rules for sharing the resulting surplus. It is easy to see that lower monitoring costs lead to expanded

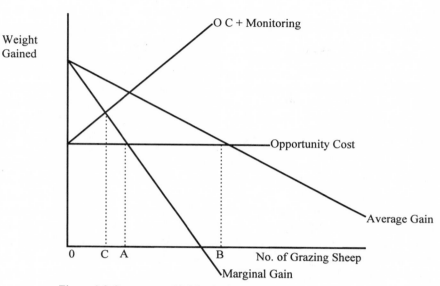

Figure 1.2 Commons with Monitoring

use of the scarce pasture, but it is not easy to see how, short of warfare, an enclosure might come about. Of course, the use of might is a solution, but not a pleasant one. But we know that quasi-property rights do emerge where long-standing custom has allowed access to a commons for a defined group (de Jasay 1996, 5-40 - 5-41). A revision of property rules—movement from an informal to a formal order—calls for payment or preannounced rules for sharing the proceeds. To minimize the costs of controversy and possible warfare, consensus must be found. The shepherd society must define itself, identify those who can make a legitimate claim in the eyes of the community, and then agree to rules for sharing the anticipated gain. From that point, transferable property rights can be defined, trade allowed, and enclosure enforced.

What might motivate a search for lower-cost monitoring and property rights enforcement? Competition from other shepherd clubs is the easy answer. Remember, each share owner in the pasture desires to produce as much wealth for himself as possible, and property rights protection is a necessary ticket to wealth. Lower-cost ways of defining, protecting, and transferring property expand wealth-generating opportunities, which make the pasture more valuable. If there are many shepherd communities, each one will have an incentive to find the low-cost way to manage the scarce asset. Competition across shepherd communities and then across multiple owners of private rights is the key to improving pastures and conserving land for more valuable purposes.

The Trip to Full Transferability

As mentioned previously, transferability of rights to natural resources is not a simple matter. In the Middle Ages, grazing communities used something called stints to manage common pasture lands. The pastures were controlled by close-knit groups who lived nearby. Stints were grazing rights, and each family received a specified number of stints that allowed the family to graze a set number of cattle, goats, or sheep. Branding, bells, or some other method for tagging animals identified ownership and reduced the cost of monitoring. Those who cheated on the system were held accountable by the community. The stint system was self-enforcing, since the wealth of each community member was linked to the stint system.

The same number of stints was provided to each family, no matter how large the family or how needy it might be. Having uniform stints reduced monitoring costs, but the lack of transferability reduced the potential wealth that might have been created under another rationing system. We know that cattle grazing today is not hampered by a system of nontransferable stints. Or is it? In many places of the world, cattle ranchers own private rights to land and cattle. They know the gains that come from expanding or contracting herd size and take steps to maximize their wealth. If cattle raising ceases to be profitable, the landowners can convert to some other activity or sell their land.

But there are other places in the world where stints are still used. Federally owned land in the Western United States is managed with a system of grazing rights that allows adjacent landowners to graze a specified number of grazing units—cattle, sheep, or goats. The grazing rights go with the land; they cannot be sold to nonlandowners, and owners of grazing rights must use them or lose them. In other places in the world, communities of farmers have used common pasture land for more than 700 years (Ostrom 1990, 61-65). For example, written records dating from 1224 describe arrangements whereby Swiss farmers moved cattle to commonly owned mountain pastures after the snow had melted (Ostrom 1990, 61-65). Rules for sharing the common property limited its use and maximized wealth. Because of its location and limited use, the common pasture land continues to be used just as it was in the Middle Ages. In other words, opportunity cost has not pushed the pasture to alternative uses.

We find systems of nontransferable property rights all about us. In most U.S. states, wild animals on public land and fish in public waters are said to be the property of the people, which means that no person can claim ownership to living fish and animals in their natural environment. Ownership occurs when animals are killed or fish are caught. Generally speaking, a system of nontransferable stints is used to ration access to the common property of the people. Bag limits and other rights to kill, which ration access to scarce species, are distributed during specified periods for some species and for open season for others. A person with a hunting or fishing license cannot transfer his limits to another person. Nontransferability reduces monitoring and enforcement costs, but reduces the value of the scarce species.

Evolving property rights structures seem to pass through stages that involve crude rationing rules that lack transferable rights before reaching a point where private ownership or shared ownership and transferability are allowed. Nontransferable rights are often found where tradition and long-established social norms reinforce rules that limit access to the commons. Sometimes this informal property rights process is reversed by statute and regulation.

Consider the case of the Makah, an isolated tribe that today lives on the northwestern tip of Washington state's Olympic Peninsula just as Makah ancestors have done for 2,000 years (De Alessi 1996, 47). For most of those years, the Makah enjoyed a whale-based economy, which centered on the grey whale species. Whaling was supplemented by fishing in the Pacific waters. In an investigation of the Makah community, anthropologist Ann Renker reported that the tribe had a centuries-old legacy of property rights protection for whales and fish supported by informal law and custom. As Michael De Alessi recently reported, "Everything from salmon fishing on rivers and streams to shellfish beds to fish banks more than sixty miles offshore were owned at one time by Makah families" (De Alessi 1996, 47).

In more recent times, the property rights rules of the Makah that conserved whales and fisheries were overriden by national and international law that gave rights managed by the International Whaling Commission. Under the international regime, expanded whaling rights were given to commercial whalers and fishermen from the United States, Japan, and Russia. What had been protected by customary property rules became a regulated commons, and it is unlikely that Russian, Japanese, and U.S. whalers care about the Makah traditions. The whale population declined until the grey whale was placed on the endangered species list. Today, the whale has recovered and, with the support of the U.S. government, the Makahs have petitioned the International Whaling Commission to allow them to catch five whales annually out of a population of 23,000. Their request is being rebuffed by some who claim that the United States does not own the whales, nor do the Makahs.

Fikret Berkes tells how effective property rules based on tradition and sharing were disrupted by colonial authorities in sub-Saharan Africa and the Pacific Islands who converted land and marine resources to common-access resources (Berkes 1996, 87-107). As Berkes puts it, "the 'tragedy' occurred only after open-access conditions had been created by external factors, after the destruction of existing communal land-tenure and marine-tenure systems" (Berkes 1996, 94).

Anderson and Leal tell a similar story about Native Americans living along the Columbia River who had established property rights and customary rules for managing the salmon long before the arrival of the Europeans (Anderson and

Leal 1995, 165-66). Understanding the spawning patterns of the salmon, the Native Americans established private fishing locations and intertribal agreements that ensured sufficient upstream migration to sustain the fishery. Things changed with the arrival of formal law. As Anderson and Leal put it: "Unfortunately, state and federal governments allowed newcomers to circumvent these rights by placing nets at the mouth of the Columbia, ultimately decimating salmon populations" (Anderson and Leal 1995, 165).

We see what appears to be a more productive reversal in the property rights institutions in a recent Alaskan development ("Hook, Line and Quotas" 1996, 57-58). The problem had to do with overfishing black cod and halibut in the Sitka region where loss of the species had led to state regulations compressing the entire fishing season into one twenty-four to forty-eight hour period, a massive tournament in which skippers would literally race to reach the fishery and, if lucky, stuff their boats with as many fish as could be carried. Size and speed of boat were obviously important.

In an attempt to remedy the problem, the state of Alaska, working with the U.S. Department of Commerce, privatized the fishery (Anderson and Leal 1991, 168-79). Marketable property rights to fish were distributed to all the owners of fishing vessels based on the average catch over the preceding five to seven years, with the collective rights being equal to an estimate of what the fishery could produce and still sustain itself. All parties to the system knew in advance that there would be fewer vessels and fishermen working after the system was in place. They also estimated that those fishermen would earn far better profits and wages than before. Instead of many boats, mile-long lines, and needless racing to the fishing grounds, more efficiently sized boats, crews, nets, and lines would be employed.

Once in place, the new system allowed a boat captain to purchase as many rights as he might deem profitable. One captain now owns 1 percent of the rights, which go with a $1 million-dollar vessel that will hold 150,000 pounds of fish, one of the largest vessels in the fleet. This captain and thirty other now prosperous captains cheer the new system. Even local banks are pleased to finance the purchase of fishing rights. But the distribution of outcomes poses a problem. As should be expected, some former fishermen dislike the new approach and hope to see it end. They claim they cannot obtain loans and have been frozen out of the business. In effect, the disgruntled fisherman are saying that they held quasi-rights to the fishery, perhaps based on custom and tradition, which were not adequately represented by the limited permits they received. Their complaints have the same echo as those of citizens in Eastern Europe where socially owned enterprises are being privatized. Transitions from social to private rights are never easy.

In spite of this understandable friction, the implication of the change is fairly easy to see. The new system, which imposes a binding constraint, encourages efficient use of equipment and management. Those best equipped to fish are able to obtain loans and purchase rights. Those who lack the competitive skills must seek another way to earn a living. Meanwhile, the fishery is protected. Rights to use the common-access resource, not the resource itself, have been made private transferable property.

A different approach to fish and wild animals is taken in other places. In the United Kingdom and parts of Canada, angling clubs own the rights to trout in specified streams (Brubaker 1995, 206-13; Leal 1996). The rights are private property. The angling clubs have an interest in maintaining viable fish populations; they limit the catch of members. For example, there are 101 salmon fishery districts in Scotland, created by an act of Parliament, but managed by owners of fishing rights (Leal 1996, 10-12). Owners of rights in each district, which may be bought and sold, form District Salmon Fishery Boards that protect and develop the fishery. The boards employ water bailiffs who enforce rules established by the boards.

Maintaining a viable fish population means that water quality must be protected. Under English common law, the angling clubs have environmental rights. Anyone who pollutes or otherwise damages a life-sustaining trout stream can be sued by the angling clubs. Over the years, the common law has protected the fish and improved water quality throughout the trout streams of England and in parts of Canada.

Private or shared property rights give the holders rights to wealth that can be passed on to kin or obtained through transfer. The normal self-interest of the rightholder causes him to look further into the future when using scarce natural resources. The more secure the rights, the longer the planning horizon. With complete transferability, planning horizons are extended indefinitely. By contrast, uncertain rights raise the temptation to cut the last tree and capture the last fish.

A traveler making his way along the coast of the South of France will be impressed by fences that stretch into the Mediterranean Sea near the Spanish border. For years, shell fishermen have owned private rights to plant and harvest shellfish in the tidelands. The property rights are defined and protected by French civil law, which, like common law, is rooted in custom and tradition. The fishermen tend their land and reap the rewards and penalties that accrue on the basis of the management of their transferable property rights.

Applying the Lessons to Water Quality

Water Quality As a Commons

Barring angling clubs and other organizations that hold a property interest in fish, water in rivers seems to be available to anyone who decides to use it. Surely this was the case when people first moved to the vicinity of a naturally flowing stream. With water there for the taking, some people logically used the river as a dump for raw sewage and other waste products that needed to be shipped away.

Ownership of land adjacent to streams limited the amount of waste that could be shipped out from particular locations, but rising population density and the ability of people to devise piping systems made it possible to increase the concentration of waste going in the river. Without the river's convenience, the people would have had little choice but to move or dispose of their waste in some more costly way. In other words, there was a demand for the river's assimilative and transportation capacities, and like all other demand curves, this one embodies the economist's law of demand. The lower the cost of using the river, the larger the flow of waste. And if no one owned the river—the common-access resource problem—users of the river faced a zero price. We all know what happens when a valuable commodity carries a zero price. People try to gain possession of large amounts of it.

Using rivers to haul off sewage and garbage may not be such a bad idea, provided other people are not unwillfully harmed by the activity or that owners of downstream rights are paid to transfer their rights to the discharger. If rivers are plentiful and people can move at low cost when they no longer can stand the stink, then it makes sense to go with the flow. While biologists may not like the sound of this, we must recognize that people ultimately determine the use of rivers and everything else, providing us with an opportunity to define pollution in economic terms. The economic way of thinking focuses on costs and benefits that are reckoned by ordinary human beings. If a person imposes unwanted costs on someone else when dumping waste, then the problem is economic. If the same discharger pays all holders of downstream rights before discharging an agreed amount of pollution, then there is no economic problem, but there may still be a biological problem.

The definition of economic pollution, which is silent on the biological and chemical aspects of pollution, speaks loudly to the human dimension of the problem. If some people care about the biological effects of discharge and are willing to take action to safeguard the natural environment, then we have economic pollution. The key is voluntary human action and a willingness to engage in voluntary exchange to alter outcomes. However, an institutional framework has to be in place for wealth-improving transactions to occur. Property rights must be defined and enforced; arrangements for contracting must exist; and people must feel secure when trading one good for another.

As a common-access resource, rivers will tend to become degraded, much like the pastures discussed earlier. That means that people will either move to higher ground, which means moving north in the western hemisphere, or they will find a way to solve the tragedy problem. Along these lines, it is interesting to note that urban land values in the western hemisphere are generally higher on the north side of cities located on rivers. That is partly explained by the common-access trait of rivers. People pollute; land values fall; and those who can afford to move head north. Then, the northern fringe gets polluted, and the story continues. At some point, expanding northward becomes more costly than dealing with the common-access problem. A review of history tells us that people have found a variety of ways to change the status of rivers from common access to common or public property, depending on the way they organize things. There are also cases where people have converted the right to use water quality to private property.

River Basin Associations That Deal with Common Access

People seeking to avoid a tragedy of the commons will naturally seek to learn first about the physical dimensions of the problem that is to be addressed. As we have seen, the size of a pasture defines the zone to be rationed just as a specified fishery determines where marketable rights apply. Few environmental problems have dimensions that coincide with political units, like counties, states, and nations. Few U.S. environmental problems span the entire continent. They are largely local. Even so, our federal statutes give a peculiar form of ownership or control of water quality to government managers who attempt to address water pollution as a national problem. Most problems to be solved surely should be addressed at the level of small ecological units. Speaking about the tendency to carry local problems to higher levels of government, Margaret McKean describes the results this way:

> [W]e have vested ownership in too large an entity (e.g., highly centralized governments or firms that are too large), creating severe problems where bureaucrats, owners, and managers can insulate themselves from the undesirable social consequences of their actions. It is often very difficult for those who suffer these consequences to complain and get corrective action if their appeals must travel upward through many layers of bureaucracy. (McKean 1996, 223-24)

By contrast, river basins or watersheds form natural units for managing water quality. People and features of nature located in and along a river basin may be linked economically, but they are surely linked ecologically. Fertilizer runoff from a farmer's fields may add to nutrient loading in a river just as surely as discharge from a municipal treatment works or a factory. People who earn their livelihood from fishing tend to be more informed about water quality and the consequences of pollution than people who live in river basin cities, but all make up a biological envelope that forms a community.

River basin associations formed by ecologically related community members are generally a mixture of process and systems. Water quality management along Germany's Ruhr River has been in place for more than a century (Bower, et al. 1981; Bower and Kneese 1984). At the turn of the twentieth century, the

Ruhr, which was then located in Prussia, was one of the most intensely used industrial river basins in the world. There were large concentrations of mining and steel manufacturing plants as well as several major cities located along the Ruhr. Practically speaking, the Ruhr became a cesspool, and no one particularly cared. The people in the area thought life was good as it was. Incomes were higher than elsewhere. The river hauled away a lot of unwanted waste; it was a common-access resource. A typhoid epidemic changed all that. Hundreds of people died from pathogens that arose from the polluted river that bit back.

The king of Prussia decided that never again would his people suffer from such a tragedy—a tragedy of the commons. He organized river basin associations and gave them the responsibility of improving and managing water quality in the Ruhr and other rivers in his kingdom. Rights to the use of water quality in the Ruhr were endowed to the Ruhrverband or Ruhr association.

All water users were required to be members of the new associations. And eventually all users had to pay for the right to discharge waste. The more water quality they consumed, the more they paid. Even cities were required to join the association and to pay if they discharged untreated sewage in the river. Fees were raised to the point that pollution declined. All who sought to locate plants on the river were required first to have their waste discharge analyzed by the Ruhrverband. In other words, the property rights to water quality were held by the association, which was a public body. The rights were a form of public property.

Depending on the characteristics of waste that might be discharged, the association would either announce a price to be paid for each unit discharged or inform the owners of the prospective plant that they could not discharge into the river. Hearing the price, a prospective firm could make a choice. The firm might find it cheaper to alter its technology and use less water in its manufacturing process, or the firm could treat its waste prior to discharging. The price to be paid for discharge rights determined the outcome.

Today, the Ruhr River basin, which is still characterized by dense population and significant industrial activity, is an attractive area with parks and camping areas provided by the association and cities along the river. The river's water quality has risen markedly over the years. As science improved, testing and treatment methods became more sophisticated. Today there are no serious water pollution problems along the Ruhr.

What are the functions of the association? It monitors water quality, regulates entry, and maintains exclusive rights to water quality use. And what about the discharge rights? They are not transferable. Their value is determined by the opportunity cost of locating elsewhere or modifying plants and water treatment facilities.

The French have taken a river basin approach to water quality management since 1969 when the national government established distinct governmental units for managing each of the country's six major rivers. Each river basin authority has responsibility for managing the rivers and for building the necessary infrastructure for improving and maintaining water quality. Interestingly enough, unlike most things in France, none of the river basin authorities is given a budget by the natinal government. They must obtain necessary funds from river users. As a result, the system of charges levied by the different authorities for withdrawal and discharge more closely resemble taxes than charges based on consumption of water quality. Persons that discharge waste are required to pay on the basis of discharge. Communities and other users that withdraw and treat water are also required to pay for the scarce resource. Administrative commissions are established for managing each of the French river basins, with members drawn from industrial, political, and environmental units. These commissions establish policy, set fees, and allocate revenues. Part of the revenues are used to construct treatment facilities and to assist water users in reducing their discharge. The French approach relies on a regional process with systems thinking reflected in the design of taxes and the use of funds.

Though no longer operating, a river basin association was formed along the Ohio River immediately following World War II (Maloney and Yandle 1983, 283-320). The problem was raw sewage from Pittsburgh and other cities along the Ohio located above Cincinnati. At first, the people in Cincinnati built larger and larger water treatment plants, hoping to get ahead of the problem. But the more they cleaned, the more sewage came their way. There were no restraints on upstream users of water quality, and the law of gravity ensured that Cincinnati would receive the cumulative results.

But Mother Nature has a way of sending a signal when things get bad enough. Gastroenteritis caused by waterborne pathogens began to affect people in communities upstream from Cincinnati. People along all the reaches of the river began to incur costs that they generated.

A multistate compact was formed by Ohio, West Virginia, Pennsylvania, and New York, and that started the Ohio River Sanitation Commission (ORANSCO), which had the responsibility for managing and improving water quality in the Ohio. The compact effectively eliminated common access and created public property rights for water quality. ORANSCO set a water quality standard to be achieved in the river and translated that to limitations that were imposed on all dischargers. A system for continuously monitoring water quality was installed, and managers of the association took steps to improve the river. Eventually, the public health problem was solved; raw sewage no longer made its way into the Ohio River. In a later chapter, we will examine closely a recently formed river basin association that operates today in North Carolina.

Public Goods and Collective Choice

The discussion of rivers and steps taken to manage them as valuable assets has skirted around a characteristic of the water quality target that attracts considerable attention from economists and policy analysts. When one level of water quality is set and maintained for a community, it is somewhat like turning on the lights in a room full of people. The level of water quality is the same for each and every person, just as with the level of light. But unlike the intensity of the light bulbs that illuminate a room, which is not affected by individual users of light, water quality can be deteriorated by individual users. A *pure public good*, like the level of illumination in a room, is characterized by nonexclusion and nondepletion. If the room is lighted for one person, it is lighted for a room filled with people; exclusion is costly. And if one person reads by the light, that person's use does not limit another person's ability to use the same light. Of course, a room can become so congested that crowding affects individual consumption. Sometimes we hear people say, "Would you move a bit? You are in my light."

Water quality is not a public good, since water quality can be degraded by one user, but setting the level of water quality for a river, like determining the level of illumination for city street lights, is a collective choice problem. Once a water quality level is set, maintaining it is a problem involving individual choice.

Economists use a simple framework for explaining how the appropriate level of a uniform rule is determined. If we know how much value each user or consumer attaches to each level of a range of water quality characteristics, then we can sum the values assigned by each person to each level and determine the collective value. For example, if there were two water quality users who assigned different values to water quality having a particular level of dissolved oxygen and one person were willing to pay $100 for the desired level and another were willing to pay $200 for the same level, then we would assign a value of $300 to that level of water quality. Each person would enjoy the same level of water quality, once it was produced.

But each person could also affect the level of water quality. One person might discharge sewage into the water, which consumes some of the dissolved oxygen as it is degraded. The other person might discharge runoff from a field where fertilizer is applied frequently. The discharge would affect the growth of algae that in turn reduces the level of dissolved oxygen. Maintaining the desired level of water quality requires rationing discharge. Individual use matters.

While economists can describe helpful theoretical devices for determining an appropriate level of water quality in collective settings, doing so in the real world is a far more perplexing problem. Publicly managed water bodies are subject to politically determined rules. Politics and interest group struggles determine outcomes. The same is true to a lesser extent for water bodies managed by associations.

The solutions to the river management problem described earlier required some collective action. Recall that an association of water quality users was offered as one institution for managing the river. Assigning public property rights to the river and placing the river under the control of a governmental unit was another solution. Again, one level of water quality would be determined for all the people living in the river basin.

The Vexing Nature of Collective Decision Making

Decisions involving public goods are almost always vexing. Anytime a larger group has to decide on one outcome that applies to every person there is almost always controversy. Consider a simple example of a preteen girls' softball team that persuades the coach to stop by a local ice cream shop before heading home for the day. The coach agrees to the stop, but in the interest of saving time sets a constraint: There will be one flavor of ice cream selected for team members. One person will go in the shop, place the order, and deliver ice cream cones to the team's parked van.

The larger the range of ice cream preferences, the more vexing the decision faced by members of the softball team, especially if the decision is made by majority rule. If, however, the voting rule calls for unanimous agreement, any team member can block the decision. Increasing the proportion of votes required for approval offers protection to team members deeply committed to one flavor of ice cream. But increasing the proportion of required votes makes it likely that many flavors will be considered before finding a winner. Even worse, it is possible that no decision will be made.

Recognizing all this, the coach may decide to select the flavor. She will be the ice cream flavor dictator. Dictated outcomes almost eliminate transaction costs, but may deliver a decision that pleases no one. Of course, the coach could take another tack. She could give each team member a dollar in change and ask each person to bid as flavors are announced. Any person can bid up to the full dollar. By summing the values of each bid, the coach could get a crude estimate of the total value for each flavor announced. The flavor receiving the highest bid would win the auction.

We can imagine other decision-making approaches that might be used in determining a collective outcome. Each approach generates different decision-making costs and different outcomes with respect to delivering the most preferred flavor for team members. Of course, decisions involving ice cream cones seem trivial compared to decisions that set levels of water quality. After all, if the ice cream choice turns out to be almost inedible for one team member, that person can grin and bear it, knowing that another cone can be purchased tomorrow. Knowing that future choice is less bounded makes a momentary disappointment more bearable. Is it possible to design a water quality management system that offers a similar possibility?

On first blush, the answer to the question seems to be decidedly negative. Once a community sets a standard and regulatory concrete is poured, it is very costly for a factory or treatment works to pull up and move to another river. But what if the river basin managers compete with other water quality managers when determining standards? That is, the managers recognize that citizens, owners of factories, fishermen, and other users of water quality can and do vote with their feet. If location decisions are made frequently for a significant number of water users, that will be enough to affect the decision makers' behavior. But the decision rule used to determine water quality standards will determine the extent to which water quality managers are exposed to gains and losses when residents in the river basin make location decisions.

If water quality standards are set politically using majority rule, preferences of minority voters will be muffled. If a super-majority voting rule is used, say a rule requiring two-thirds or three-fourths for approval, part of the insulation that covers strongly held preferences will be stripped away. If consensus is required, we can be more confident that the optimal decision will be made. Of course, the ideal outcome is one where each person voluntarily agrees to the same standard.

Something close to voluntary agreement may evolve if a river-basin management association is formed and required to act like a private firm. That is, the association, as river "owner," must obtain enough revenue from charging for water quality use to cover all its costs. Acting like a private firm does not avoid the challenge of setting one water quality standard to be met throughout a section of the river, but the fact that there are other river basins to choose from brings an element of competition and a strong desire to serve the needs of customers. After all, disgruntled citizens and firms that discharge waste can and do relocate, and relocation implies agreement with the rules of the receiving river basin association.

Just as with retail shops from which ordinary consumers can take their business elsewhere, the ability to shop for locations causes water quality managers to search for the ideal bundle of benefits for people in their regions. But what if there is just one water quality standard and one approach dictated for achieving it for every river and stream in an entire country? The single approach eliminates choice, erodes incentives to search for and find ideal outcomes, and causes river basin managers to behave more like administrators than entrepreneurs.

Solutions Based on Private Action

There is another approach that can be taken for achieving a desired level of water quality that avoids the collective choice problem and the knotty challenge that comes when it is desirable to determine how much each person in a group values particular units of water quality. Private rights to reasonable use and enjoyment of water quality can be assigned to all who own or occupy property adjacent to the river. This approach, which is referred to as a system of *riparian rights*, forms the underlying logic of English common-law rules brought to

America for managing water quality. These rules formed a basis for environmental outcomes in the Eastern United States for decades before there were statutes that regulated the use of rivers, lakes, and streams. In the arid western states, various systems of *appropriative rights* emerged, which gave ownership of water flows—not water quality—to the first party to stake a claim. After that, water quality rights much like the riparian system took hold. Riparian and appropriative rights are based on property rights. How would this decentralized approach address the management of water quality in a river? The common-law theory, which is conceptually simple, is sketched out here. A more detailed discussion will be given in chapter 4.

The legal theory begins with property rights. Any downstream holder of riparian rights can have a cause of action against an upstream discharger, if the upstream party causes water quality adjacent to the downstream owner to deteriorate in ways that impose unwanted costs. Similar logic applies to air pollution, odors, vibrations from factories, disposal of harmful waste products, and any other action that might damage another person's property and its enjoyment.

To illustrate, suppose a new paper mill is constructed on a river that flows by a farmer's pasture. Prior to building the mill, the owners know about common-law rules. But when the mill operates, waste from the paper-making process is discharged into the river, and some of the unoxidized waste passes by a farmer's land. The uninvited polluted water is consumed by the farmer's cows, which become sick. The farmer has a cause of action against the mill operator. If he chooses to act, the farmer can bring a private nuisance action (or violation of riparian rights) against the upstream paper mill. In bringing the action, the farmer must provide evidence that he has been damaged by the pollution and also prove that the named defendant is the source of the pollution. He can sue to recover for damages suffered and for injunctive relief; that is, request the court to direct the mill to cease polluting. The action is based on a system of private rights.

The common-law approach for dealing with the common-access problem has a number of interesting features that go beyond the public goods issue. However, we should first notice that the public goods problem is not a part of the common-law approach. There is no collective choice of water quality to be maintained at every point in the river. Individual property owners or occupants of land determine the level of water quality. The value of the river is revealed by private action, which is all voluntary. Only holders of rights can bring a private nuisance or riparian rights action, and they must demonstrate damages. The remedy can involve payment of damages and an injunction requiring the polluter to stop its harmful action. Of the two remedies, injunction is the more powerful and is most consistent with protection of property rights (Calabresi and Melamed 1972, 1089-1128). The amount of damages paid is determined by the court and must be based on some objective standard, such as a diminution in the value of land. Such calculations do not take account of subjective costs endured by the damaged party, and they cannot account for the fact that the transaction was involuntary. An injunction requiring the polluter to stop polluting or shut down recognizes the security of property and notifies all future polluters that they must gain approval of their operations from parties who might be affected before they pollute.

With the prospects of legal action from damaged parties always present, polluters understandably work to avoid suit. The interaction of actual suits and efforts to avoid them generates a spontaneous order that defines water quality.

Voluntary exchange is another feature of the common law of private nuisance. In the story of the paper mill and the farmer, the mill operator, knowing the common-law rule, can approach the farmer before building the mill and purchase the right to affect the quality of the river. If downstream rightholders agree to the offer, property rights will transfer from the riparian owners to the mill operator and with them the basis for bringing a common-law suit. In setting the terms of trade, the value of the water quality to the mill operator determines willingness to pay for discharge rights. The value of raising cattle or simply of having clean water pass by one's property at a particular location determines the willingness of the farmer to accept the terms of mill operator's offer. In other words, market value and opportunity cost enter the calculations. On this basis, we can say that markets determine water quality outcomes under common law.

Common law rights extend beyond individual farmers and landowners and include larger numbers of citizens who might be adversely affected by pollution. When multiple parties are affected simultaneously and similarly by an upstream discharger, the affected parties have a basis for bringing a public nuisance suit at common law. To do this, the parties might join together or might contact a public defender, like an attorney general, and describe their cause of action. The attorney general can, in turn, bring suit on behalf of the affected community. Again, damages or prospects of imminent harm have to be demonstrated, and the right of action is based on citizenship and ownership. Here we see a public goods problem; the multiple parties will seek one outcome—damages and injunction against the polluter. The outcome is the same for one and all. Group consensus regarding the desired outcome is determined by private action. Some person or persons in the affected group decides to organize an action. If enough petitioners are persuaded to go along with the action, then the attorney general may move against the polluter. Again, private action determines the outcome.

Comparing Characteristics: Public Versus Private Action

We have described two approaches for solving the common-access resource water quality problem. The first involved forming a club or transferring the problem to a unit of government. This approach immediately encounters a public goods, collective choice problem and raises the question of the appropriate scale of action. Somehow the community must determine the level of quality to be set for the entire river or for defined reaches of the river. Once set, the water quality club—be it governmental or otherwise—must monitor outcomes and protect the rights of the club members. Depending on the rules adopted, the club or governmental unit may define individual property rights that may or may not be traded. Incentives to conserve and to accumulate wealth are conditioned by the rules.

The second approach is more evolutionary and less deterministic. At the outset, no single water quality goal is set. The resulting water quality is determined by the private action of persons who live along the river. Each property owner, and each citizen, has environmental rights that cannot be infringed without legal consequence. Potential polluters know about the system of rights and infringe them at their peril. Persons who have the greatest incentive to protect their property rights must organize methods for monitoring the river. If they are harmed, they have a cause of action. The threat of action disciplines potential polluters. Communities can bring an action as well. Again, individuals must monitor environmental quality and organize actions when it is logical to do so.

Both approaches have positive and negative features. There are tradeoffs to consider. The collective approach has the problem of arriving at one outcome. Collective decision making is costly and occurs less frequently than private decision making. But the collective approach can ensure a common level of water quality; it can also set water quality parameters that have nothing to do with property damage. In other words, it is possible for the target to be too low or too high. The collective approach relies on agents to act on behalf of club members or citizens, and agency cost tends to be higher than for the market alternative. If private parties are unhappy with a collectively determined outcome either way, they have the burden of forcing the entire group to accept a different standard.

The private, common-law approach has the advantage of constantly taking account of individual values. Any person in the community can bring an action, or the entire community may do so. The resulting water quality outcome can change, either way, depending on the economic values assigned to water quality. Pollution limits that have nothing to do with economic values are not likely to emerge under common law.

The common-law approach depends on custom, tradition, and the threat of law suits, and law suits are costly. The collective approach depends on collective decision making, monitoring, and enforcement, and those activities are costly as well. Ultimately, both approaches depend on making effective use of environmental information. Finding ways to minimize the cost of bringing information to bear on private decisions is a fundamental challenge to be met by either system. Arguably, those closest to the problem, like the farmer with his cows, have access to the best information. But in some cases, the information needed is highly technical and farmers may not be well equipped to monitor and measure environmental effects. Larger associations may have an advantage there. But if there is a demand for information, we should expect providers to emerge. In other words, under the common-law system, individual landowners might need to call on consulting firms to measure and monitor outcomes. With reliance placed on common-law environmental protection, private firms would emerge to monitor streams and provide certified data. If information is sufficiently valuable, private action will address the problem.[5] Imagine how this might be done in this digital age when vast amounts of almost free information are made available to people worldwide. One can picture a continuously updated database that provides water quality information for defined segments of rivers, streams, and lakes. Persons holding environmental rights could access the information and determine quickly the status of their rights. Any significant reduction in water quality could trigger a complaint to upstream polluters whose discharges would also be monitored continuously. If appropriate remedies did not follow, the downstream rightholder could bring suit, demanding damages and injunction to stop the harmful action.

Notes

1. Garrett Hardin's classic description of the commons problem begins with the notion that there is a set of human problems for which there is no technical solution; that is, we cannot look to technology to solve them. The commons problem has to be resolved by building an institution—rules are to be followed by all participants. Hardin 1968, 1243-48.

2. Hayek indicates that the existence of shared values enable us to count on people "doing the right thing," without formally specifying what the "right thing" is. That is, the rules and their nuances are not necessarily written. This possibility is a precondition in Hayek's discussion of spontaneous order, which he then carries forward to the extended order. Hayek begins his last book with this point: "To understand our civilization, one must appreciate that the extended order resulted not from human design or intention but spontaneously: it arose from unintentionally conforming to certain traditional and largely moral practices, many of which men tend to dislike, whose significance they usually fail to understand, whose validity they cannot prove, and which have nonetheless fairly rapidly spread by means of an evolutionary selection" (1988, 6).

3. The states were Arizona, California, Idaho, Kansas, Louisiana, New Mexico, Texas, and Oregon.

4. For a related action, see *Olympia Oyster Co., Inc., v. Rayonier Incorporated*, 229 F. Supp. 855, 1964.

5. Just as private landowners pay for security services and locks and doors because others can gain by taking property, owners must bear some costs to protect valuable resources.

References

Anderson, Terry, and Donald R. Leal. 1991. *Free Market Environmentalism.* San Francisco: Pacific Research Institute for Public Policy.

————. 1995. Fishing for Property Rights. In *Taking the Environment Seriously,* edited by Roger E. Meiners and Bruce Yandle. Lanham, Md.: Rowman & Littlefield Publishers.

Berkes, Fikret. 1996. Social Systems, Ecological Systems, and Property Rights. In *Rights to Nature,* edited by Susan S. Hanna, Carol Folke, and Karl-Goran Maler. Washington: Island Press.

Boorstin, Daniel J. 1970. *The Decline of Radicalism: Reflections on America Today.* New York: First Vintage Books Edition.

Bower, Blair T., et al. 1981. *Incentives in Water Quality Management: France and Ruhr Area.* Washington: Resources for the Future.

Bower, Blair T., and Allen V. Kneese. 1984. *Managing Water Quality: Economics, Technology, Institutions.* Washington: Resources for the Future.

Brubaker, Elizabeth. 1995. *Property Rights in the Defence of Nature.* London: Earthscan Publications Limited.

Calabresi, Guido, and A. D. Melamed. 1972. Property Rules, Liability Rules, and Inalienability. *Harvard Law Review* 85: 1089-1128.

Ceplo, Karol. 1995. Land-Rights Conflicts in the Regulation of Wetlands. In *Land Rights: The 1990s Property Rights Rebellion,* edited by Bruce Yandle. Lanham, Md.: Rowman & Littlefield Publishers.

Dawkins, Richard. 1987. *The Blind Watchmaker.* New York: W. W. Norton & Co., Inc.

De Alessi, Michael. 1996. Tender Loving Hunters. *Science* (June 22): 47.

de Jasay, Anthony. 1996. Before Resorting to Politics. In *The Political Economy of the Minimal State,* edited by Charles K. Rowley. Cheltenham, Eng.: Edward Elgar.

Ensminger, Jean. 1996. Culture and Property Rights. In *Rights to Nature,* edited by Susan S. Hanna, Carl Folke, and Karl-Goran Maler. Washington: Island Press.

Greve, Michael S. 1996. *The Demise of Environmentalism in America.* Washington: American Enterprise Institute Press.

Hanna, Susan, Carl Folke, and Karl-Goran Maler, eds. 1996. *Rights to Nature.* Washington, D.C.: Island Press.

Hardin, Garret. 1968. The Tragedy of the Commons. *Science* 162: 1243-48.

Hayek, F. A. 1973. *Law, Legislation and Liberty.* Chicago: University of Chicago Press.

————. 1988. *The Fatal Conceit.* Chicago: University of Chicago Press.

Hogue, Arthur R. 1966. *Origins of the Common Law.* Indianapolis: Liberty Fund, Inc.

"Hook, Line and Quotas." 1996. *U.S. News & World Report* (November 4): 57-58.

Klein, B., R. G. Crawford, and Armen Alchian. 1978. Vertical Integration, Appropriable Rents, and the Competitive Contracting Process. *Journal of Law & Economics* 21: 297-326.

Leal, Donald R. 1996. *Community-Run Fisheries: Avoiding the "Tragedy of the Commons."* Issue No. PS-7. Bozeman, Mt.: Political Economy Research Center.

Leoni, Bruno. 1991. *Freedom and the Law.* Indianapolis: Liberty Fund, Inc.

Libecap, Gary D. 1989. *Contracting for Property Rights.* Cambridge: Cambridge University Press.

Locke, John. 1961. *Two Treatises on Government.* New York: Hafner Publishing Co.

Maloney, Michael T., and Bruce Yandle. 1983. Building Markets for Tradable Pollution Permits. In *Water Rights,* edited by Terry Anderson. San Francisco: Pacific Institute for Public Policy Research.

Marzulla, Roger J. 1995. Presumed Guilty: Wetlands Criminal Prosecutions. In *Farmers, Rangers and Environmentalists,* edited by Roger Clegg. Washington, D.C.: National Legal Center for the Public Interest.

McKean, Margaret A. 1996. Common Property Regimes As a Solution to Problems. In *Rights to Nature,* edited by Susan S. Hanna, Carl Folke, and Karl-Goran Maler. Washington, D.C.: Island Press.

Ostrom, Elinor. 1990. *Governing the Commons.* Cambridge: Cambridge University Press.

Ostrom, Elinor, and Edella Schlager. The Formation of Property Rights. In *Rights to Nature,* edited by Susan S. Hanna, Carl Folke, and Karl-Goran Maler. Washington, D.C.: Island Press.

Smith, Adam. 1976. *The Theory of Moral Sentiments.* Indianapolis: Liberty Fund, Inc.

Chapter 2

Limiting Polluter Behavior

When I was a sophomore in high school, back in 1949, a buddy in my home-room had a wonderful after-school job. He worked for the local paper mill, which was located on a large river that flowed through our town. My friend's job seemed simple enough, and it paid well. Each day, he sat on the bank of the river near the mill's discharge point and sampled the river water, recording its level of dissolved oxygen and other chemical characteristics. The paper mill owners were worried about water pollution.

Bear in mind that this was in an era of common-law and state and local environmental management, years before the federal government seriously entered the water pollution control business. At the time, there were no federal statutes guarding the nation's rivers and streams, and there were no rigorous state statutes. The mill had other reasons for bearing the cost of protecting the local river. Most likely, the mill was looking after its own long-run interests. Why was Mead Paper Company worried about the condition of the Ocmulgee River?

I must admit that I really don't know why Mead was worried about the river. I have to rely on multiple theories to answer the question. The first theory to be discussed here relates to externalities, which are the economic effects imposed on other rightholders against their will, in this case, by polluters. The theory of externalities leads to a discussion of what appears to be market or process failure and political solutions that are proposed for dealing with the problem. The story then becomes complicated by political considerations. If the body politic is to apply a systems approach to a market problem, we must make some assessment of what drives politics and the extent to which politicians may be relied on to improve market outcomes.

The next body of theory discussed relates to social forces that cause polluters to be made aware of and accountable for their actions. This is followed by another theoretical approach for resolving externality problems. The chapter's final component focuses on regulatory remedies that attempt to solve the externality problem.

Externalties: Harmful Side Effects without Payment

When a paper mill discharges wastes into a river that flows by land owned or occupied by other people, it is possible for the dirty water to reduce their health or the value of the land; that is, to infringe on the landowner's *riparian rights*. Recall, riparian rights provide owners of land adjacent to a stream the right to beneficial use of an uninterrupted supply of water of undeteriorated quality. If water quality has been *unreasonably* reduced by an upstream user, it is possible that cost has been imposed on downstream water right holders, a cost often referred to as a negative externality. A negative externality is said to exist when the dirty water imposes involuntary costs on the landowner. For the externality to be recognized at law, the costs imposed must be of sufficient size for an objective observer to recognize them. (A positive externality is present when discharge into a river lowers the cost of water quality use, improves the water quality or raises the value of downstream property. For example, the discharge may be cleaner than the receiving water.)

A simple externality analysis is usually shown in terms of a supply and demand diagram, like the one in Figure 2.1. Let the supply curve in the figure represent a paper mill's cost of producing and shipping paper products. The supply curve captures all costs paid by the mill owners. The costs include labor, rent, interest on borrowed money, electricity, supplies—everything that has to be purchased to produce paper. The curve's upward slope indicates that it is more costly to produce more paper in a given time period. Notice that the cost of using the river was not mentioned when listing all the costs embodied in the supply curve, and for good reason. At this point in our story, no one sends a bill for using the river.

The demand curve in the figure captures the value of different amounts of paper per period of time to consumers who purchase the product. The demand curve tells us that the mill must lower its price if it wishes to sell more paper in a given week or month. The demand curve also illustrates the reverse—the higher the price, the less paper will be sold.

The market clearing price for paper, P_1, is also shown in the figure. At that price, the mill covers the additional cost of producing the last unit, and the amount produced equals the amount demanded. At P_1 we have an equilibrium. Meanwhile, the mill is discharging waste into a nearby river that imposes costs on downstream landowners. The cost imposed on downstream landowners is not captured in the supply curve, unless the downstream landowners send a bill.

There is a second upward sloping line, MSC, in Figure 2.1 that captures all of the costs of producing paper, including the externality imposed downstream.

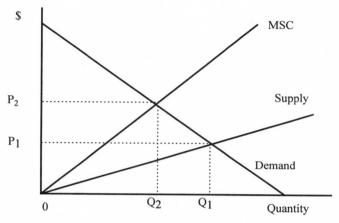

Figure 2.1 Externality Analysis

MSC stands for marginal social cost and includes the costs shown in the supply curve plus the external costs associated with each additional unit of paper produced. The amount of externality is equal to the vertical distance between the supply curve and MSC.

Externalities and Market Failure

This traditional display of external cost shows an equilibrium point where MSC crosses the demand curve that corresponds to a higher price than P_1. If the mill owners had to bear the cost of the externality, the owner would charge a higher price for paper, and produce and sell less of it. (P_2Q_2 would be the equilibrium.) If the externality is left unattended, too much paper will be produced, and its price will be too low. The "too much paper" outcome is called a *market failure* by many economists. Market failure means that prices and costs generated through the market process have not captured the costly effects of the pollution discharge by the mill. Some analysts argue that government action is required when market fails. But this assumes that the results of government action, including all costs, is superior to an unaltered market failure.

The analysis of market failure shown in Figure 2.1 was carefully developed in the 1920s by a British economist, A. C. Pigou (Pigou 1920, 183-94). Pigou's solution for too much pollution called for a tax to be imposed on the polluter that was just equal to the external costs generated by the polluter. If properly calculated, the tax would cause the polluter to receive a regular bill for using the river. Price would rise, and output would fall. The externality would be internalized by the producer. The problem would be solved by a sensitive central government, at least in the eyes of Pigou and his many followers.

Pigou's influence on the economic analysis of public policy is astounding. Today, there are carbon taxes in Scandinavian countries, bottle taxes across the United States, emission taxes on industry in California, and various fuel taxes in many states that attempt to adjust for smog production (Brannlund 1995). In each case, public authorities can claim to be adjusting for market failures; they are attempting to place a price on environmental use. Every industrialized country has taken the Pigovian approach in a larger sense. They have centralized the control of the environment and more often than prescribing taxes, have developed detailed rules that attempt to regulate polluter behavior.

What economists call Pigovian taxes are deceptively simple. Just calculate the correct tax (the difference between supply and MSC), impose it on polluters, and all will live happily ever after. But think of the complex information that must be gathered to accomplish this feat. Reference to Figure 2.1 reminds us of the difficulty in determining the appropriate tax with any degree of precision. Somehow the government authorities must estimate the demand for paper and the prices people are willing to pay for different amounts of output. When that is done, an assumption falls into place—the estimated demand curve will not change.

Next, the politician must have an estimate of the amount of damage imposed on people downstream (Macaulay 1972, 187-224). Estimating damage in the absence of market-generated information is no simple matter. For example, what if a person downstream can take actions to avoid the harm of dirty water at a cost of $5,000, yet the estimate of damage without taking offsetting action is $10,000? It is the $5,000 damage that is relevant to the policymaker, not the $10,000. But the $10,000 estimate is easier to obtain than the $5,000 estimate. If the tax is based on $10,000, the paper mill and its customers will pay more than the social cost of producing paper. The river will be too clean.

The situation becomes even more complicated when there are many receivers of waste, and each one assigns a different level of harm to the water pollution. As the scale of control increases, this cost rises exponentially. Consider the complication that comes when a national government attempts to set an appropriate tax for each producer that pollutes water, and all users of their products, and all downstream water users to take care of multiple externalities across a vast geographic area and many rivers.

Pigovian Taxes and Moving Targets

Suppose all these technical complications could be resolved and government officials determined the appropriate per-unit tax, individually tailored and placed on the harmful waste discharged by all paper mills and other producers. Would the problem be solved? There are two answers to the question. At a technical level, the answer is yes. But in a world of human action, the answer is no.

Think for a moment about the forces that generated the call for taxation. Politicians became concerned when constituents complained about pollution. The concerned citizens wanted cleaner rivers. They had no way of knowing what the optimal pollution would be; they just wanted to see clean water. When the politicians decided to impose a tax on polluters, the constituents were understandably pleased. Let the polluter pay; it only makes sense.

But once the appropriate tax is calculated and imposed, some level of pollution continues to make its way into rivers. Reference to Figure 2.1 reveals a nonzero pollution outcome. All along, the constituents have not been charged a price for their enjoyment of river. When the river becomes cleaner, they continue to receive benefits at no higher cost to themselves.

People who live along affected rivers come and go, but the tax-paying paper mills have a way of staying put. When the price of something we value is zero, we tend to want a relatively large amount of it. In fact, economists tell us that we seek to consume the valued resource until the last unit consumed is approximately equal to the value of what we give up in exchange for the unit. A zero price goes with zero enjoyment of the last unit. With pollution still in the water, though it be the optimal amount approved by Pigou, the mobile population along rivers will likely call for more pollution control, which means a higher tax or some form of regulation.[1] Of course, political action is not costless, so the concerned population may not clamor for complete elimination of pollution, but that outcome is clearly the more desirable one from their standpoint. Unless the Pigovian solution calls for zero discharge, the solution tends to be politically unstable. A reading of the Federal Water Pollution Control Act of 1972, clearly communicates this point. The statute called for *zero* pollution in the nation's rivers and streams by 1985. That goal obviously has not been and cannot be met. That goal, and only that goal, which everyone had to know was an impossibility, satisfied the dedicated environmentalists who influenced the writing of the statute.

What we have here is a commons problem with a one-sided solution. There is a demand for water quality, which is scarce and unrationed. Part of the demand relates to industrial production. Paper mills want to discharge waste into the river to produce paper. People along the river wish to enjoy nature's bounty. There is competition for use of the commons. If one group is required to pay a price for using the commons, we can predict that their use will decline. But the competing community, which pays nothing, will understandably want to expand its use of the commons. The one-sided solution leaves an unstable outcome. When all users of the environment pay rightholders for the benefits they receive, the environment becomes protected by a system of rights. When only one group pays, the rights system tends to break down again. A commons is a commons as long as a group of people have free access.

Free access and political standing make it possible for a disgruntled group to seek out polluters and demand political action, which is possible when a systems approach to pollution control is in force. At common law, a plaintiff must demonstrate damages to obtain relief in court. Loose assertions about environmental quality and the need to protect it will not do the job. Ownership of damaged property or losses of recognized rights must be shown. Information relevant to the harm must be provided. The common law protects rightholders—those who seek to preserve the environment and those who wish to use it for production—from being disrupted by those who simply do not like what they see.

Suggesting that solutions to the commons must be two-sided carries us back to common-law rules and property rights. If a downstream landowner has invested in land with expectations of receiving a predictable level of water quality, the landowner has incurred a cost that relates to his demand for environmental quality. He has paid for environmental rights. That takes care of one side of the commons problem. Investment in land that carries riparian rights precludes other investments that might have been made with the same funds; the landowner is bearing an opportunity cost for environmental quality. Under common law, to avoid litigation, a mill operator who desires to degrade water quality by discharging waste must first gain the approval of the downstream holder of environmental rights. The mill may do so by purchasing or leasing the rights (Davis 1971, 738). That takes care of the other side of the problem. Having purchased rights, the mill owner is bearing the opportunity cost of environmental quality he seeks to use. If the landowner held some rights after selling some to mill, then the rights being held carry an opportunity cost. In any case, both transacting parties are bearing the cost of their environmental preferences.

If, on the other hand, the mill operator decides to discharge waste in violation of the downstream owner's rights, the party downstream has a cause of action against the polluter. Expectations of losses at trial introduce opportunity cost for polluters. Common-law rules yield a two-sided solution through its process approach. But what if the polluter anticipates merely paying damages if brought to trial, which is a crude and lower-bound estimate of the opportunity cost imposed on the landowner and the amount the mill would have paid had it purchased the rights before hand? Obviously, the mill operator would prefer to use the river until stopped by suit and then pay. Aware of this possibility, common-law judges set damages at a level that exceeds the payment that might have been forthcoming in a voluntary setting, including interest. Better still, the court may enjoin the polluter from using any water unless pollution is controlled and force recognition of downstream rights.

The Political Economy of Pigovian Taxes

Imposing a tax on the polluter offers a systems-based approach to the pollution problem. It is possible, but at the same time highly doubtful, that Pigovian taxes can be found that reflect a best effort by politicians to deal exclusively with environmental costs. But the political economy of the situations raises serious doubts about the frequency of such outcomes in a majoritarian democracy. The logic for taking a pessimistic view reflects assumptions about politicians: Politicians want to keep their jobs; therefore, they seek to serve the interests that support them.

Think for a moment about Pigovian taxes and the interest groups that might favor or oppose them. Then, consider the relative strength of organized interest groups and their ability to provide meaningful support to politicians who seek to serve the public interest by pricing away external costs. Some environmental organizations would likely support Pigovian taxes, and perhaps downstream landowners who believe the taxes will improve their lot will lend their support. But not all environmental organizations support taxes on pollution. Some believe that setting a price on pollution means the acceptance of pollution as a legitimate feature of life, which is repugnant to many committed environmentalists. There are a few economists who like the idea of putting prices on environmental use. But industries seldom favor taxes that increase the price of their products; they are likely to alert consumers that their products could become more costly, to enlist them in the anti-tax camp. We are left with relatively weak support for the politician who simply seeks to serve the public interest by imposing the "efficient" tax on polluters. But the story doesn't end here. Politicians who seek to serve other interests may still push for taxes that wear the clothing of Pigou.

The special interest theory of politics claims that politicians will, more often than not, take actions that provide well-identified benefits to narrowly defined special interest groups. Suppose producers of corn and corn products find that they can also produce ethanol, a substitute for gasoline. Suppose that ethanol is asserted to be cleaner burning than petroleum-based gasoline. The ethanol producers organize and seek special tax treatment for their fuel. Instead of asking for a higher tax on gasoline, they ask for a subsidy or a lower tax on ethanol-based fuels. The larger the substitute or lower the tax, the lower will be the relative price of ethanol. The market for ethanol will expand, and ethanol producers will capture the benefits of a Pigovian-type tax that claims to deal with externalities.

Similar logic can be applied to taxes placed on the sulfur content of fuels, such as coal and oil. Producers of natural gas, nuclear power, and other substitutes for carbon-based fuels will appreciate a tax that reduces the relative price of their products. They may support a Pigovian tax on carbon.

Another theory of political behavior says that politicians constantly seek new sources of revenue that can be spent to serve interest groups that favor the politicians. Citizens generally favor taxes that are placed on someone other than themselves. This seems to be the case even though consumers ultimately pay all taxes, one way or another.[2] A tax that seems to address a pollution problem generates revenues that can be spent on politically popular activities. The revenue-maximizing politician who wants funds to spend on unrelated projects may support Pigovian taxes, even though that support is not based on environmental considerations.

By combining public interest, special interest, and revenue-maximizing theories of political behavior, we have expanded the support base for Pigovian taxes. Along with some environmental organizations, receivers of pollution, and a few economists, we now have producers of competing products, and politicians who seek to reduce the tax burden that falls directly on citizens. This gives a much stronger case for Pigou's tax plan.

Escaping Market Failure

The entire discussion of Pigovian taxes was based on the assumption of market failure. Somehow the polluter was able to discharge waste without paying a penalty at least as large as the cost imposed on people downstream. But what about my friend who worked after school for the paper mill? Is there something here that speaks to market failure, and just how reliable is the motivation of firms to protect environmental assets?

The paper mill that employed my friend was owned by Mead Corporation, a company headquartered in Ohio. The mill in question was located in the middle of Georgia. Why might Mead spend money to monitor water quality in a distant river? Is it possible for the desires of people along a river in Georgia to be systematically communicated to the headquarters of a firm in Ohio? And how would those expenditures be shown in Figure 2.1?

Referring again to Figure 2.1, we note the firm's supply curve that captures all the cost of producing paper. The wages paid to my friend and the cost of running the laboratory for analyzing river water is included in the supply curve. And what does the addition of the precautionary costs do to the gap between marginal social cost and supply? Logic tells us the gap is narrowed. Indeed, if water quality monitoring completely eliminates costs that might be imposed downstream, the gap disappears. The supply curve is marginal social cost.

Most likely, the paper mill took precautionary actions because of a combination of forces. Common-law rules may have formed one force. The mill owners did not want to be sued by downstream landowners; lawsuits are costly and place the firm's reputation as a good citizen at stake. Raising the topic of reputation introduces another important constraint on firm behavior. Firms like Mead have made large investments in their brand name, or *brand name capital*, and they seek to get a return on those investments. The larger the firm's customer base and the more extensive its product line, the larger the risk to reputation that comes from pollution or any other action viewed as improper in the eyes of consumers. Some consumers of Mead products will punish the firm if the brand name becomes tarnished.

The power of consumer response to information that links a firm to environmental degradation is seen in recent activities undertaken by the Geneva, Switzerland, International Organization for Standardization, which issues voluntary standards for manufacturers worldwide. Best known for its ISO-9000 standards that relate to manufacturing quality control, the organization has also developed environmental management standards (ISO 14001) that call for taking a fully integrated management approach aimed at eliminating pollution. To qualify for any of the ISO standards, a firm must develop costly plans and then stand periodic audits to assure that its programs are functioning effectively.

Home Depot, a major national seller of building supplies, has announced that it will require all of its suppliers to be ISO-14001 certified. The firm's action reflects its perception of consumer interests. If consumers want more assurance that manufacturers are taking steps to reduce pollution, the market process will deliver. Other firms, such as Hitachi, adopt ISO standards for plant operations around the world. Multinational firms sometimes show more concern for environmental quality in distant locations than do the people in those locations.

Another story of efforts to satisfy consumers and protect reputational capital is found in the saga of McDonald's Corporation's efforts to provide "environmentally correct" packaging for its many hamburger and sandwich products (National Pollution Prevention Center 1995). In the 1970s, McDonald's responded to environmentalists' concerns about timber cutting for the production of paper by switching from a paper hamburger carton to a polystyrene clamshell. Concerned about its public image, the firm made the switch after obtaining the results of a thoroughgoing full-cycle study by the Stanford Research Institute. The study attempted to take into account the full environmental consequences—cradle to grave—of providing paper or plastic containers. Shortly after McDonald's made the conversion, scientists sounded the alarm about the chlorinated fluorocarbons (CFCs) used as a blowing agent in producing polystyrene. The CFCs were linked to destruction of the ozone layer (Dupont 1993; Holed-Up 1995, 63). With its highly visible 12,400 restaurants in fifty-nine countries and 18 million daily store visits by customers in the United States, McDonald's was fearful about the loss of its reputation for providing high quality, clean, and safe products.

Environmental groups placed pressure on the firm to do something about the clamshell, labeling the company McToxic. Trying to respond, the firm installed incinerators at a number of its restaurant for eliminating all solid waste. The firm was then labeled McPuff. Wrestling with the public image problem, McDonald's then developed regional polystyrene recycling centers, which were made available to other firms that lacked recycling capability. All along, however, pressure was building for the firm to eliminate polystyrene. The former paper container began to look more attractive.

Finally, when school children nationwide—the heart of the firm's market—entered the fray, McDonald's threw in the towel. Working with the Environmental Defense Fund, a large environmental group, the firm conducted more research, developed other recycling programs, pressured its suppliers to do the same, and finally adopted a paper container. With that, the pressure ended, and the blemish about to form on the firm's reputation was removed. However, it is still not clear that paper is environmentally superior to polystyrene. The full cycle analysis of paper versus polystyrene, which takes into account energy costs, natural resource use, and final disposal, is just not convincing. Paper products do not degrade in landfills. Polystyrene does. In addition, the discarded plastic provides a liner that helps to prevent leaching from landfills. In any case, reputations matter, and market forces do cause nationally prominent firms to become very sensitive to environmental issues.

Another example of how market forces are generating demands for improved environmental management is seen in the golf course certification program developed by the New York Audubon Society.[3] In this case, Audubon put its brand name at risk. The environmental problem relates to the heavy use of pesticides, herbicides, and fertilizers used to provide the near-perfect greens desired by golfers. When combined with the heavy use of irrigation and sprinklers, use of concentrated chemicals can lead to contamination of surface and groundwater. In the absence of other constraints, golf course operators have an incentive to go after the last weed when manicuring their courses. The incremental cost of chemicals is low, and the perceived value of extended lush fairways is high.

In an effort to provide better information to golf course operators, the Golf Course Superintendents Association developed a stewardship strategy, which provided guidelines for chemical use and information on alternative ways to provide improved greens. Then, in 1990, the Audubon Society of New York began to work with the U.S. Golf Association to improve environmental quality. The effort led to the Audubon certification program. Golf course operators who see value in having the Audubon seal of approval petition Audubon and document the details of their environmental management program. The documentation includes information on chemical use, water conservation, and maintenance of wildlife habitat. Audubon Society staff work with golf course managers to improve overall environmental management. A similar effort is underway for advanced planning and certification of new golf courses. Managers of certified golf courses display the Audubon logo and in some case provide each golfer with a flyer telling about their environmental practices. The cooperative effort is voluntary and the steps being taken to protect environmental assets is evidence of market forces at work.

Market forces are also delivering environmental protection in less complex ways. Campbell Soup Company pays a premium for tomatoes with low nitrate residues, which gives farmers an incentive to reduce their use of chemical fertilizers. Campbell Soup is apparently responding to concerns expressed by those who buy its food products or is acting in advance of the kind of criticism it knows could arise.

Investors in the stock of polluting firms are also interested in the environmental behavior of firm managers. Managers who are careless with rivers and other features of the environment may also be careless when producing and delivering products. Profit maximization implies careful use of all resources over time. Investors generally assign negative value to news of law suits that affect firms in their portfolios. Negative reactions lead to sell orders, which cause stock prices to fall. When stock prices fall, the managers of affected firms find it more costly to obtain additional capital; investors can punish polluting firms. The firm's reputation, its fear of common-law suits, and investor monitoring give three reasons for polluting firms to discipline their behavior.

Recent empirical work illustrates how financial markets react to news about pollution. U.S. firms are required by federal law to provide annual data on the number of pounds of more than 600 chemicals emitted from their plants. Shameek Konar and Mark A. Cohen gathered data on this annual listing of emissions, known as the Toxic Release Inventory, and matched the data to the discharging firms that were listed on major U.S. financial stock exchanges (Konar and Cohen 1997). Using financial markets analysis, which isolates the effects of an event on the movement of specified stock portfolios relative to the market as a whole, the researchers found that firms associated with chemical releases on the annual list experienced losses in share values. Looking at data for a later period, the researchers found that those firms that previously suffered the largest reductions in share values reduced their emissions significantly in the next period. In other words, financial market monitoring matters.

There is one last motivation that causes factory managers to take better care of the environment. Factory managers and employees generally live in the vicinity of the factory; indeed, some will likely live downstream from the firm. If the pollution that spews from a factory contaminates drinking water supplies and in other ways diminishes the quality of life for employees, managers and owners will eventually bear some of the cost. The extent to which this concern causes managers to reduce pollution nudges the supply curve in Figure 2.1 closer to the marginal social cost curve. Some firms require managers to live next to their plants to help demonstrate their environmental commitment.

Protection of reputational capital, avoidance of common-law suits, fear of investor punishment, and concern for community yield a set of forces that can push profit-hungry management in the direction of environmental protection. But even the most diligent factory management efforts can fail to protect environmental assets. There will be spills and accidents that impose unwanted costs on downstream owners and citizens. Environmental insurance provides a standard approach for managing this risk, yet insurance carries costs and imposes special demands on clients. Standard commercial insurance for environmental risks requires periodic inspections of facilities, training programs for employees, and other accident-reducing steps to be taken. When firms take all the actions mentioned and also purchase insurance to cover environmental liabilities, the associated costs become embodied in the firm's supply curve. This moves the curve all the closer to marginal social cost and the elimination of "market failure."

When Are Market Forces Most Reliable?

It is obvious that some industrial firms will take action to protect common-access resources, like rivers, but how reliable are these forces? Will all firms respond to the forces we have just discussed? Are some firms more responsive than others?

Our theory-based discussion spoke of common-law suits, reputation, investor monitoring, community protection, and insurance as motivating factors for cost avoidance, or profit maximization. Those motivations will be weakest for polluters that are not challenged by market forces: publicly owned sewage treatment plants and hospitals, military and defense establishments, and all governmental units. Indeed, the threat of common-law suits is completely missing for public units; they enjoy immunity from such actions. Brandname reputation carries less weight with them, since many public units are monopolies that do not compete directly for consumer patronage. There is no stock market monitoring of the U.S. Army that punishes it for inflicting groundwater damage at one of its bases, and most public units carry no environmental insurance. In short, all else equal, publicly owned and operated facilities will be less careful with the environment than privately owned units.

Looking further, we can conclude that private firms that do not need brandname capital or public reputations and that are privately owned will not experience as much market pressure for reputational and financial capital. These are likely to be less responsive to environmental concerns than their market-exposed counterparts.

All of the factors that push in the direction of environmental protection rely heavily on actions taken by consumers, investors, or private citizens. If none of these are concerned about pollution, the management of firms will likely show little concern.

Can we depend on consumers and widely dispersed citizens to demonstrate concern for environmental quality? Based on research and casual observation, we know that incomes have a great deal to do with environmental concern. The higher the level of income, all else equal, the more people value the environment. Rising incomes are one of the most important forces leading to environmental cleanup. At the low-income end of the social spectrum, it is all people can do to provide the basic necessities to their families. Food, shelter, and basic health are assigned far more importance than improving water and air quality. In the lowest income cases, life expectancies are too short to reap the benefits of a cleaner environment. As incomes rise, and basic necessities are provided, individuals become more concerned about the world in which they live. Longevity increases, and with longer life expectancies, people become more concerned about avoiding environmental diseases that have long gestation periods. In addition, the environment where they will spend their retirement years becomes more relevant. Natural resources, parks, forests, and scenic beauty become more important.

Empirical research on the linkage between income growth and environmental quality undertaken by Gene Grossman and Alan Krueger sheds some interesting light on the topic (Grossman and Krueger 1991). Using data on air quality, income, and other variables for a sample of forty-two countries, the economists isolated the relationship between levels of income and levels of pollution. Income levels in the sample were as low as $1,000 annually and as high as $17,000. The results of their statistical modeling indicate that environmental quality falls in the earlier stages of industrialization when per capita incomes are less than $5,000 annually. After that, environmental quality systematically rises with income growth. Other research on income growth and environmental quality for developed countries indicates that a 1 percent increase in income leads to a 2.5 percent increase in the demand for environmental improvements (Coursey 1992). The relationship between income growth and demand for environmental quality, the income elasticity of demand, is about the same as the relationship between income and demand for Mercedes and BMW automobiles. This implies that richer is better, at least for the environment.

Firms located in higher-income communities face a higher likelihood of common-law suits and complaints over pollution than will firms in lower-income communities. We should expect similar levels of attention to be paid by investors in the stocks of polluting firms. Reputational capital will be more important and therefore riskier in higher-income communities.

Consideration of these market forces helps us to understand why nature seems to have been mistreated in early industrial periods, and why improvements came in later periods. Critics of the reliability of market forces often point out that in past periods, say, during the industrial revolution, rivers were despoiled, forestland denuded, and air quality was allowed to deteriorate. They suggest that any relaxation of government regulation of the environment today will lead to similar outcomes here and now. Consideration of rising incomes, shorter work weeks, and longer life expectancies suggests that command-and-control regulation is less important today than twenty or thirty years ago. At the same time, we find that community attention to environmental concerns is found most frequently in higher-income countries and regions, giving politicians added incentive to act. In short, both market and political forces are fed by rising incomes.

Professor Coase: Another Approach to the Problem

When the "market failure" story is fleshed out with institutional detail, the failure disappears; any pollution that remains leads us to speculate that the cost of eliminating that part may be greater than the resulting benefits. Human ingenuity, the mainspring of the market process, constantly drives toward elimination of relevant costs, but any path taken will itself be costly. In that sense, there is a supply of and demand for solutions to problems like pollution. When the value of taking one more step is greater than the cost, that step will be taken. But there is always friction in every system, whether it be mechanical or social. In this case, the friction is transaction costs. People have to organize, communicate, make agreements and enforce them, and all this is costly. If transaction costs were eliminated, the world would be a very different place.

Ronald Coase, a Nobel laureate in economics, studied the Pigovian solution and arrived at a very different way of looking at the pollution problem. His analysis led him to conclude that were it not for transaction costs, that is, the costs involved in dealing with one another, there would be no pollution problem. Yes, there would be pollution, but the amount would be agreed upon voluntarily by producers and receivers of pollution.

The Coasian story, like that of Pigou, can be told in terms of a paper mill located on a remote river—a common-access resource—that seeks to minimize the cost of producing paper. The location of the mill is not a random occurrence. The river is an important input to the production process. The river provides water used in producing paper and then provides carriage for waste discharged from the production process. In other words, the mill operators value the river. Indeed, they probably paid more for the land because of the river.

Like all production inputs, use of the river is determined by its cost to the mill. If river use comes without a bill—a common-access resource—the mill will use larger amounts. In fact, the river will tend to be used until the last unit of its capacity provides zero benefit to the mill. Production theory tells us that all the previous units of use provide positive, but declining, benefits. This outcome is shown in Figure 2.2 where the mill's demand for the river's assimilative and waste transportation capacity is labeled marginal benefit. The MB curve slopes downward, indicating that the initial benefits are relatively large. If river use is

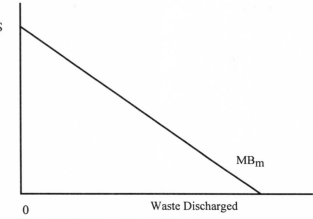

Figure 2.2 Discharge Demand

free, the mill will tend to discharge waste at the point indicated by the intersection of the MB curve with the figure's horizontal axis.

The value of the river to the mill is determined by what the mill would have to do if the river disappeared. The mill would still need to have water for its production process and would still have to get rid of its waste products, which means that some kind of disposal system would be built. If we read the MB curve from right to left, starting at its low point and reading toward the vertical axis, we observe a rising marginal cost curve. Benefits denied are costs incurred. Notice that it is very costly for the mill to reduce its discharge to zero. It is relatively cheap for the mill to remove those last units of waste that were discharged where the MB curve cuts the horizontal axis.

Now suppose there are people who live downstream from the mill in a remote location on the outer fringe of a large city. It is a charming location, set on hills that slope down to the river. The spot was carefully selected by a developer who constructed a community complete with recreational facilities and a boat dock. The developer assigned value to the river, even though it was a common-access resource. And condominium units were built and located in ways that maximized the value of the river. Figure 2.3, which shows a reverse image of Figure 2.2, describes the condominium community's demand for river services. The curve here is labeled marginal benefit to the community. In spite of its reverse image, which becomes useful later, the curve is read exactly like the one in Figure 2.2. Since units of the river can be consumed at no additional cost to the developer,

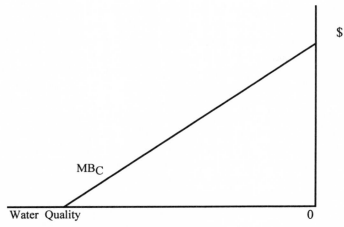

Figure 2.3 Water Quality Demand

the developer will construct units until the last unit built derives zero benefit from the river's location. Notice again that denial of benefits imposes a cost on the development. If the river deteriorates slightly, there is relatively low cost, but if the entire river disappears or becomes a waste dump, then the costs imposed reach their upper limit.

At the outset of this story, the paper mill imposed no cost on the downstream community; the waste discharged to the river is assimilated as it moves downstream. The downstream community is aware that the mill exists somewhere upstream, but is not bothered by the mill's operation. Everything is fine until the mill increases its production, which comes when demand for its product increases.

Any increase in demand causes the mill's demand for the river to rise also. In terms of Figure 2.2, the mill's MB curve shifts outward and to the right. Increase production taxes the assimilative capacity of the river. Eventually, with rising demand for paper and more daily discharge, the river begins to deteriorate. Now, we move to the downstream community.

People who live in the community gather on weekends to enjoy tennis, swimming and boating. On one of these happy occasions, residents, much to their distress, see odd colors in the water, notice a peculiar odor, and then see a few dead fish. Their getaway from the city has been invaded by pollution. Some of the marginal benefits enjoyed previously have been taken away. In terms of Figure 2.3, we have moved up the community's MB curve.

We can capture this circumstance graphically by combining Figure 2.2 and 2.3 in telescope fashion to form Figure 2.4. Notice the two curves have their original labels. The curves intersect, and the laws of gravity yield a particular meaning to the graphical display. Special attention should be focused on the origins of the two combined figures. The leftmost origin denotes zero discharge from the mill. The rightmost origin signifies zero water quality for the community. Expansion of water quality for the community means reducing discharge by the mill, and vice versa.

Since waste travels downstream, the mill's activity will overwhelm the community's desire for water quality. In Figure 2.4, the mill continues to discharge waste at the point where its MB curve intersects the horizontal axis. At that point, all of the marginal benefits of the river have been denied to the community. In terms of the figure, the community has been pushed up its MB curve to the point of zero units of water quality. The mill has consumed all of the water quality valued by the community.

Closer inspection of Figure 2.4 tells us that the mill's pollution has taken considerable value from the community, but that use of the river has added considerable value to the production of paper. Is paper production more valuable than water quality to the community? The next part of the story addresses this question.

It is election time, and a politician seeking a seat in the House of Representatives hears about the voters who live along the river and makes an appointment to visit the clubhouse one weekend. The community is pleased to hear from the politician. They have a problem they hope the politician will solve.

On the evening of the politician's visit, the time comes when she is asked to talk about her platform. After telling about her desire to cut taxes, improve welfare programs, reduce red tape and make the streets safer for citizens, she stops to take questions. Immediately, a member of the community rises and asks the big question: "Where do you stand on the environment? Have you seen the polluted mess outside?"

The politician will, no doubt, say that if she is elected, she will sponsor a bill that gives environmental rights to communities like this one. No polluter should have the right to destroy the environment. There will be no more indiscriminate discharge of waste, if she is elected.

Having given the right answer to the question, the politician receives support from members of the community. True to her promise, she sponsors a river protection act that contains the details she described to the community. The act becomes law. The community celebrates, and the paper mill cuts its waste to zero. A glance at Figure 2.4 reveals the implications of the mill's waste reduction. The mill now discharges zero waste and incurs a high cost for handling the waste in another way. The cost incurred is read from the mill's MB curve, at the point where the curve intersects the vertical axis. The community,

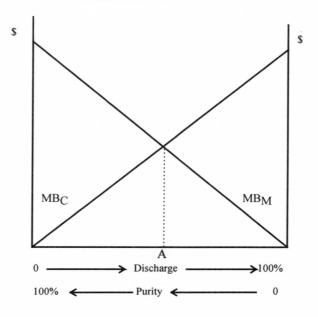

Figure 2.4 Coase Analysis

on the other hand, has reclaimed its original level of water quality. With zero discharge affecting the community, the community owners enjoy marginal benefits of zero, the point where the community's MB curve intersects the figure's left-most origin.

Notice that the marginal benefit to the mill of being allowed to discharge a small amount of waste is much larger than the loss of benefit to the community. There are potential gains from trade. This is where transaction costs enter the picture. If those costs are small enough, the mill operator may be able to entice the community to accept a little waste in the community's river. Remember, the federal statute transferred ownership to the community.

Suppose the mill operator calls a key member of the community and asks: "Would you allow us to discharge some waste into your river?" An emotionally triggered response might not be repeatable. After all, the community has just recovered from the days when pollution practically destroyed the local environment. But a more dispassionate analysis may yield another response. Suppose the mill operator says: "We will be happy to pay you for each unit we discharge, and we will maintain records of discharge monitored by a certified environmental engineer. If we violate the terms of a contract, you can haul us into court." An examination of Figure 2.4 tells us that the mill operator can pay enough to purchase discharge rights from the community over a fairly large zone of the figure.

For the sake of our analysis, suppose the community agrees to sell the mill some discharge units. They use the funds generated to make community improvements that are worth more to them than the slight deterioration of the river. As transfers are made between the two parties, the action moves the outcome along the horizontal axis of Figure 2.4. When the point is reached where the marginal benefits of discharge to the mill are less than the losses of benefits caused by the discharge to the community, trade ceases. The mill cannot outbid the community for use of the river beyond level A. Since the outcome is based on voluntary agreement between the affected parties, we call it an optimal outcome. We recognize that the cost of transacting had to be small enough to allow the trading to take place.

The solution we have found is based on several important institutional traits. Of key importance, property rights to the river were assigned to one of the trading parties, and the rights were enforced by statute. But the statute allowed for exchange between parties, so long as all affected parties agreed to the outcome. Finally, the mill operator agreed to an enforceable contract that was based on outcomes assured by a third-party auditor. We are now halfway into the Coase analysis. Coase's crucial point is yet to be made.

Let us return to the politician who visited the riverside community and promised to pass a property rights statute if elected and revise the story's outcome. There was another politician running for office who did not visit the community. He visited the paper mill. This politician spoke to a gathering of mill employees and managers and told them that their future was threatened by a group of unreasonable environmentalist who wanted to shut down an American factory and destroy the free enterprise system. To the sound of cheers and applause, the politician said: "If you send me to Washington, I will make it safe to produce paper in this country. I will push through a statute that gives rights to discharge to all firms that produce valuable products for the marketplace." The mill operators and its employees' union offered their support for the campaign. And the politician won in a close race with the woman who supported a new environmental ethic.

When the new statute was passed that opened the valves of America's polluting industries, the paper mill operators gave a sigh of relief. They had been concerned about the possibilities of demonstrations and petitions; they could now pollute and relax. Discharge continued to be released at the point in Figure 2.4 where the mill's MB curve cuts the horizontal axis. Members of the community installed air conditioners and odor-reducing devices, and built fences to block the view of the dead fish in the river.

An examination of Figure 2.4 tells us that the mill received little benefit for the last units of waste it discharged, and the community suffered considerable harm as the river reached its point of biological death. There are obvious gains from trade, if the community can entice the mill to reduce its discharge by a small amount.

Let a spokesmen for the community call the mill operator and say: "We know you own the river, and we despise what you are doing. But it's yours. Would you consider reducing your waste by a small amount? Just take out the big chunks. We will pay you for each unit of waste removed." Examination of Figure 2.4 tells us again that the community can outbid the mill for water quality to a point. In fact, it is to the same point that was reached when the community owned the river, and the mill was doing the bidding.

In telling this story, it is natural that one would sympathize more with one party than the other. Some people relate more to the community that had enjoyed water quality until the mill spoiled it. Others relate to the mill and its employees that had enjoyed the use of the river until the community moved in and complained. The point, however, is not to argue one side or the other, but to see that each party imposed cost on the other. This is one of Coase's key points. Externalities flow both ways. There is no such thing as a one-sided externality problem.

The final point in the story relates to the outcome generated when the two parties engaged in trade. The environmental outcome is the same, no matter which party holds the rights. The deeper implication of this outcome relates to the value of the two activities. Bidders for more valuable use of the river are able to outbid the less valuable uses. Put differently, the low-cost avoider of the problem makes the largest adjustment. In addition, the system is forward-, not backward-looking. Instead of looking at the current users and finding solutions that fit the needs of existing technologies and plans, the more dynamic approach encourages all users to focus on the future: What is the lowest-cost way to organize my use of the environment? Can I find a new approach that enables me to bid more for the resource? Putting it this way makes another point: Trade based on property rights brings a solution that minimizes society's costs for managing valuable water quality.

Externalities, Pigou, and Coase

We have now discussed pollution as a negative externality—those unwanted costs that can be imposed on unwitting parties who have no direct voice in the polluter's decision. We have also discussed two very different approaches to the problem. Pigou's solution speaks of market failure and the need for a central authority to fine-tune markets so that the appropriate level of pollution would emerge. The Pigovian approach calls for collection of complicated and rapidly changing information, translating the information into a tax, and imposing the tax on the polluter. We discussed some of the problems with this approach and indicated that in spite of the problems, Pigovian-style taxes continue to be debated and used.

We then turned to the Coasian analysis of the same problem. Instead of speaking of market failure, this analysis looks to markets for the solution.

Where transaction costs are low and property rights are clearly assigned, the market process can lead to an optimal solution. The Coase solution takes a decentralized, process approach where parties involved in the problem assemble their own information and use it in formulating contracts, just as in any other market. Obviously, the parties would have experts available to them to assist in making technical assessments. The Coase solution is also dynamic. If conditions change, the parties can revise their agreement in the next contracting period. They do not have to wait for elections and changes in national statutes.

In its barest form, the Coasian approach seems to fit small-numbers cases where people involved in a problem can bargain to a solution. The Pigovian approach seems to fit larger-numbers cases, where there are just too many parties to rely on contracts and trading. But before jumping to conclusions about the relative merits of the two approaches, we should recognize that large-numbers cases can become smaller-numbers when the individual participants form associations, clubs, or firms, like the river basin associations described earlier. A community can form a governing body, set a quality constraint, and delegate responsibility for trading with a group of polluters, who may also form an association. Of course, there are problems with any collective decision making, but clubs, firms, and associations are usually smaller than national governments, which suggests that the Coasian approach may have a large domain for action.

We might consider a blending of the two approaches. Politicians charged with protecting a broad public interest are constitutionally authorized to write statutes and rules to control pollution. Their actions may involve setting a tax on pollution discharges. But any rule they write and enforce, such as legal limits on pollution dumped, is akin to a tax (Posner 1971, 22-50). Action by politicians can be termed "Pigovian." At the same time, politicians may set a minimum floor for environmental quality and then allow communities, states, and regions to discover and implement their own approaches to controlling environmental quality within the limits of the political constraint. We can term the communities that choose to use property rights and common-law remedies "Coasian," which yields a blend of Pigou and Coase. The blended solutions were seen in the management of the Ruhr, the French river basin associations, and in the early Ohio River and Sanitation Commission.

Finally, we should think about common-law judges who rule on environmental controversies involving damages sought from polluters by receivers of the pollution. If the judges reach their decisions by weighing the benefits produced by the polluter against those provided by the receiver of the pollution, instead of simply enforcing well-established environmental rights, then the judges are blending Pigovian logic with the logic of Coase. Pigou called for political action aimed at reducing the social cost of pollution. Coase called for common-law courts to protect property rights.

River Basin Management: How Does It Evolve?

The stories about river basins and their focus on biological envelopes shared one common trait: An organized community of water quality users emerged after sensing or experiencing an emergency. A constraint imposed by nature was translated into a constraint built by human beings. Having some binding constraint on water quality use is a necessary first step toward the invention of some system for allocating future use. Once the constraint has been identified and imposed, the next step involves a decision regarding how to allocate shared use. It is at that fork in the road that we again encounter systems, process, and combinations of the two.

Communities are continually encountering environmental quality problems that call for action. But before they move to some formal system, improvements can be found by rallying the interest of all water quality users, informing them of the situation, and then getting voluntary actions underway to postpone a tragedy of the commons. Informal actions that avoid the transaction costs of forming an association or passing a statute may well be the most cost-effective approach.

An example of informal action was observed in 1996 in Vermillon County, Illinois, where questions were raised about the safety of the local water supply (Shipman 1996, 4). After the news media made a major story of the issue, community leaders formed an Environmental Working Group that included farmers, business leaders, local elected officials, and managers of the local water works. The group set a goal of reducing sediments and chemicals that were polluting the North Fork Vermillon River. After defining the appropriate dimensions for a 120,000-acre watershed, the group engaged in testing to determine the origin of the unwanted nitrates and other pollutants. The results indicated there was no single major culprit. Runoff from city streets and parking lots were as much to blame as nutrient runoff from farmers' fields.

The group took steps to inform community civic clubs, garden club members, hunters, and farmers. One group, Pheasants Forever, allocated part of its budget to assist landowners with the purchase of seeds for forming filter and buffer strips. Test plots were identified in the watershed so that pollution reduction outcomes could be monitored. The local American Farm Bureau office led part of the effort and the University of Illinois Cooperative Extension Service developed a newsletter and watershed fact sheets.

In one year, some 200 acres of filter strips were seeded to reduce field runoff, and 300 more acres were planned for the year ahead. Drawing on a combination of creativity and community work, the informal, grassroots effort is reaching a collective water quality goal that could lay the foundation for taking a more formal approach in the future.

A much more formal management approach is seen in North Carolina's Tar-Pamlico River Basin Association, which was formed in 1989 to manage water quality in the Tar river's 4,300-square-mile basin (Riggs 1993; Yandle 1993,

185-207). The Tar and its tributaries form 2,300 miles of stream that ultimately discharges into the Pamlico Sound and Atlantic ocean. Again, a serious ecological episode triggered actions that recognized the economic/ecological linkages within a well-defined biological envelope. In this case, it was a series of fish kills in the Pamlico Sound, one of the most productive fisheries on the Atlantic coast.

North Carolina citizens, both on their own initiative and as a part of federal government requirements, earlier had passed statutes and employed people to manage water quality. A systems approach was in place. Following the fish kills, the affected fisherman, instead of bringing suit against a vast number of poorly identified parties, petitioned North Carolina's Environmental Management Commission to designate the Tar River and Pamlico Sound as nutrient-sensitive waters. The designation brought with it a binding constraint on pollution that was well below the current levels. At the time, all of the direct dischargers were in compliance with their government-issued permits. This meant that each direct discharger of wastes would have to take extremely costly additional steps to reduce discharge. The cost of those steps was estimated to run between $50 and $100 million. Even then, the problem would not be solved. Most of the uncontrolled pollution came from numerous nonpoint source polluters, such as farmers, cities, and construction activity. Recognizing this, the state water quality managers gave the polluting community ninety days to find an alternate solution. Failing this, the community would face the cost of implementing the new plan. Incentives for finding a lower-cost solution were large and pressing.

Some of the managers of treatment works and industry in the area took the initiative to hold meetings attended by other dischargers, environmentalists, and government officials. After debating alternatives, the group decided to form a river basin association made up of all direct dischargers who wished to join. Membership would require payment for discharge based on the level of nutrients in the discharge. In addition, each new member would pay a membership fee that would go to fund a computerized model of the workings of the entire basin.

To accommodate the association's new beginning, federal and state regulators agreed to relax the individual permit requirements for members. A polluter could discharge untreated waste provided the river improved. This meant that if one discharged more waste, some other discharger would have to cut back even more. The makings for a market emerged. Rights to pollute would be transferable among sources.

The association then began to operate. At one of the early meetings, the members agreed to hire a consulting firm that would inspect all facilities, tighten controls, and fine-tune the discharge. For the first time, complete information was on the table. The previous systems approach provided no incentive for polluters to share information, since each one had to meet an individual standard irrespective of treatment costs. When the consultants work was done, the first target for pollution reduction was met. Dischargers with high treatment costs cut back; lower-cost operators expanded their treatment; faulty equipment and leakages were repaired. Under the new system, it paid to keep all operating systems in good repair. Under the old system, an operator had no problem as long as his discharge stayed within the limits of the discharge permit.

The second phase of the project involved using the fees paid by members for discharging to pay farmers to alter their farming practices. The funds from the association supplemented grants that were being made to farmers through state and federal programs. Contracts enforced under common law were written between the coordinating state agency and farmers who built settlement ponds, planted buffer strips, and took other steps to reduce nutrient runoff. The cost estimate for solving the pollution problem by trading with farmers and managing all facilities collectively came to $11.7 million, compared to the $50 to $100 million for meeting the state's plan.

In November 1996, contracts with farmers involved more than 1 million dollars in funds from state, federal, and association sources.[4] Of this total, some $300,000 had come from the Tar-Pamlico River Basin Association. In addition to these funds, each farmer is required to provide at least 25 percent of the cost of the achieving the new management practices covered by the contract.

Today, the Tar-Pamlico River Basin Association is the only official water pollution trading community in North America. Trades continue to be made between the association and farmers. The operation combines systems and process approaches for addressing an environmental problem. Discharge property rights have been defined. Common-law rules supplement regulation and cooperation. Since 1989, the tragedy of the commons has been avoided.

Who benefits from all this? The fishermen immediately come to mind. Fish kills have been eliminated. The position of the fishermen is restored with brighter future prospects. The taxpayer/owners of treatment works, the point-source dischargers, are better off. They have avoided the higher cost of installing more sophisticated technologies at every plant. Farmers who voluntarily engage in trades are clearly no worse off and arguably are better off. They are being paid to produce nutrient runoff reductions. People along the river who value its environmental qualities are better off, and the river is better off.

With all this on the positive side, who could be opposed to operations like Tar-Pamlico? Why do we not see approaches like this sweeping the country?

Supporters of command-and-control include some government employees who share responsibility for making centralized control work. They understand the status quo, in some cases developed it, and find it easier to deal with permits than with monitoring water quality. Some dischargers that invested large sums in treatment plants in order to meet their federal pollution discharge permit requirements are reluctant to walk away from their investments. And command-and-control protects some dischargers from the entry of new competitors who must obtain permits and install costly equipment. If entry can be purchased simply by obtaining low-cost reductions from farmers and others, the secure position of firms in place is threatened. Some environmentalists oppose changes that make it easier for polluters to meet environmental goals. They prefer systems that penalize industrial and other facilities that in any way use the environment. Finally, the Tar-Pamlico approach is management by exception, requiring relaxation of a major federal statute. Inertia of rest delays change, especially when those who reach too far in their efforts to change the system can be sued for compromising a federal law.

Notes

1. Opinion surveys regularly indicate that the public thinks more needs to be done about the environment, even where improvements have been so great that there is little evidence of any problem.

2. An interesting exception to this is found in the failure to pass of a November, 1996 Florida referendum on placing a one-penny-per-pound tax on sugar produced by Florida sugar firms for the avowed purpose of mitigating the effects of pollution in the Florida Everglades. The tax, which would have raised an estimated $37 million annually, would have been lightly felt by a many people. A campaign opposing the tax pointed out that Florida sugar cane growers were already paying $233 to $322 million annually of $685 million being spent by state government to deal with the problem (Blumel 1996).

3. On this, see *The Audubon Cooperative Sanctuary Program for Golf Course,* Golf Course Superintendents Association of America, Internet, 1996, Bob Costa, "Golf and the Environment: Initiating Change," *Golf Course Management,* Lawrence, Kansas: Golf Course Superintendents Association of America (February 1996), p. 176, and "Environmental Activists Tee Off," *Golf Course Management,* Lawrence Kansas: Golf Course Superintendents Association of America (February 1996): 22-40.

4. This is from data provided by Noah Ranells, North Carolina Department of Environment, Health, and Natural Resources (November 4, 1996).

References

Blumel, Phillip. 1996. *Is the Proposed Sugar Tax a Good Thing?* Tallahassee: James Madison Institute (October).

Brannlund, Runar. 1995. *Where Have Eco-Taxes Worked? The Swedish Experience.* Brussels: Centre for European Policy Studies (December).

Coursey, Don. 1992. *The Demand for Environmental Quality.* Department of Economics Working Paper. St. Louis: Washington University.

Davis, Peter N. 1971. Theories of Water Pollution Litigation. *Wisconsin Law Review* 3: 738.

DuPont Freon Products Division (A). 1993. Harvard School Case 9-389-11. Boston: Harvard Business School (October 18).

Grossman, Gene M., and Alan B. Krueger. 1991. *Environmental Impacts of a North American Free Trade Agreement.* Working Paper No. 3914. Cambridge: National Bureau of Economic Research.

Holed-Up. 1995. *The Economist* (December 9).

Konar, Shameek, and Mark A. Cohen. 1997. Information As Regulation: The Effects of Community Right to Know Laws on Toxic Emissions. *Journal of Environmental Economic Management* 32: 109-24.

Macaulay, Hugh H. 1972. Environmental Quality, the Market and Public Finance. In *Modern Fiscal Issues,* edited by Richard Bird and John G. Head. Toronto: University of Toronto Press.

National Pollution Prevention Center. 1995. *McDonald's/EDF: Case Study.* Ann Arbor, Mich. (March).

Pigou, A. C. 1920. *The Economics of Welfare.* London: Macmillan and Company.

Posner, Richard A. 1971. Taxation by Regulation. *Bell Journal* (Spring): 22-50.

Riggs, David W. 1993. *Market Incentives for Water Quality: A Case Study of the Tar-Pamlico River Basin, North Carolina.* Clemson: Center for Policy Studies (December).

Shipman, Kay. 1996. Illinois Group Focuses on Improving Water Quality. *Farm Bureau News* (October 28): 4.

Yandle, Bruce. 1993. Community Markets to Control Agricultural Nonpoint Source Pollution. In *Taking the Environment Seriously,* edited by Roger E. Meiners and Bruce Yandle. Lanham, Md.: Rowman & Littlefield Publishers.

Chapter 3

Seeking Special Favors in a Systems-Managed Economy

River basin associations like Tar-Pamlico are a rare institutional species in the United States, and common law and other process-based systems for managing environmental assets are almost forgotten. Why is this so? Is it really the case that all environmental problems are more effectively and efficiently controlled at the level of the national government? Does the national scale best fit each and every problem? Common sense and logic suggest otherwise. We are left with the challenge of explaining why command-and-control regulation has been the dominant approach taken for protecting environmental rights for almost thirty years. To meet the challenge, we must rely on theories that attempt to explain the way the world works.

This chapter begins with a discussion of theories of regulation and then focuses on one principal theory that seems to provide the strongest explanation for command-and-control dominance. Armed with a powerful explanation for taking a systems instead of a process approach, we then turn to a special interest theory of regulation and apply it to a series of environmental issues. This last theory, now known as the theory of Bootleggers and Baptists, provides a logical supplement to an explanation of why property rights and market approaches tend to lose out when political bodies focus on environmental regulation.

Examining theoretical arguments leads naturally to a review of some evidence that is provided in the discussion. Then, before the conclusion, a section is devoted to an assessment of the command-and-control record itself.

Learning Theory the Hard Way

In 1976 I took my first assignment in Washington, joining a small unit in the Office of Management and Budget and the White House dedicated to an early regulatory reform effort. The unit was a part of the President's Council on Wage and Price Stability and had the misnomer of Government Operations

.... ch. Unlike others on the council staff involved in efforts to limit price increases, our small unit was involved in reviewing newly proposed federal regulations and preparing formal White House comments to be included in regulatory proceedings. Scanning each day's *Federal Register* for important announcements and commenting on selected major proposals supplemented an Executive Order mandate that required executive branch agencies to submit major rules for our review.

Our unit was led by James C. Miller III, an energetic deregulator who later served as chairman of the Federal Trade Commission and then as director of the Office of Management and Budget in the Reagan administration. Miller assigned me to handle regulations from the EPA, the Federal Trade Commission, the Department of Transportation, and several less active agencies. Fresh out of the classroom teaching market economics, I was eager to meet the challenge. As I saw it, the job would be a snap. Ignorance of basic economics had to be the only explanation for the prevalence of so many costly and often ineffective regulations. I would explain how economics could be applied, and the regulators would rise up and call my name blessed, or so I thought.

In a matter of days, I learned otherwise. Those who developed rules for the regulatory agencies were not only well versed in basic economics, they often knew how to apply it and when not to, and when they did, they knew not to expect regulatory outcomes to be determined by economic considerations. The problem I faced was not as simple as teaching bureaucrats how to apply basic economics in the regulatory process. It was then that I began to seriously study theories of regulation and public choice economics, ideas that I had formally studied for years. The problem had more to do with political economy than economics.

Three Theories of Regulation

Theories of regulation that purport to explain the way government goes about addressing perceived problems begin with the *public interest* theory. This theory claims that government is in the business of seeking efficiency, attempting to correct market inadequacies, and focuses on the country's broad general welfare. Accordingly, politicians and regulators lie awake at night trying to find ways to improve the functioning of the economy, cautiously searching for ways to compensate for inadequately informed consumers and workers and, if possible, seeking to regulate only where the benefits of the action, somehow measured, are greater than the cost. When in doubt, the driven politician avoids doing anything, leaving the problem to the market where ordinary people will find a solution.

The next theory, the *capture theory*, states that publicly interested politicians and regulators will do their best to improve the well-being of all people taken together, but that they lack information on how to do this. Faced with a social problem, the politicians seek advice and information, which logically puts them into contact with the sector to be regulated. Who else could possibly be better informed? Those to be regulated welcome the opportunity to meet and talk with their future regulators. Indeed, the regulated can be pleasant and reasonable people, often willing to provide guidance in the form of proposed rules. As the process unfolds, the regulated capture the regulators. It's all downhill from there.

The capture theory goes some distance in explaining why regulations frequently seem to protect the interests of a regulated sector, while still providing some public interest benefits. But the theory does not explain which of several competing special interests will be successful in gaining influence. The *special interest* or *economic theory of regulation* steps to the plate to meet that challenge. First developed by the late Nobel laureate George Stigler, this theory portrays politicians as brokers who simply auction their services to the highest bidder (1971, 3-21; Peltzman 1976, 211-40; Posner 1974, 335-58). If telecommunications is to be regulated for some reason, then the cable-TV operators, broadcasters, telephone and others in the business struggle to offer the highest reward to the politicians who favor them. Those with the most to gain, or most to protect, who have low organizing costs and specialized capital, to mention a few features, are seen as being the most successful in the struggle. The special interest theory attempts to predict which of several interests will gain, and which firms or organizations in the winning sector will gain the most.

Polluters' "Profit" and Political Response

How does this help us to understand the prevalence of command-and-control and the near-nonexistence of property rights and markets for managing environmental resources? A major step in the direction of answering this question was provided by Nobel laureate James Buchanan and Gordon Tullock in a 1975 article in the *American Economic Review* (1975, 139-47). Buchanan and Tullock focused on the dominance of command-and-control and offered a very logical explanation. Command-and-control regulation always generates an output restriction; the total amount of goods produced by a polluting industry is reduced. Note the emphasis on industry. If industry output is reduced by government fiat, then price will rise, just as if the industry were cartelized. Indeed, the result is an industry cartel managed by the pollution control authority. If the resulting price increase is larger than the associated increase in cost generated by pollution control expenditures, then polluters make a profit from pollution control.

Consider the picture after command-and-control is in place. Industry price is higher and profits, at least for some members of the industry, are higher as well. Typically, higher profits attract new competition. But in this case, competitors cannot enter or expand output without permission from the pollution control authority. To make the story even more compelling, consider the typical pattern of U.S. command-and-control regulation. New sources are required to meet a higher standard than are existing or old sources. In addition, the entry of new sources is easily monitored by regulators, who stand at the door of the industry. Existing firms obviously have a much stronger political voice than undeveloped firms that might want to enter an industry.

Let us alternately compare the incentive effects of this regime with others that rely on common-law protection of environmental rights, emission fees, performance standards, and tradeable pollution permits. First, consider common law. At common law, a party damaged by a polluting firm may bring an action against the polluter. If damages are proved and evidence linking the damage to the polluter is demonstrated, the court can award damages and/or grant an injunction stopping the pollution. The court cannot impose an award for damages on an entire industry or issue an industry-wide or nationwide injunction. There is no way for an industry to gain from a common-law action. Dischargers that comply with common-law rules may gain briefly, however, when scofflaws are brought to justice. But any gains that play across a competitive industry will soon be dissipated by competitive expansion of clean output. Can a discharger gain an advantage by attracting a common-law suit? Hardly. And can an industry lobby every common-law judge in the country and gain some special treatment by the courts? It is unimaginable. Simply put, common-law remedies encourage firms to avoid imposing real harm on the actual receivers of pollution, and punish those that do.

Now, consider the other regulatory alternatives—emission fees, performance standards, and tradable pollution permits. Assume the same level of pollution reduction is mandated, but the industry is told it can accomplish the reduction in any way it desires, just so long as the environment is protected. Firms that discover new ways to reduce pollution can do so. Competition among firms pushes toward improved, lower-cost environmental management. Those that find better approaches can expand, relative to firms that are less successful. Ultimately, the industry will achieve the reduction, but entry and exit will not be blocked. Any extra profits made along the way will be temporary.

What about emission fees or taxes? If the pollution control authority announces a price to be paid for polluting that corresponds to a desired level of pollution reduction, then each firm in an industry will attempt to beat the price. They will search for lower-cost ways to produce products using less environmental quality. Again, competition will ensue. Firms that discover lower costs will pay fewer fees. Those firms that do not will pay to discharge. Profits that result will reward innovative firms and attract the entry of cleaner producers. The extra profits will be temporary, worn away by relentless competition.

And what about marketable permits? Let the control authority call for a mandated reduction in pollution to be met by using permits that authorize a specified level of discharge. Let the permits be transferable among dischargers.

Firms that face higher treatment costs will seek to buy permits from firms with lower control costs. All firms will have an incentive to discover lower treatment costs. After a period of trading and cleanup, the industry will settle down and produce a new level of output, but with less pollution. Innovative firms will earn higher returns because of their efforts. Other firms will get by with less profit. The profits will be temporary.

Command-and-control gains industry support over alternative pollution control strategies for several reasons. First, it can be profitable. Second, uniform, technology-based standards imposed across an entire country make it easier to know what the rules will be at any location. Life can be simpler that way, and certainty, which is always valued by business firms, increases. Finally, those who fear a "race to the bottom" with states trading environmental quality for jobs, will be comforted knowing that the same standards apply across all states and regions. But the latter benefit can be obtained with performance standards, which are seldom if ever used in federal regulatory programs. And the idea of racing to the bottom no longer seems to fit a world where citizens are almost always aroused when mention is made of locating an incinerator, landfill, or some new polluting industry in their state or region. We simply cannot have it both ways—a population that would gladly trade away the environment for industrial growth and a population that struggles against all actions that appear to degrade the environment. If there is to be a race in this day and time, the race will more likely be run to the top, not the bottom.

We should also consider the incentives of regulators who must implement and enforce pollution regulations. Tailoring one suit to fit all is much simpler than monitoring and certifying every plant in an industry. Instead of having to focus on the environment and its progress, regulators can simply define technology-based standards and ensure that they are applied. Monitoring permit compliance is less costly than monitoring environmental outcomes. Using taxes or emission fees is complicated by the problem of determining environmental prices in the first place and then altering them when economic conditions change. Command-and-control seems more attractive to regulators, the regulated, and the environmental community.

We are left with one principal explanation for command-and-control: the special interest theory of government. This does not say that the public interest is not served. It simply says that in attempting to serve the public interest, special interest forces hold sway, sometimes to the point that the overall costs of the episode can swamp the value of the delivered benefits. Unfortunately, the command-and-control approach attracts attention to inputs, not outcomes. Incentives to monitor environmental quality are weak at best.

Commenting on the general shift in American law to federal regulation that began in the New Deal period and continued as command-and-control in the environmental era of the 1970s and 1980s, Michael Greve spoke of how industries were cartelized via regulation:

Cartels cannot be built on the rules that order and protect private markets, such as the right to exclude and freedom of contract. For this reason, New Deal regulation did not stop at the threshold of property and contract, as traditionally conceived. But cartels do need barriers, both to protect against outsiders and to police relations among the interests within. The purpose of the regulatory arrangement thus entailed, first, a natural stopping point: regulation went only so far as to protect its intended beneficiaries—the members of the cartel—from harmful effects. The cartel nature of regulation entailed, second, standing rules that permit lawsuits by members of the regulated industries but not by outsiders and members of the public. . . . And it entailed, third, judicial deference to administrative expertise. (Greve 1996, 10)

But as Greve points out, while environmental regulation is applied at the level of specific industries and thus yields regulator-managed cartels, the regulation goes on to encompass all industries (Yandle and Young 1986, 59-69). In that sense, environmental regulation, as compared to the older industry regulation, is unlimited. As a result, Greve concludes

There can no longer be boundaries in the form of property claims or harm-based standing barriers: no one can be an outsider, and no one an owner. There is still deference to statutes, but it is deference to the values they embody, not to the bargains they strike. (1996, 11)

Bootleggers and Baptists

Saying there is industry support for certain kinds of regulation does not fully explain the final delivery of particular rules through the political process. Indeed, it is impossible to imagine politicians proclaiming to the world that command-and-control is desired so that some firms will gain additional profits. A better story than that must accompany proposed laws that mandate technologies for all firms in an industry.

The theory of Bootleggers and Baptists, which I described a number of years ago, seems to fit the bill (Yandle 1983, 12-16; 1989, 29-35; 1989). I often explain this theory by asking a group to perform the following thought experiment. Imagine that you and your spouse live in Philadelphia at the turn of the century. It is 1895, and your family has run a butcher shop for three generations. You have a well-established business, a group of loyal customers, and you earn a good living. Your family's reputation for providing safe, fresh meat products is unblemished. You have a lot to celebrate. Indeed, it is the end of the week. You and your spouse are sitting at the kitchen table talking about the good life you enjoy. You look forward to opening the shop on Monday morning.

Monday rolls around, and the shop is ready for the first customer. One of your oldest and best customers arrives. After a short greeting, the customer says, "I hate to tell you this, but I will not be doing business with you anymore." Taken by surprise, you inquire if there's a problem with the meat or the service. "No," your customer responds, "It's not that. There's a new store in town run by a firm named Swift. They bring meat from Chicago, which is good and much cheaper than yours. I simply can't pay 30 percent more to shop with you."

Amazed, but somewhat relieved, you indicate that meat slaughtered in Chicago can't be shipped and sold safely in Philadelphia. The customer responds, "Haven't you heard about the new refrigerated rail car?"

Customer after customer comes to the shop that day with the same message. Almost overnight, a celebrated business turns into a failing venture. You and your spouse find yourselves once again at the kitchen table that night. Only this time, you are attempting to sort things out, to determine what you might do to survive in the butcher shop business.

At this point in the story, a number of alternatives surface. The business can shift to other products—cheese, vegetables, flowers, even clothes. After all, the business has a reputation and a group of loyal customers. Then, there's the possibility of outdoing Swift. Why not duplicate the Chicago operation in Philadelphia? After some investigation of the idea, the shop owners quickly realize that Chicago has specialized features, such as being nearer the supply of beef and having excellent rail capacity that Philadelphia cannot duplicate. The thought of becoming a Swift agent enters the minds of the owners. If they can't lick them, why not join them?

Finally, the owners realize that every other small butcher shop in Pennsylvania faces the same problem. Why not call a meeting of butcher shop owners and discuss the mutual problem? Just such a meeting is held; a trade association is formed. The mission: Save the butcher shops. But how? What about government?

A delegation of association members sets a meeting with a state senator, who gladly greets them in his office. When asked what he might do, the butchers tell their story. "We want to save our businesses. We cannot compete with the Chicago packers. Isn't there some way you, Senator, can ban out-of-state meat?" The senator is sympathetic, but reminds the butchers that there are many people who would like to eliminate competition and make more money. He simply cannot sponsor a butcher shop protection bill. The story has to be better than that. Finally, a member of the delegation thinks about food safety and the potential threat posed by unsafe meat. Unfortunately (or fortunately), there is no evidence of a problem. But the potential is always there. "Senator," he says, "We are not really worried about our own well-being. We are concerned about public health. We ask you to sponsor legislation that ensures safe and wholesome meat products for the citizens of our state; especially for the children."

After some discussion, the senator sees the situation clearly. A safe meat law is proposed, one that requires all foreign-produced meat to be inspected by

Pennsylvania meat inspectors, at the point of slaughter and packing, with a fee charged to the producer. A new safe food commission is established, and quite logically, prominent members of the butchers association are made members. Who else would know meat better?[1]

Back to the Theory

The theory of Bootleggers and Baptists says that diverse interest groups often seek the same end. Lacking diverse groups, a single interest group will come up with alternate motivation that fits another group's interest. Bootleggers sell illicit liquor when they have the opportunity. Baptists and other religious groups oppose the Sunday sale of liquor by legal outlets. The bootleggers like that idea, too. But the bootleggers never have to petition the state legislature or march in the streets to gain their way. The Baptists do that for them. And who monitors to make certain the legal outlets are shut tight on Sunday? The Baptists. The result: A regulatory cartel delivered and enforced by a group that takes the moral high ground. Both the bootleggers and the Baptists achieve their goals.

But how can we apply this theory to environmental statutes and regulation? Who are the bootleggers? The Baptists? Command-and-control regulation, unlike common law and other forms of regulation, imposes uniform, technology-based rules on all existing plants, and sets higher standards for new plants than older ones. Entry is restricted. Profits can rise. We understand why polluters might prefer this to other control instruments. But who else prefers this most costly form of pollution control? Environmental organizations, with a few notable exceptions, have historically favored command-and-control and fought valiantly to forestall the use of emission fees, taxes, performance standards and tradeable permits. When proposals have been put forth to relax technology-based standards in favor of flexibility and cost-effective control, environmentalists have been quick to accuse the politicians of getting soft on polluters. And when told that command-and-control is costly and often ineffective, environmentalists have still rallied to the cause, sometimes suggesting that cost is no object when the environment is at stake.

The Evidence

Theory is one thing, stories another. Is there evidence that firms are actually better off under command-and-control regulation? Two significant studies address the problem, one directly and the other indirectly. Economists M. T. Maloney and Robert McCormick sought to determine if the stock values of firms rose or fell in association with stricter command-and-control regulation (Maloney and McCormick 1982, 99-124). For their study, they considered the U.S. copper industry and the final announcement of emission guidelines that affected the domestic industry. They then investigated the U.S. textile industry and the

Occupational Safety and Health Administration's cotton dust standard. In both cases, the researchers developed stock portfolios of all major firms in the two industries, observed the stability of the portfolios relative to broad market averages, and then identified the movement of the portfolios in association with the announced rules. In both cases, the portfolios of the affected industries rose significantly with the announced regulation. Some might not consider this evidence to be persuasive, but it is of interest that in the background documents on the copper industry standards, EPA indicated that if the rule was made final, there would never be another new copper smelter built in the United States. In other words, the regulatory agency knew that the final rule would block entry into the industry. It is little wonder that shareholder wealth improved with the regulation.

Another relevant study examined the voting patterns of members of Congress on various parts of the 1977 Clean Air Act (Pashigian 1985, 551-84). This study focused on features of the act that set higher standards for lesser developed regions of the United States, which meant lower, less expensive standards for the industrialized regions. Common sense suggests that dirtier regions would have to clean up more. The statute required just the reverse. Using variables that related to special interest demands located in the states of the voting politicians, the research rejected the hypothesis that politicians were driven by environmental concerns. In fact, the research implies that politicians were more interested in softening the effects of the rules on dirtier plants than in protecting environmental quality.

Other research that has attempted to model voting behavior in the passage of clean air legislation and the allocation of Superfund resources for hazardous waste cleanup fails to show a strong relationship between the health risks to be addressed and political actions taken in the name of addressing those problems (Yandle 1984, 63-69; McNeil et al. 1988, 4-9). But the documentation of the 1977 Clean Air Act's requirement of scrubbers for electric utilities for cleaning coal, even if clean coal was used, is one of the most impressive stories of costly and less effective pollution control (Ackerman and Hassler 1981). The story was coauthored by Bruce Ackerman, who at that time served in the general counsel's office of the Environmental Protection Agency. The agency and others struggled to obtain a performance standard that would allow coal-burning electric utilities to find the lowest-cost way to achieve mandated reductions in sulfur dioxide emission. But those who struggled on the other side, environmentalists and the United Mine Workers, were more effective. The senior senator from West Virginia chaired EPA's oversight committee; command-and-control, technology-based regulation took the day. The possibility of cleaning the air by switching to natural gas or low sulfur coal was lost.

Jonathan Adler's recent survey of the Bootlegger and Baptist phenomenon provides an interesting story involving a coalition of hazardous waste treatment companies (HWTC) and environmental organizations (Adler 1996, 26-34). It makes sense that both the HWTC and environmental organizations would support tough environmental regulation that require the processing of hazardous waste. That is, in fact, what happened; environmental organizations even testified on behalf of the HWTC in congressional hearings. But the twin effort went even further when the coalition attempted to preclude operators of cement kilns from using hazardous waste as fuel, which elminates a significant part of the waste disposal problem. They have also opposed Superfund cleanup standards that would allow low-risk sites to be sealed off, using HWTC members from disposing of contaminated soil. But the most telling action came when the HWTC and some environmental organizations (1) attempted to block pollution prevention efforts that, if successful, would reduce the need for the services of the hazardous waste cleanup industry, and (2) fought the use of waste taxes as a means of financing Superfund cleanup.[2] Of course, taxes placed directly on the production of hazardous waste would provide strong incentives to reduce the waste and also the demand for HWTC services.

In related work on the passage of the first Superfund statute, my coinvestigators and I examined portfolios of stocks for the chemical, petroleum, insurance, and waste management industry to see if the stock values rose or fell significantly when certain specific features of the statute were voted on by Congress (Dalton et al. 1996, 75-87). We found that the waste management portfolio experienced statistically significant gains as the statute became tougher. The portfolios of the chemical and petroleum industry became significantly more risky and in some cases experienced significant losses. In other words, Superfund was value enhancing for waste handlers. Efforts to limit pollution would obviously work against the interests of the waste management industry.

Most Bootlegger and Baptist episodes require some digging to discover the invisible coalition of environmental and other interest groups. This was certainly not the case when the North American Free Trade Agreement (NAFTA) was being debated in the early 1990s (Yandle 1993, 1-11; Yandle 1993, 91-103). At the time, NAFTA protagonists were heralding the widening of a market that would encompass 350 million consumers, extending trade from the Klondike to the Yucatan. Gains from trade appeared large, and the hope for improving environmental conditions in Mexico hinged on the prospects of rising income.

U.S. workers and owners in import-sensitive industries were dedicated and vocal in their opposition to NAFTA. As they saw it, NAFTA would open America's gates to a flood of lower-cost goods that would devastate an already suffering industrial base. Such self-serving arguments were to be expected from representatives of organized labor. But the unexpected came when American labor unions began to insist that the environment was their true concern. In their view, NAFTA would place even more environmental pressures on rivers, lakes and other natural resources along the Mexican border. In addition, post-NAFTA adjustments in the United States would bring new environmental impacts as industry and agriculture adjusted to a more competitive world. The labor interest groups were joined by major environmental organizations in what came to be a frustrated attempt to require an environmental impact analysis of NAFTA that would have scrutinized every major sector of the U.S. economy. Finally, NAFTA was signed and ratified, but not without a major Bootlegger and Baptist effort to stop the opening of markets in the name of environmental protection.

The Bootlegger and Baptist effect is not peculiar to the United States. The phenomenon has also been observed in colonial land consolidation practices espoused by colonial conservationists in Kenya in the 1950s and 1960s (Ensminger 1996, 179-203). At the outset, policy planners who sought to improve land use in Kenya faced a perplexing problem. Small parcels of agricultural lands were allocated on the basis of tradition, with families often farming multiple plots located at some distance from each other. Rules of common property, developed over the centuries, dictated the who and what of land use. Risk diversification was the rationale for part of the system. Another part was related to rules of inheritance that formed part of social bedrock. In the eyes of European agriculturists, the system made little sense. It seemed apparent that a system of private fee simple property rights for consolidated tracts of land would improve production, avoid the tragedy of the commons, and improve the well-being of the Kenya natives.

The land reforms, which ultimately failed, established a land titling process that limited to five the number who could receive land rights by inheritance. It was hoped that the new system would reduce land fragmentation, encourage the farming of economic units, and provide a basis for more market-based land transactions. But the land reform, which seemed so beneficial, required breaking down a cooperative communal system that relied on kinship and cooperation. The failure to see portfolio diversification as a rationale for fragmented plots, and neglect of the importance of custom and tradition, doomed the land reform effort.

Retrospective studies of the land reform efforts report that "a number of authors have examined the political motivations of the colonial officials who promoted [the land reform]. Although couched in the economic logic of efficiency and agrarian development, there is good reason to believe that consolidation also allowed the British to use land reform as a means of rewarding their friends, that is, the loyalists who fought against the Mau Mau during Kenya's war for independence" (Ensminger 1996, 192). Efficiency was the "Baptist" theme; lining the pockets of colonial managers was the "bootlegger" element.

Spotted Owls and Regulation

Stepping away from air and water quality and land for a moment, we can find other evidence of Bootlegger and Baptist effects. Efforts in the early 1990s to protect the habitat of the northern spotted owl is one of the more controversial episode involving the Endangered Species Act (Welch 1995, 151-197). As the saga unfolded, more than five million acres of federal land in the Pacific Northwest were placed off limits for timber harvesting. As a result, countless jobs were slashed and the economic viability of many lumber towns was eroded away. The effects on major timber companies was directly related to the extent to which they relied on federal lands for their supply. But at the outset, the large restriction on cutting was bound to have a significant price effect. Profits soared for some firms and plummeted for others.

In June, 1992, an interesting front-page story in *The Wall Street Journal* told how Weyerhaeuser had employed wildlife biologists to search for spotted owl habitat (1992, 1-A). As the story explained, the biologists were making owl calls, hoping to get a response. Identification of owl habitat meant that a large amount of land would be placed off limits. Why would the nation's largest timber product company be searching for owls? As the story indicated, the biologists were not searching on Weyerhaeuser land; they were searching on federal land. The story put it this way: "Weyerhaeuser says it has restricted logging on 320,000 acres to comply with federal and state rules protecting the birds. On the other hand, logging restrictions to protect the owl have put more than five million acres of federal timberland in the Pacific Northwest out of loggers' reach—and driven lumber prices through the roof." Going on, the story indicated that "Owl-driven profits enabled the company to earn $86.6 million in the first quarter, up 81% from a year earlier."

As the saga continued, other news reports told of higher prices for timber and homes, and also gave glowing reports of timber company profits and stock price increases. When President Clinton came into office, there was some question as to whether or not the restrictions would continue. In early February, 1993, Clinton indicated that he would protect wildlife in the logging areas. *The New York Times* reported that lumber futures prices "soared the permitted daily limit for the twelfth straight day and set an all-time high" following the Clinton announcement (*The New York Times* 1993, C15). Finally, the Clinton administration announced a timber summit for the purpose of resolving the spotted owl controversy. Uncertainty gripped the market. Would the President reverse his stand and reopen federal lands for logging?

USA Today reported two versions of the outcome in the same day's paper. On page one, the story read, "President Clinton dealt a blow to the Northwest timber industry Thursday, ordering a severe cut in tree harvests to protect the northern spotted owl" (*USA Today* 1993, 1A-2A). The financial section of the same paper put the outcome in different terms: "Paper stocks were higher. President Clinton announced plans to drastically reduce logging in the Northwest forests the next 10 years to protect the spotted owl. The logging cuts will likely mean higher paper prices, which helps paper companies' profits" (*USA Today* 1993, 3B). The note went on to report the significant increases in stock prices recorded for timber and paper companies that day.

None of this implies that major timber companies would seek to establish an endangered species act as a way to make more profit. But the story does suggest that some timber companies would likely support efforts to keep the spotted owl on the endangered species list long after the population of owls has increased. But the timber companies do not have to worry about lobbying for this outcome. Environmental organizations will do the lobbying for them.

Taking Another Approach

Is it possible to provide spotted owl protection and avoid the Bootleggers and Baptists problem? The current approach penalizes owners of private land who find the endangered owl in their forests. They lose the right to cut their timber. Obviously, the incentive goes against species protection. The owl is the last thing one wishes to find in a private forest. But what if people were rewarded for providing owl habitat? Suppose landowners were paid a bounty for every fledgling they document? And suppose the taxpayer funds, like most budgets, were limited (Tibbetts 1995, 16-20)?

The agencies with the budget would seek the most productive locations first and then announce the reward system. Payment would require documentation, which would provide data on population gains. At some point, the targeted population would be obtained, and the goal of species protection achieved. Restrictions on public land are an entirely different matter, since the land use is politically determined. However, even there, contracts entered in good faith should be honored. Sudden breach of contract should be accompanied with payment to the damaged party. Again, a budget constraint would induce greater care in determining which lands are the most valuable habitat and how those lands should be managed. In addition, rewards could be provided to the agency responsible for protecting habitat, which would give incentives to conserve scarce resources while achieving the goal. The introduction of market process thinking into the systems approach would certainly alter outcomes and enhance the integrity of government.

Taking a Look at the Statute Law Record

Command-and-control dominance does not mean the absence of gains in environmental quality. Indeed, as this section will show, substantial reductions in certain pollutants are well documented. But selection of the most costly instrument for achieving environmental gains means that more could be accomplished if market forces were unleashed. While saying this, we should be aware that there is no simple way to compare command-and-control outcomes with alternatives that might have been used. Command-and-control, which sets specific prior constraints on behavior, has been applied systematically across the entire country. The possibility of having natural experiments that could be compared was generally eliminated. While there are exceptions to the rule that offer glimmers of insight, the best we can do is to consider the statute law record and discuss how common law might have been applied. In chapter 4 we will see how common law worked when polluters violated common-law rights.

Assessing the Record

After the passage of the 1972 Clean Water Act, regulations spawned by that legislation were imposed on each state. By statute, each state had to classify streams and other waters and develop a permitting procedure for all facilities that discharged waste in lakes, rivers, streams and oceans. The law effectively federalized the rights to all state water quality. Along with the permitting requirement came technology-based, end-of-pipe standards for all major industries and for publicly owned treatment works. To obtain a permit, the facility operator had to show the use of specified technologies. The EPA-mandated effluent guidelines, which focused on inputs rather than outcomes, were designed to bring significant reductions in water pollution and therefore improvements in water quality. Along with mandates to be met by industrial and public facility dischargers came huge federal subsidies for upgrading municipal treatment works. The focus again was on end-of-pipe controls from point sources of pollution. Pollution that came from farmer's fields, construction sites, and runoff from city streets and parking lots—the so-called nonpoint sources—were largely untouched by the new regulations. Since 1972, some $20 billion has spent annually to satisfy the requirements of federal programs.

In his 1993 survey of studies reporting the effects of the federal water pollution control program, Robert Nelson reported on water quality conditions in 1972, the year when the first major Clean Water Act was passed (Nelson 1993, 8-9). Citing Conservation Foundation data, Nelson tells us that 64 percent of the stream miles and 84 percent of lakes and reservoirs were meeting the 1972 water quality fishable and swimmable goal when the statute was passed. Of course, many rivers are cleaner today than in 1972, and water quality generally has not deteriorated. A recent report by the Pacific Research Institute for Public Policy provides an excellent summary of many gains in water quality (Hayward et al. 1996). For example, considerable strides have been made in cleaning the waters of the Great Lakes, which show significantly lower levels of phosphorous, PCBs, DDT, and lead. And most of us can point to a river in our own regions that is cleaner today than in 1972. But we should expect no less when $20 billion or so is spent each year and with more than $60 billion transferred to local sewage treatment plants from federal taxpayers for the purpose of cleaning up the discharge.

Making end-point comparison is surely helpful and important when assessing the state of our biological envelope, but finding improvement does not necessarily say that federal statutes cause it all. Production of goods, the mix of production, and the kinds of inputs used have changed substantially over the last two decades. The United States is no longer a smokestack economy. While manufacturing and agriculture continue to be major components of the economy, service is now the dominant sector. At the same time, the public sector—all levels of government—has not done as well as the private sector.

In 1989, the Council on Environmental Quality reported on the record for water pollution reductions for various U.S. sectors (U.S. Council on Environmental Quality 1989, 32-35). The report indicated that industrial discharge had been reduced by 71 percent. More than 80 percent of all industrial plants were in compliance with the law. BOD levels, a common measure of water pollution, were down significantly for industry, with municipal treatment works contributing 73.2 percent of the problem nationwide, and agriculture producing 21.6 percent. For suspended particulates, municipal waste accounted for 61.5 percent; industrial waste, 26.6 percent; and agriculture, 13.3 percent. The pollution problem has become primarily a government problem.

The 1970 Clean Air Act took an approach much like that of the Clean Water Act. It too required states to develop implementation plans that included a permitting program for all major emission sources, with different standards and specified technologies for old and new sources and for regions that had more or less deteriorated air quality. With the passage of the statute, common-law remedies became secondary to federal rules for resolving interstate air quality problems.

In his 1990 assessment of the record for air pollution, Resources for the Future president Paul Portney gave a comparison of gains in air quality prior to the formation of EPA in 1970 and the record of accomplishments since then. Portney states:

> If air quality had been deteriorating prior to 1970 but then began to improve, some contribution on the part of the amendments passed that year might be suggested. While air quality data extending back into the 1960s are less reliable than today's, they do tell an interesting story. According to data from the EPA, average ambient total suspended particulate levels fell about 22 percent between 1960 and 1970. During the period 1966 to 1971 annual average ambient SO2 concentrations fell by an even larger 50 percent. While we must be leery of trends based on such a small number of sites, these data are important because they suggest that air quality was improving as fast or faster before the Clean Air Act as it has since that time. . . . [T]his conclusion should give us pause in reflecting on the likely effects of the Clean Air Act. (Portney 1990, 50-51)

Again, there is little doubt that some major dimensions of air quality have improved since 1970. This is especially true for auto tailpipe emissions, which are now 90 percent less than they were from 1970 vintage cars, and for SO_2, which has been largely reduced from coal-fired boilers and utilities. But

Portney's cautious assessment suggests that we should consider what might have happened had state and regional control and common law been relied on more fully to deal with the problem.

Any frustration observed in federal efforts taken to improve air and water quality is nothing when compared to the record on hazardous waste cleanup—the Superfund program. In some cases, the problem site has an owner; in others, the problem relates to abandoned sites, which simply need to be cleaned. With viable owners, the problem involves a well-identified pollution source and a relatively small number of aggrieved parties. These features suggest hazardous waste problems would head to a common-law court, provided evidence of harm could be demonstrated. But where there are damages and no one to sue, the community involved is left to determine if it makes sense to clean away the waste at public expense.

Discussion of Superfund is almost always accompanied with distressing stories about Love Canal, a hazardous waste site near Niagara Falls, N.Y., that triggered political demand for a federal cleanup program (Ives 1996). To some, the Love Canal debacle is compelling evidence that common law fails to meet the environmental protection challenge. A review of the history of the event leaves a decidedly different impression.

Love Canal came into being in the late 1890s when William T. Love attempted to build a direct current electricity supply for a planned city (Deegan 1987, 329). The canal was built to supply water to hydroelectric generators. Love's venture failed; his land and the canal were purchased by Hooker Electrochemical Company, later named Hooker Chemicals and Plastics Company. Hooker's chemical production generated large amounts of waste. In 1942, the firm began using Love Canal for disposing of waste and later acquired ownership of part of Love Canal and used a dammed and sealed part of it for storing waste products. By 1952, the firm had dumped some 21,000 tons of waste in the canal (Clark and Hager 1980, 56).

In 1946, the Niagara Falls Board of Education approached Hooker Chemical, expressing an interest in purchasing the Love Canal parcel for the purpose of building an elementary school. Hooker refused to cooperate with the Board. In 1952, the Board approached Hooker again seeking to purchase the parcel and indicating that condemnation proceedings would be used if Hooker refused to sell voluntarily. Hooker documented the waste stored in the canal and sold the parcel to the city for one dollar. The deed of transfer indemnified Hooker for all potential future liabilities and claims. The transfer also called for continued testing of the chemical waste site. With the passage of time, the Board of Education built a grammar school in the vicinity of the canal and sold the unused land to a residential developer. Documentation of the chemical wastes disappeared in the transaction.

Twenty-four years after Hooker had sold the land and following heavy highway construction and an unusually wet winter, residents of the Love Canal community began to experience problems with soil upheavals, chemical burns and contaminated groundwater. Homes were invaded by chemical wastes; grass and other vegetation died. Panic swept the residential community. In 1978, Love Canal was declared a national disaster area, the elementary school was closed, 800 families were evacuated, and Hooker Chemical Company was targeted as the villain.

Hooker Chemical has since been acquired by Occidental Chemical Company, but the legal liability has followed. Facing lawsuits from all directions, Occidental has paid $20 million to settle major suits. At trial, the firm was found not guilty of deliberate wrongdoing. The firm was not judged to be liable for the harm suffered by the community; it was penalized and admonished for not having warned the community as construction expanded and the risk of harm increased. The Board of Education faced no suits and bore no cost for failing to pass on the restrictive covenants on land use when the Board sold the land. Hooker appears to have behaved responsibly in first resisting the sale of the land and later, when forced to sell, including risk information in the deed of transfer. Its main failure was, years later, not protesting vigorously when things were done to the property that the school board had promised would not be done.

Following in the wake of Love Canal, Congress debated and passed major legislation that formed Superfund. In the debate, the Hooker episode was mentioned as justification for a federal program for preventing future Love Canals. By implication, common law and community action cannot be relied on for protecting environmental rights and assets. But the Love Canal episode suggests that something other than common law and community action stand at fault. Instead, the problem seems to relate to the immunity from suit enjoyed by school boards and other public entities. Common law and any other institutional safeguards break down when an organization or person is able to act irresponsibly without penalty. In addition, it might be agreed that chemical companies are far more attractive political targets than school boards when matters of pollution are at stake. Love Canal was an episode that should not have happened. It involved a failure on the part of a seller (the school board) to provide material information it possessed (from Hooker) to various buyers. The legal breakdown then involved failure of an unwitting and damaged party to sue the seller. Instead, the legal machinery of the federal government brought action against the first seller, who had taken normal precautions to inform a buyer of risks. Common-law logic still comes through, in spite of these unusual circumstances: the failure of an informed observer to give warning of foreseeable harm to an unsuspecting person. Common sense and rules of just conduct call for a warning.

If the Love Canal episode can be called a mistake, as opposed to being evidence of systematic failure of common law, is it possible that the remedy—Superfund—is also a mistake? Since the 1980 Superfund program was initiated, the EPA has investigated 38,000 potential sites to determine whether or not they should be cleaned (Probst et al. 1995). More than 3,500 emergency actions have taken to deal with high risk sites; and 1,320 sites have entered the full Superfund program for complete cleanup. At present, around 100 sites have been cleaned. On average, twelve years are required to jump the bureaucratic hurdles, handle the litigation, and proceed with cleaning away hazardous wastes. Congressional Budget Office estimates of the cost of cleaning all current and future Superfund sites runs from $106 billion to $460 billion, with a healthy portion of the cost going to pay attorney fees generated from litigation to settle who pays the cost (Probst et al. 1995, 18).

Water quality protection is one of the principal reasons for having the Superfund program. Abandoned and other hazardous waste dumps pose a risk to ground- and surface-water contamination. Toxic and other wastes that leach into sources of drinking water can be dangerous to human health, if the concentration of contaminants and degree of human exposure is sufficiently high. However, the Superfund program is fraught with many private-sector sites that pose little risk to human populations, but the statute requires that a clean site generates runoff that meets the nation's drinking water standard. In other words, the standard to be met is extraordinarily high. While meeting the standard cannot be avoided, paying the cost of cleanup can be. The statute looks first for payment from those parties that had anything meaningful to do with the formation of the site, even to those who did no more than transport a truck load of drums for someone else. The statute's liability rule calls for strict joint and several liability. Any private party that contributed anything to a site can be required to pay the full cost of cleanup. Then, having been required to pay, that party can sue all others for cost recovery. Superfund is a Mecca for law suits but a failed attempt to clean up waste sites.

In 1987 the EPA examined each of thirty-one regulatory programs and compared the risks of each to the regulatory effort required by the statutes that mandate the programs (U.S. Environmental Protection Agency 1987). The thirty-one regulatory areas were evaluated for four types of risk: Cancer risk, noncancer health risks, ecological effects, and welfare effects. After considerable work was done by seventy-five EPA staff members, the report concluded that "the rankings of risk . . . do not correspond closely with EPA's statutory authorities" and "do not correspond well with EPA's current program priorities" (U.S. Environmental Protection Agency 1987, xix).

Listed among environmental programs that posed high risk but received low effort and protection were indoor radon, indoor air pollution, nonpoint source pollution, and accidental releases of toxic materials. In EPA's judgment, more effort should be exerted to address these problem areas. In contrast, the report listed Superfund, municipal nonhazardous waste site cleanup, and cradle-to-grave regulation of toxic chemicals as high budget items that deal with low risks.

Research findings in 1991 showed that as many as 20,000 annual lung cancer deaths were associated with radon gas in homes. By comparison, 500 cancer deaths at most are predicted to be associated with all the nation's hazardous waste sites (Main 1991, 95-101). The federal government was then spending $100 million annually on radon control and some $6.1 billion annually to clean up hazardous waste sites.

Examination of the public sector side of the hazardous waste problem reveals a more troublesome picture. Some of the riskiest problems are found on closed military bases, at nuclear-processing facilities, and on other federal facilities that operated for many years with considerable abandon. After all, the federal government was the environmental policeman.

The problem's magnitude is staggering. For example, the Department of Energy has 10,000 potentially contaminated sites, the Department of Defense more than 21,000; the Department of the Interior some 26,000; and the U.S. Department of Agriculture some 3,000 sites (Council on Environmental Quality and Office of Management and Budget 1995, 17). In some cases, especially for the Department of Energy, the cleanup effort is in its infancy, and efforts in many cases are fraught with documented waste and inefficiencies. In October 1995 a federal interagency report indicated that as much as $389 billion would be needed over the next seventy-five years to address the problems of hazardous and radioactive waste sites located on federal property (Council on Environmental Quality and Office of Management and Budget 1995, 32).

Common law cannot discipline and punish the federal government. Sovereign immunity provides a shield from such actions. How might common law deal with Superfund sites located on private land and deal with the many other problems now addressed by EPA? The EPA's own risk assessment suggests that private parties seeking common-law remedies for many problems would get no further than the judge's chamber. When scientific evidence fails to identify harm to people, to the ecological system or to welfare, there is no basis for a common law action. However, in cases where evidence of harm or potential harm is compelling, private parties could and do call on common law for protection. We will revisit this topic in chapter 6.

Subsequent amendments to the major statutes have left the bright lines of command-and-control intact and common-law remedies somewhere off in the distance; common law technically survived for intrastate controversies. In a market sense, common law and statute law were placed in competition for resolving environmental quality issues within the states. We find statute law prevailing but with common-law pleadings being filed along with the more popular, and generally simpler, statute-based complaints. The resulting blending of law can lead to strange interpretations of common-law rules.

Final Thoughts

This chapter began with the question, Why are property rights-based approaches not sweeping the nation? The answer to the question required an exploration of theories of regulation and use of a theory that explains how taking a systems approach can be far more attractive to some important special interest groups than using the market process. As the chapter unfolded, we then turned to the theory of Bootleggers and Baptists and used it to explain how environmental and other public interest groups sometimes seem to assist opposing interest groups. On its surface, command-and-control regulation seems always to be hard on industry, but on closer examination we find differential effects that can reward some in an industry while imposing heavy penalties on others. No industry would start a new regulatory movement hoping to shoulder a new burden. But once regulation is in the works, it is logical to expect that some forms of regulation are more attractive than others.

The chapter ends by applying common-law thinking to endangered species and hazardous waste, which are just two of the major problems addressed by statute law. Common-law logic causes us to reexamine the issue; to focus on outcomes, not inputs to the problem; and to ask a fundamental question: What is the real purpose of the rule being imposed?

As noted before, common law, which focuses on problems where they lie, is heavy with realism. Real people incurring real harm are protected by the law. Those who impose unwanted costs on other rightholders are penalized. Common-law remedies apply only to the parties to a controversy, but common-law precedents do become embodied in future court decisions.

While common-law protection of environmental rights surely has its limits, it is clear that common-law thinking can assist in the design of remedies for problems that may be too complex and diffuse for common law, strictly speaking, to solve. The next chapter provides considerable detail on how common law has worked to provide environmental protection, and where the common process seems to be headed.

Notes

1. The story here parallels actual historic events. States did regulate meat products, but when the national producers became entangled in a multitude of state regulations, they sought federal regulation. Federal regulation did two things for them: (1) it eliminated the crazy pattern of state regulation, and (2) it raised barriers for the importation of foreign meat products. The gain from the latter was more than enough to offset the cost of meeting uniform federal regulation (Weiss 1964, 107-120).

2. It should be noted that Superfund is fed by taxes placed on feedstocks and crude oil, which are, of course, inputs that may find their way into the hazardous waste stream. Obviously, a tax placed directly on hazardous waste would be far more effective in reducing waste. (Yandle 1989, 3-10; Yandle 1989, 751-764).

References

Ackerman, Bruce A., and William T. Hassler. 1981. *Clean Coal/Dirty Air.* New Haven: Yale University Press.

Adler, Jonathan H. 1996. Rent Seeking behind the Green Curtain. *Regulation* (Fall): 26-34.

Buchanan, James M., and Gordon Tullock. 1975. Polluters' "Profit" and Political Response. *American Economic Review* 65: 139-47.

Clark, Mark, and Hager, Mary. 1980. Fleeing the Love Canal. *Newsweek* (June 2): 56.

Council on Environmental Quality and Office of Management and Budget. 1995. *Improving Federal Facilities Cleanup.* Report of the Federal Facilities Policy Group. Washington, D.C.: (October).

Dalton, Brett A., David Riggs, and Bruce Yandle. 1996. The Political Production of Superfund, *Eastern Economic Journal* (Winter): 75-87.

Deegan, John Jr. 1987. Looking Back at Love Canal. *Environmental Scientific Technology* (November): 329.

Ensminger, Jean. 1996. Culture and Property Rights. In *Rights to Nature,* edited by Susan S. Hanna, Carl Folke, and Karl-Goran Maler. Washington, D.C.: Island Press.

Greve, Michael S. 1996. *The Demise of Environmentalism in American Law.* Washington, D.C.: American Enterprise Institute Press.

Hayward, Steven, Job Nelson, and Sam Thernstrom. 1996. *The Index of Leading Environmental Indicators.* San Francisco: Pacific Research Institute for Public Policy.

Ives, Angela. 1996. *Love Canal: An Environmental Economics Analysis.* Clemson: Center for Policy Studies (December).

Main, Jeremy. 1991. The Big Cleanup Gets It Wrong. *Fortune* (May 20): 95-101.

Maloney, Michael T., and Robert E. McCormick. 1982. A Positive Theory of Environmental Quality Regulation. *Journal of Law and Economics* 25: 99-124.

McNeil, Douglas W., Andrew W. Foshee, and Clark R. Burbee. 1988. Superfund Taxes and Expenditures: Regional Redistribution. *Review of Regional Studies* (Winter): 4-9.

Nelson, Robert H. 1993. How Much Is Enough? In *Taking the Environment Seriously,* edited by Roger E. Meiners and Bruce Yandle. Lanham, Md.: Rowman & Littlefield Publishers.

The New York Times. 1993. Fear of Limits on Logging Pushes Lumber to a High. (February 10): C15.

Pashigian, Peter B. 1985. Environmental Regulation: Whose Interests Are Being Protected? *Economic Inquiry* 23: 551-84.

Peltzman, Sam. 1976. Toward a More General Theory of Regulation. *Journal of Law and Economics* (August): 211-40.

Portney, Paul R. 1990. Air Pollution Policy. In *Public Policies for Environmental Protection,* edited by Paul R. Portney. Washington, D.C.: Resources for the Future.

Posner, Richard A. 1974. Theories of Economic Regulation. *Bell Journal* (Autumn): 335-58.

Probst, Katherine N., Don Fullerton, Robert E. Litan, and Paul R. Portney. 1995. *Footing the Bill for Superfund Cleanup.* Washington, D.C.: The Brookings Institute.

Stigler, George J. 1971. The Economic Theory of Regulation. *Bell Journal* (Spring): 3-21.

Tibbetts, John. 1995. An Endangered Species of Law. *Planning* (September): 16-20.

USA Today. 1993. Clinton Proposed Remedy. (July 2-5): 1A-2A, 3B.

U.S. Council on Environmental Quality. 1989. *Environmental Trends* Washington, D.C.: Government Printing Office.

U.S. Environmental Protection Agency. 1987. Vol. 1, *Overview.* Washington, D.C.: U.S. EPA (February).

The Wall Street Journal. 1992. Owls, of All Things, Help Weyerhaeuser Cash in on Timber. (June 24): 1-A.

Weiss, Roger W. 1964. The Case for Federal Meat Inspection Examined. *Journal of Law and Economics* (October): 107-120.

Welch, Lee Ann. 1995. Property Rights Conflicts Under the Endangered Species Act: Protection of the Red-Cockaded Woodpecker. In *Land Rights: The 1990s Property Rights Rebellion,* edited by Bruce Yandle. Lanham, Md.: Rowman & Littlefield Publishers.

Yandle, Bruce. 1983. Bootleggers and Baptists: The Education of a Regulatory Economist. *Regulation* (May/June): 12-16.

———. 1984. Sulfur Dioxide: State Versus Federal Control. *Journal of Energy and Development* (Autumn): 63-69.

———. 1989. Bootleggers and Baptists in the Market for Regulation. In *The Political Economy of Regulation,* edited by Jason F. Shogren. Norwell: Kluwer Publishers.

———. 1989. *The Political Limits of Environmental Regulation.* Westport: Quorum Books.

———. 1989. Can Superfund's Fatal Flaws Be Fixed? *National Environmental Enforcement Journal* (October): 3-10.

———. 1989. Taxation, Political Action, and Superfund. *Cato Journal* (Winter): 751-764.

————. 1993. Is Free Trade an Enemy of Environmental Quality? In *NAFTA and the Environment,* edited by Terry L. Anderson. San Francisco: Pacific Research Institute for Public Policy.

————. 1993. Bootleggers and Baptists—Environmentalists and Protectionists: Old Reasons for New Coalitions. In *NAFTA and the Environment,* edited by Terry L. Anderson. San Francisco: Pacific Research Institute for Public Policy.

Yandle, Bruce, and Elizabeth Young. 1986. Regulating the Function, Not the Industry. *Public Choice* 51: 59-69.

Chapter 4

Common-Law Protection
of Environmental Rights

My interest in common law developed more than ten years ago from an association with two close colleagues. Both Bob Staaf and Roger Meiners were trained in economics and law. While they had completed their law degrees after receiving Ph.D.s in economics, I had moved from an M.B.A. degree to the Ph.D. in economics. Until Bob and Roger became my colleagues, I knew nothing about common-law rules and how the common law worked, and I did not realize that the common law forms the legal foundation in America for all market transactions. I did not recognize that common law is the legal counterpart to free markets; nor did I appreciate the distinction between politics and law.

Long discussions with Bob and Roger led me to embark on a research project that carried me back to tenth-century England and the roots of common law (Yandle 1991, 225-41; 1993, 263-85). After several years of reading and writing on the topic, I rediscovered what many legal historians already knew: Our system of property rights, contracts, claims for damage, and rights all stem from the "law of the land," which is the honored name for the old common law. Statutes and ordinances passed by politicians are not held to be a part of the "law of the land," even though we may call them by that name.

My education in common law was assisted by many others as I attended conferences and seminars with legal scholars, philosophers, and economists who, like me, were excited about the topic. My main interest in all this concerned the markets that might emerge for environmental rights. Finally, I realized that markets for environmental rights had existed for centuries—they were part of the ordinary world of common law. They had evolved naturally over many years with the recognition and enforcement of privately held property rights, which include what we now label rights to environmental quality. Like many others, I was relatively well-informed about statutes and regulation, but ignorant about common law.

What is the source of common law? Answering the question requires us to go beyond the technology of law, which involves lawyers, courtrooms, judges and their decisions. Finding the source takes us to ordinary people who instinctively seek to protect themselves and their families from harm and, beyond that, to build communities that have a sense of fairness and just conduct. This natural law interpretation suggests that all real law begins in the minds and hearts of ordinary men and women who have a sense of right and wrong that is fundamentally based on survival instincts. Common law evolves from a social setting where judges seek to understand this sense of fairness and then base their decisions on the norms of the community. Judges are said to discover the law by observing custom, tradition, and common-sense approaches to problems. Decisions that reflect a community's values and norms are accepted and enforced by the community. Those that do not are rejected.

Justice Oliver Wendell Holmes saw the common law as ever evolving, always adjusting to the reason of the times, assuming new content, and taking on new forms, all in a seemingly unconscious process (1881, 32). Expanding on this point, Justice Holmes said, "The truth is, that the law is always approaching, and never reaching consistency. It is forever adopting new principles from life at one end, and it always retains old ones from history at the other, which have not yet been absorbed or sloughed off. It will become entirely consistent only when it ceases to grow" (Holmes 1881, 32). Holmes saw the common law through the lens of evolution, constantly adjusting and adapting to a changing environment.

The common-law theory that applies to pollution is a part of the law of property and torts, a body of law that protects life and property from harm caused by others. Based on rights, the common law emerges in rulings announced by judges on a case-by-case basis. The law is formed from specific controversies, claims for actual damage, and requests for injunctions against the threat of damage.

The rules of tort law that relate to the environment are found in a component of common law that deals with nuisance and trespass. The latter property right violation is associated with uninvited physical invasion of property, while the former relates to harms, like odors or contamination of a stream, that do not reflect a physical crossing of a property boundary.[1] Common-law rules are based on an initial endowment of environmental rights to property owners and communities of people. These are negative rights. The rightholder has the right not to have pollution damage his property, person, or community.

The 1611 *William Aldred's Case* (77 Eng. Rep. 816 [1611]), involving a homeowner who lived downwind from a hog farm, illustrates the underlying logic. In the case, the defendant gave a benefit/cost argument, saying that his hog farm provided food, a socially valuable commodity, and that odor went with the operation. He suggested that people who enjoyed the farm product should not be so sensitive about odors. The court rejected the argument and gave a ruling that influences common-law rights to this day. Translated from the Latin, the ruling said, "One should use his property in such a manner as not to injure that of another" (Id. at 817). In other words, one whose activities impose damages on the property of another is strictly liable for the harm that is done. A comparison of benefits and costs is irrelevant. If rights are not protected by the rule of law, then rights have no meaning.

The remainder of this chapter, which explains more about common law and how it works, is based in part on work by Roger Meiners that was first reported in our book, *Taking the Environment Seriously* (Meiners and Yandle 1993, 73-102; Meiners 1995, 269-94). The chapter tells the common-law story by discussing a series of cases that illustrate how common law works to protect the environment. Reactions to the chapter generally follow one of two paths. Some will say the stories are interesting but not relevant to today's world. They will raise problems like air pollution from automobiles that, because of the immense number of parties, do not lend themselves readily to common-law remedies, or speak of unsettled issues like global warming and protection of the ozone layer where property rights have never been defined. The fact that common law does not work for some problems is enough to convince some to discard it for all problems. They seek one approach for all problems.

Others will be surprised that common law worked rather well when allowed to, and they may be even more surprised to learn that a growing number of legal scholars are calling for a reincarnation of common law as a basis for environmental protection. In contrast to the first group, which sees common law as a flawed instrument for protecting the environment, those observing its strengths suggest that common law should be reinvigorated and applied across a large range of environmental problems, but not used for every problem. The economic way of thinking suggests we should consider all the tools in our toolbox when addressing a problem, matching specific tools to specific features of the problem. I believe the common law offers a powerful set of incentives that encourage those who care the most, property owners, to seek low-cost remedies for a large array of environmental problems. The case stories in this chapter provide part of the rationale for my belief.

The chapter proceeds as follows: The next section provides a brief sketch of rights in general and how property rights, long protected by common law, were placed off-limits when the several states formed the union. After tracing the development of property rights in a constitutional context, the section then discusses common law and the legal framework used for centuries to protect individual rights. Section three forms the major element of the chapter. That section presents capsule summaries of a series of pre-1970 common-law cases for the purpose of illustrating how common-law rules dealt with pollution. A series of recent cases that illustrate a significant reemergence of common law are described toward the end of the third section. All along, the discussion focuses on property rights and the interplay between approaches that might be termed systems or Pigovian and those that would be labeled process or Coasean. Some final thoughts conclude the chapter.

What Are Environmental Rights and How Do They Evolve?

The English Roots and Natural Law

The English law that gave us *William Aldred's Case* is the original basis of American law. When the nation was founded, much English law, especially the common law, and the rights and duties it provides for all citizens, had already been incorporated into the constitutions of the states that formed the union. Thus, common law made a seamless transition and continued to operate in the individual states, functioning under the federal Constitution. It is a modern myth that our rights were created by the Constitution (the "supreme law of the land"); the writers of the Constitution presumed *inalienable rights* that citizens hold simply by virtue of being free persons in a free nation. As one great British legal scholar expressed over a century ago, "personal freedom does not really depend upon or originate in any general proposition contained in any written document" (Dicey 1982, 123).

The Constitution created the basic framework of government, expressly limited the powers of government, and provided safeguards against invasions of certain rights. But the Constitution did not grant us all the rights we have as citizens. We are presumed to have a host of individual rights; this concept is often called *natural law*. Some natural law is expressed through the common law; but the elements of natural law were simply presumed to be understood by the judiciary. "Thus the Framers [of the Constitution] believed that liberty and personal security are the ultimate purposes of society; they favored limited government and dispersal of power, feared the tyranny of political majorities, and . . . subscribed to the belief that individuals have fundamental and inalienable rights with which government may not interfere" (Siegan 1971, 12).

Most governments in the history of the world grant some rights to their citizens, while the state is presumed to be the source of all law. The United States is one of the few governments created by a free people, long accustomed to the rule of law, who understood that they possess inalienable rights. One of those inalienable rights had to do with property, which could not be taken or damaged without compensation. And what we now call environmental rights held by landowners was one of the property rights.

Nuisance As a Common-Law Cause of Action

How did common law work to protect ordinary people from unwanted pollution? At common law, rightholders to land have the right to enjoy the benefits of land ownership or usage and to exclude from their land unwanted and unreasonable invasions by people or pollution. The law of trespass and nuisance provides causes of action, and common-law courts provide remedies that include injunctions and damages. The notion that property right-holders can call the sheriff to chase unwanted people from their land is hardly controversial, since the common-law basis for doing so is still more or less intact. However, the idea that landholders could and did protect their property from pollution is not widely recognized; many people believe that we would all succumb to pollution were it not for federal regulation and EPA protection.

Long before EPA existed, the *nuisance* cause of action provided the basis of common-law environmental protection. For example, people owning land along rivers had the right to beneficial use of the water that passed their property. If an upstream user discharged damaging waste into the stream without obtaining permission from the downstream owner, to protect their riparian rights, the downstream party had a cause of action against the polluter based on the tort of nuisance. When convinced by evidence that the polluter had damaged the party downstream, the court moved against the polluter. The offending party was generally ordered to cease polluting and to pay damages.

While sometimes difficult to apply, since scientific evidence of harm is required, the concept of nuisance is generally commonsensical. As Justice Sutherland said, "Nuisance may be merely a right thing in a wrong place like a pig in the parlor instead of the barnyard" (*Village,* 1926). But as Dennis Coyle reminds us, we must know a bit more about the pig and the parlor: "If I keep my own pig in my parlor, it is not a nuisance. If my pig prefers *your* parlor, but you do *not* prefer my pig in your parlor, then it is a nuisance" (Coyle 1993, 833). Causes of action for nuisance claims can be either public or private, but nuisances may be combined public and private nuisances.[2] Peter Davis draws on Prosser's 1955 statement of torts and defines a private nuisance this way:

> An unreasonable interference with the interest in the use and enjoyment of land. . . . It is distinguished from trespass in that the interference is with use or enjoyment, rather than with the interest in exclusive possession. (1971, 740)

A *public nuisance* is an action that causes inconvenience or damage to the public health or public order, or an act which constitutes an obstruction of public rights (*Stoughton* 1955; *Enchave* 1948). For example, a firm that discharges emissions that damage the health of citizens in a city could be charged with public nuisance. Normally, only public officers (attorneys general or district attorneys) have standing to sue to abate public nuisances. However, individuals who show they suffer harm distinctly different from that suffered by the general public may also be granted standing to sue to abate a public nuisance.

Public nuisances are not limited to protecting interests in land. Claims of nuisance may arise from conducting certain businesses. For example, in *Ballenger v. City of Grand Saline*[3] the court of appeals heard a suit in which residents living near a "chicken house" complained of offensive odors. The city sought a permanent injunction to abate the operation of a wholesale chicken business, alleging various nuisances, including noise and odor.[4] The court of appeals upheld the lower court's decision that the operation was "in fact and in law" a public nuisance, and that the city was entitled to permanently abate the activity.

In cases such as *Ballenger*, the defendant could argue that the complaining party had "come to the nuisance" and could sometimes prevail. That is, common-law rules provide safeguards against persons buying land next to a chicken house at bargain basement prices and then suing to shut down the chicken house in the hopes of obtaining a windfall.

Just as public nuisance provides a basis for protecting the general rights held by a community of people, private nuisance applies to harmful actions that damage one or a small number of land holders. *Private nuisance* is defined as a *substantial and unreasonable interference* with the use and enjoyment of an interest in land (*Ryan*; *Hederman* 1955). The interference may be intentional or careless. As applied to pollution, the typical case involves a defendant operating in a way that is offensive or harmful to the plaintiffs. The legal issue posed in such cases is whether the "act" of the defendant is an intrusion that is "sufficiently noxious" to give rise to a finding of nuisance.

While private nuisance claims have been traditionally limited to protecting the interest to land, modern courts have been more generous, holding that the action protects a wide range of comforts normally associated with occupancy of land. Case law also allows for consequential damages to the "possessor of land interest" to allow recovery for injuries to his own health (*Vann* 1936) and for loss of services of family members (*U.S. Smelting Co.* 1911; *Towaliga Falls Power Co.* 1909).

Environmental statutes have displaced some of the protections previously afforded by common-law rules. Actions that might in the past have been considered nuisances may be permitted under various environmental regulations. For example, pollution that crosses from one state to another is generally controlled by statute and is not actionable at common law. In a specific instance of this transition in legal regimes, acid mine drainage that damaged marine life was held immune from a public nuisance claim because the discharges were administratively sanctioned under state law.[5]

The ability of the property holder to enforce common-law rights forms a crucial link to all market transactions, including those related to the environment. When two parties bargain over the use of land, the resulting terms of their agreement always relate to a transfer of rights. If the rights are not enforced, transfer cannot obtain. When enforcement is lax, people will not transact. The rights to land, houses, automobiles, clothing, food, and practically everything else in the world are transferable. So are environmental rights. At common law, a person desiring to make an alternative use of the downstream parties rights may lease or purchase them. Benefits and costs matter in this setting. The party that assigns the higher benefit to environmental use can obtain the rights from one who assigns low value. Market transactions are accommodated and the resulting contracts are enforced by common law. The Coase solution discussed in chapter 2 can loom large in addressing pollution problems through the market process.

The Shift from Law to Balancing Benefits and Costs

Unfortunately for fans of a process regime that relies on market transactions, the common law is not as simple and straightforward as *Aldred's Case* might suggest. A lot has happened since 1611. Over part of the span of history, common-law judges tended to enforce the property rule—holders of environmental rights could not be forced to accept unwanted pollution. However, along the way, some common-law judges began to weigh the utility of the damaging party's activity against the harm imposed; in some cases, the defendant prevailed. In other controversies, courts used a negligence standards, deciding that though a nuisance might have been generated, the event was clearly an accident that occurred after all reasonable precautions had been exercised. No damages were due. In still another category of exceptions to strict enforcement of rights and liability, some courts shielded defendants from private nuisance actions when the defendant's action was authorized by statute or other government action and when the harmful activity provided valuable public benefits.[6] The observed shift from strict enforcement of rights to public interest considerations clearly put judges in the position of making policy decisions, a role that is more logically assigned to elected politicians who answer to the public. In that sense, the rule of politics replaced the rule of law. In terms developed earlier, property rights were made less certain and the ideas of Pigou became mixed with those of Coase.

We see this in the culmination of a series of nineteenth-century Pennsylvania actions involving the pollution of a stream by coal. The actions began with the 1880 case of *Sanderson v. Pennsylvania Coal Co.* (94 Pa. 302). In the final round of appeal, ruling for the coal company, the court said:

We are of the opinion that mere private personal inconveniences, arising in this way and under such circumstances, must yield to the necessities of a great public industry, which although in the hands of a private corporation, subserves a great public interest. To encourage development of the great natural resources of a country, trifling inconveniences to particular persons must sometimes give way to the necessities of a great community. (113 Pa at 149, 6A. at 459)

If environmental rights are viewed as "trifling inconveniences," then there is little hope for protection through common-law courts or elsewhere. But this concern may not be as large as first appears. Common-law courts rule on controversies before the court; they do not write regulations that affect an entire country. And while one state court may move away from protection of individual environmental rights, others can be solidly enforcing those rights.

Such was the case at the time of the *Pennsylvania Coal* case. Pennsylvania courts were balancing benefits and costs, considering public interest arguments, and deciding against small property owners. At the time, the Pennsylvania approach was described as the norm in the *Restatement of Torts (1934-1939)*. However, scholars reviewing the period find that many jurisdictions were sticking to strict enforcement of property rights. The fact that different theories can be applied to similar facts may seem unsettling at first, but further consideration leads to a more optimistic view of common-law flexibility.

Each state has its own body of common law and its own common-law courts. If judges in one court make brashly innovative rulings, there is no binding reason for other courts to follow suit. On the other hand, experimentation by one court may lead to the discovery of lower-cost ways for protecting environmental rights. If all common-law courts were required to rule in identical fashion, common law would be no different from federal statutes that impose uniform standards on all economic activity. New approaches would be discovered less frequently.

The important evolutionary character of common law is seen clearly in the 1900 New York case of *Strobel v. Kerr Salt Co.* (164 N.Y. 303, 58 N.E. 142), which made reference to *Pennsylvania Coal*. *Strobel* involved pollution from a salt operation that imposed damages on downstream farmers and mill operators. The lower court referred to *Pennsylvania Coal* and denied damages. In other words, the external costs imposed on property owners were irrelevant when considered in light of the value of industrial development. On appeal, the higher court sided with the plaintiffs, indicating that the public interest arguments about employment accepted by Pennsylvania courts had never been adopted as common-law rules in New York. The higher court awarded damages to the plaintiffs. Environmental rights were protected.

During the same period, we find strict protection of environmental rights in Wisconsin, which illustrates one of the virtues of having a laboratory of courts hearing environmental cases. In *Middlestadt v. Waupaca Starch & Potato Co.* (92 Wis.1; 4, 66 N.W. 713, 714 [1896], cited in Davis, 1971, 743), the court heard a private nuisance case involving damages received by an owner of riparian land. The court ruled against the factory in favor of the landowner:

[A] riparian owner of property is entitled to have the water of a stream flow to and through or by his land in its natural purity and . . . anything done which so pollutes such water as to impair its value for the purposes for which it is ordinarily used by persons so circumstanced, causing offensive odors to arise therefrom and injuriously affecting the beneficial enjoyment of adjoining property, may be restrained at the suit of the injured party.

When the federal government assumed ownership of U.S. environmental quality in the 1970s, converting important aspects of the environment to public property, the old common-law regime began to play second fiddle to statute law; its usefulness at times seemed almost forgotten. Statute law always takes precedence over informal, judge-made law unless the statute in question specifically "saves" the right of individuals to bring common-law suits. With the passage of each major environmental statute, large areas of common law were pushed to one side, even though saving clauses were often included in the statutes. Today, common-law remedies are often available, but are used less frequently as a principal vehicle for obtaining relief from environmental damages. A person bothered by pollution more often than not seeks a regulatory remedy provided by statute. Proof of statutory violations can be much simpler than proof of damages at common law. A polluter that dumps more pollution than its permit allows has automatically violated the law. Under common law, it must be shown that the pollution causes damages. Outside a few common law scholars, few people seem to know that they have, or once had, environmental rights.

How Common Law Works

The story to be told in the rest of this chapter is how the common law worked to provide environmental protection before the advent of federal regulatory control that largely replaced common-law protection for the environment, and then how common law has reemerged. The common law of environmental protection occurred in the application of various parts of the common law to violations of personal rights. This happened before modern environmental law was invented, so we look to the record of common-law cases that occurred over the years. We now call this environmental protection, but at the time, most of these thousands of cases were simply seen as persons or communities protecting their rights to healthy air, water, and land.

We now move to a review of some common-law cases concerning environmental quality of the natural environment. Cases will be summarized to give a flavor of the general state of the law. The cases come from courts around the country, which indicates that while common-law details varied from state to state, the essence of the rules were much the same in all states.[7]

Water Pollution

In 1987 "The Final Report of the National Groundwater Policy Forum" stated that "the federal government must have primary responsibility for groundwater quality, with state assumption of implementation under federal oversight" (*Groundwater Protection,* 36). That policy recommendation simply summarizes the law since passage of the Clean Water Act in 1972 and other statutes since then. The federal government controls how much of what substances may be dumped into waters and requires the states to enforce its policies.

After decades of centralized control, few can remember that a generation ago the federal government played little role in water quality. Instead, citizens, communities, and states protected their own waters through enforcement of common-law rights and various state and local water quality regulations. The primary common-law rights that were enforced were the right, under tort law, not to suffer a nuisance or a trespass. Most states also enforced riparian law, which provides that all who have property that abuts a waterway or body of water have the right to normal use of the water, but may not substantially reduce the use and enjoyment of the water by other and downstream users. Cases during the past hundred years indicate how the common law enforced water rights (Davis 1971, 738).

In the case of *Carmichael v. City of Texarkana* (94 F. 561, W.D. Ark., 1899), the Carmichaels owned a forty-five-acre farm in Texas, with a stream running through it, that bordered the state of Arkansas. The city of Texarkana, Arkansas, built a sewage system, to which were connected numerous residences and businesses. The sewage collected in the city was deposited "immediately opposite plaintiffs' homestead, about eight feet from the state line, on the Arkansas side." The Carmichaels sued the city in federal court in Arkansas.

The court found that the "cesspool is a great nuisance because it fouls, pollutes, corrupts, contaminates, and poisons the water of [the creek], depositing the foul and offensive matter . . . in the bed of said creek on plaintiffs' land and homestead continuously" thereby "depriving them of the use and benefit of said creek running through their land and premises in a pure and natural state as it was before the creation of said cesspool." The Carmichaels were forced to connect their property to a water system to obtain water for "their family, dairy cattle, and other domestic animals, fowls, and fish." The cost of the water hook-up and use was $700; they claimed that the value of their property was reduced by $5,000; the reduced enjoyment of their homestead over the past two years was valued at $2,000 and the dread of disease was valued at $2,000. Besides the claim for damages, the Carmichaels also sued in equity for a permanent injunction against "said open sewer, cesspool, and nuisance."

Judge Rogers found that the city was operating properly under state law to build a sewer system, but that there was no excuse for fouling the water used by the Carmichaels, regardless of how many city residences benefited from the sewer system. Citing other cases, the court found that the action at law for damages was proper as was the request for an injunction. The court cited 2. Add.Torts, 1085:

> If a riparian proprietor has a right to enjoy a river so far unpolluted that fish can live in it and cattle drink of it and the town council of a neighboring borough, professing to act under statutory powers, pour their house drainage and the filth from water-closets into the river in such quantities that the water becomes corrupt and stinks, and fish will no longer live in it, nor cattle drink it, the court will grant an injunction to prevent the continued defilement of the stream, and to relieve the riparian proprietor from the necessity of bringing a series of actions for the daily annoyance. In deciding the right of a single proprietor to an injunction, the court cannot take into consideration the circumstance that a vast population will suffer by reason of its interference.

Judge Rogers held, "I have failed to find a single well-considered case where the American courts have not granted relief under circumstances such as are alleged in this bill against the city."

The story of a farmer's problem with a paper mill discussed in chapter 1 was based on the facts in *Whalen v. Union Bag & Paper Co.* (208 N.Y. 1, 101 N.E. 805 [1913]), a New York case that illustrates how strictly riparian rights could protect water quality. A new pulp mill, which cost $1 million to build, polluted a creek. A downstream farmer, Whalen, sued the mill for making the water unfit for agricultural use. The trial court awarded damages of $312 per year and granted an injunction against the mill to end harmful pollution within one year. Noting the economic value of the mill and its 500 jobs, the appellate division denied the injunction and reduced the damages to $100. On final appeal, the court of appeals (New York's highest court) reinstated the injunction:

> Although the damage to the plaintiff may be slight as compared with the defendant's expense of abating the condition, that is not a good reason for refusing an injunction. Neither courts of equity nor law can be guided by such a rule, for if followed to its logical conclusion it would deprive the poor litigant of his little property by giving it to those already rich.[8]

To make clear that its decision went beyond a case involving serious destruction of water quality, the court cited an earlier Indiana holding:

> The fact that the appellant has expended a large sum of money in the construction of its plant, and that it conducts its business in a careful manner and without malice, can make no difference in its rights to the stream. Before locating the plant the owners were bound to know that every riparian proprietor is entitled to have the waters of the stream that washes his land come to it without obstruction,

diversion, or corruption, subject only to the reasonable use of the water, by those similarly entitled, for such domestic purposes as are inseparable for and necessary for the free use of their land; they were bound also to know the character of their proposed business, and to take themselves at their own peril whether they should be able to conduct their business upon a stream . . . without injury to their neighbors; and the magnitude of their investment and their freedom from malice furnish no reason why they should escape the consequences of their own folly.[9]

This holding did not mean that there could be no pollution. It meant that there was no excuse for uninvited pollution. To avoid water rights litigation, the mill owner could have contracted for riparian rights from downstream landowners or bought the land along the stream (Davis 1971, 777-80).

In some cases, as mentioned in the introduction, defendants in a nuisance controversy would attempt to deflect the charges by claiming that they exercised reasonable care in operating their facilities, hoping that the court would apply a negligence standard and rule in the defendant's behalf. The case of *Kirwin v. Mexican Petroleum Co.* (267 F. 460, D. R.I., 1920) illustrates this effort by the petroleum company and shows how the court still ruled to protect common-law property rights.

The plaintiff ran a shore resort called "Kirwin's Beach." The defendant

did discharge and suffer to escape from its plants, steamers, barges, etc., into the waters of the Providence River, large quantities of oil and kindred products, which were carried by the winds, currents and tides of the Providence River upon plaintiff's beach, fouling and polluting the beach and waters, and rendering the same wholly unfit for bathing, whereby the value of plaintiff's property and business is destroyed.

Judge Brown upheld the right of the action and stated:

Land located on the shores of the Providence River and Narragansett Bay have a special value, owing to the riparian rights of access to the waters. This right of access is a private right, incidental to ownership of the upland. The general public does not have the right to cross or occupy private lands to gain access to the shores below the high-water mark, at which private ownership terminates.

Kirwin could sue for the value of the lost business, under an action of private nuisance, in compensation for the loss of use of the beach. The public, via the state attorney general or local public prosecutor, would have a right to sue for the public nuisance that was caused by the fouling of the water and of the beach to the high tide line.

The oil company claimed that it could not be held responsible because there was no negligence (carelessness) shown on its part. The judge held that to be irrelevant.

A nuisance may be created by the conduct of a business with all the care and caution which is possible, and with appliances in perfect order and most carefully operated. . . . It is the general rule that negligence is not an element in an action for a nuisance, and need not be alleged. Actions for nuisance, properly speaking, stand irrespective of negligence. (Bigelow 1875, 473)

At common law, a plaintiff must provide scientific evidence of damages in arguing for damages or an injunction. Simply crying foul and asking for relief is not enough. In *Missouri v. Illinois* (200 U.S. 496, 26 S.Ct. 268 [1906]), Supreme Court Justice Holmes considered such a case.

The city of Chicago pumped its sewage into a canal originally built in 1848, under an 1822 act of Congress that allowed it to cross federal lands. The canal was greatly expanded in 1900, reversing the flow of the Chicago River—away from Lake Michigan so it would flow inland toward the Mississippi—and, as the city grew, drawing more water from the lake. Flushed with water from Lake Michigan, the canal carried the sewage, "1,500 tons of poisonous filth daily into the Mississippi," via the Desplaines and then the Illinois Rivers. Other cities similarly dumped sewage into the Mississippi.

The state of Missouri asserted that the Chicago sewage was the cause of typhoid in St. Louis. The court noted that enough water from Lake Michigan was mixed in the sewage that, where the canal dumped into the Illinois River, "it is a comparatively clear stream to which edible fish have returned. Its water is drunk by the fishermen, it is said without evil results." The court accepted that sewage could cause typhoid, which killed 100-400 people per year in St. Louis between 1890 and 1903. But the court also reviewed a test of the ability of bacilli to live in water that flows long distances (it being over 350 miles from Chicago to St. Louis); scientists testified that it was unlikely that the bacilli could survive in the river for that long. Finally, because other towns closer to St. Louis (including Missouri towns) dumped sewage into the river, there were multiple sources of filth that could be the source of the bacillus. There was no reason to single out Chicago for the expense that St. Louis must incur to filter the water it draws from the river.

In a related case, *Sanitary Dist. of Chicago v. U.S.* (266 U.S. 405, 45 S.Ct. 176 [1925]), Justice Holmes heard a dispute involving the secretary of war and Chicago's use of water from Lake Michigan for handling raw sewage. The U.S. government, at the request of the secretary of war, sued Chicago for diverting water from Lake Michigan in excess of the 250,000 cubic feet per minute that had been authorized by the secretary. The higher diversion rate, used to flush sewage from Chicago into a canal that eventually flowed to the Mississippi, lowered the water level. If continued unabated, the practice would lower the water levels in Lakes Michigan, Huron, Erie, Ontario, St. Clair, and the rivers connecting them, which was creating an obstruction to the navigable capacity of those waters. Chicago defended the water diversion as needed to flush the sewage to protect public health.

The court held that there was no question that the federal government regulates navigable waters; hence the secretary, as ordered by Congress, could decide such matters as proper levels of diversions of such water bodies. The secretary gave Chicago its first permit in 1899. Subsequently the 250,000 cubic feet per minute limit was established. Chicago, pumping about 500,000 cubic feet per minute, complained also that it would have to spend $100 million to improve its treatment works if not allowed to increase its flow. The court dismissed Chicago's defense, granting the secretary an injunction to stop the excess flow in sixty days.

Chicago's sewage disposal problems did not end with the 1925 case. Continuing its use of lake water as a way to avoid construction of sewage treatment facilities, the city eventually encountered another common-law suit. In *Wisconsin et al. v. Illinois et al.* (278 U.S. 367, 49 S.Ct. 163 [1929]), Chief Justice Taft oversaw an action that illustrates the use of special masters, qualified persons appointed by the court to assist it in determining an appropriate action. After the previous ruling by the court, Chicago asked the secretary for a new permit to draw water at an annual average rate of 8,500 cubic feet per second, subject to certain conditions. The permit required Chicago to begin constructing some primary treatment plants to reduce the strain on the canal. Wisconsin and other states sued Illinois and Chicago for its continued draw of water from Lake Michigan, despite the previous court decision. When the case was filed, the court appointed a special master, Charles Evans Hughes, with authority to take evidence and report to the court his findings of fact, his conclusions of law, and his recommendations.

The plaintiffs contended that the water draw had lowered the Great Lakes and connecting rivers by six inches, causing serious harm to navigation. Further, they noted that Chicago had requested that the permissable water draw be increased from 8,500 cubic feet per second to 10,000 cubic feet per second, which would reduce the lake and river levels by another inch.

The court reviewed the federal legislation giving the secretary the power to control lakes and rivers for navigation purposes and again found the delegation of power to be proper under the Constitution. However, the court this time gave prominent attention to property rights.

> Though Congress, in the exercise of its power over navigation, may adopt any means having some positive relation to the control of navigation and not otherwise inconsistent with the Constitution, it may not arbitrarily destroy or impair the rights of riparian owners by legislation which has no real or substantial relation to the control of navigation or appropriateness to that end.

The court denied the right of the secretary to allow Chicago to increase drainage to 8,500 cubic feet per second for sanitary purposes. The secretary was authorized by Congress to consider navigation, which included navigation on the canal, but the increase in water draw was not related to navigation and so was improper. To reduce future problems, Chicago would have to build new treatment plants to reduce their water need; the special master (Hughes) would see that the city took care of its needs and would not increase its water draw. The city was ordered to return gradually to the old water-draw level.

The story did not end with this ruling. In *Wisconsin v. Illinois* (289 U.S. 395, 53 S.Ct. 671 [1933]), Wisconsin and other states accused Chicago and Illinois of not building sewage treatment facilities that would allow it to reduce the water draw from Lake Michigan, as ordered by the court in 1929. Chicago's response involved the Great Depression and the difficulty in financing the required treatment plants. Not accepting the Depression hardship argument, the court ordered Chicago to proceed with the remedy previously ordered.

As explained earlier, common-law rights may be traded; a downstream right holder may choose to sell or lease his rights to an upstream discharger. This Coasean process allows for a market determination of water quality by private parties. We see the process at play in *International Paper Co. v. Maddox* (105 F. Supp. 89 W.D. La., [1951]). In this controversy, International Paper (IP) had a plant on Bodcaw Bayou, Louisiana, built in the 1930s, that fouled the waters of the bayou. IP paid forty landowners along the bayou for "perpetual right to discharge . . . effluent"; the cost of this was several hundred thousand dollars. Maddox made a living running a fishing camp in the Bayou (at least twenty miles downstream); his livelihood was injured by the pollution. He sued for damages or, in the alternative, for an injunction against further pollution. Expert testimony was that, over the years, IP had improved its water treatment, so it was not killing as many fish as before, but the quality of fishing and quality of the bayou had been injured. The court awarded Maddox $8,000 damages for loss of value of business and reduction in property value due to loss of prior pristine waters. Under appeal, in *International Paper Co. v. Maddox* (203 F. 2d 88 5th Cir., 1953), the higher court affirmed the decision, stating that the pollution was a nuisance for which plaintiff could receive payment for temporary damages as well as for permanent damages. The fact that IP was making continuous improvements to pollution control, some of which had been hampered by inability to get certain equipment during World War II, did not affect the right of the plaintiff to be compensated for losses.

Air Pollution

Although there are fewer common-law cases dealing with air pollution than with water pollution, the actions carry similar themes. Reaching back to the nineteenth century and coming forward, common-law actions dealt with things as simple as offensive smells, dust, and vapors, and as complex as sulfur dioxide emissions and benign microscopic particles that invaded private land.

In *Baltimore & Potomac Railroad Co. v. Fifth Baptist Church* (U.S. 317 [1882]), a private nuisance case brought by a Washington, D.C., church, the railroad was charged with annoying the church congregation during services with loud noises, smoke, cinders, dust and offensive odors. The church sought damages based on the harmful effects to its property and congregation. While evidence of harm was presented, the railroad countered by noting its operation was authorized by Congress and its operations were well within all laws of the city. The court held for the church and the case was appealed to the Supreme Court, which noted

> It is no answer to the action of the plaintiff that the railroad company was authorized by act of Congress to bring its track within the limits of the city of Washington, and to construct such works as were necessary and expedient for the completion and maintenance of its road, and that the engine house and repair shop in question were thus necessary and expedient; that they are skillfully constructed; that the chimneys of the engine house are higher than required by the building regulations of the city, and that as little smoke and noise are causes as the nature of the business in them will permit. . . . Grants of privilege or powers to corporate bodies, like those in question, confer no license to use them in disregard of the private right of others, and with immunity for their invasion. (at 330)

The Court awarded the church damages based on the depreciation of the value of the property and the inconvenience suffered by the congregation.

Georgia v. Tennessee Copper Co. (206 U.S. 230, 27 S.Ct. 618 [1907]) illustrates how common law dealt with a complex technical issue that led to the invention and application of new pollution control equipment. In a public nuisance action, the state of Georgia, on behalf of its citizens, sued two companies that operated copper smelters in Tennessee near the Georgia border. Justice Holmes noted that a public nuisance had been created because the "sulphurous fumes cause and threaten damage on so considerable a scale to the forests and vegetable life, if not to health, within [Georgia]." The plaintiffs argued that they had recently constructed new facilities that reduced the scope of the problem, but the Supreme Court held for Georgia. The Court held that the companies would be given a reasonable time to build more emission control equipment, but that if such equipment did not adequately reduce emissions so as to protect plant life in Georgia, the state could ask the Court for an injunction to shut the plants down.

In 1915 the parties returned to the Supreme Court. Defendant companies showed that their new equipment, which was very expensive, reduced emissions by more than half. Georgia argued that this was not enough and demanded that the plants be closed. The Chief Justice appointed a scientist from Vanderbilt University to spend six months, at company expense, studying the emissions and the likely effect of new controls. In the meantime, the Court ordered the companies to cut back production so as to reduce emissions further. Based on the evidence presented by the scientist, the companies either would be allowed to continue operation with more emission control equipment in place, or, if that could not reduce emissions sufficiently, would be ordered to shut down.

When deciding on a controversy before the Court, common-law judges reflect on community norms and standards, which may vary from place to place. Unlike statute law and regulation, common law does not lend itself to a "one suit fits all" approach. The facts surrounding the case matter. Because of this, common-law judges hearing a similar set of facts, like those in *Tennessee Copper*, can arrive at different decisions.

Commonwealth v. Miller (21 A. 138 [1891]), an early Pennsylvania case, illustrates this point. In this public nuisance case, the state brought action against an oil refinery "because of the [e]mission therefrom of certain noxious and offensive smells and vapors, and because the oil and gases stored and used therein are inflammable, explosive and dangerous." The court heard the evidence but decided in favor of the polluter for the following reasons:

> The right to pure air is, in one sense, an absolute one, for all persons have the right to life and health, and such contamination of the air as is injurious to health cannot be justified; but in another sense it is relative, and depends upon one's surroundings. People who live in great cities that are sustained by manufacturing enterprises must necessarily be subject to many annoyances and positive discomforts by reason of noise, dust, smoke, and odors, more or less disagreeable, produced by and resulting from business that supports the city. . . . The defendants had the right to have the character of their business determined in light of all the surrounding circumstances, including the character of Allegheny as a manufacturing city, and the manner and use of the river front for manufacturing purposes.

In other words, the common-law court saw the industrial zone of Allegheny as a safe haven for industry and found no persuasive evidence to require what might be called an industrial park to become environmentally clean.

Those who believe that to be effective, environmental law must always favor the environment will understandably dislike this outcome. But taken in the context of the time when the decision was rendered and considering the alternatives available to industry in 1891, the decision contains more than a kernel of reasonable logic. When community customs and norms lead to the development of industrial areas where property owners voluntarily operate in a polluted environment, the plaintiff who did not prove damages was defeated. However, if the plaintiff had proven damages, strict protection of property rights calls for a decision favoring the plaintiff, no matter how great the inconvenience and cost imposed on the polluter.

While common-law courts might at times compromise the environmental rights of property owners, the effect of such decisions only involved the single plaintiff, not every similarly situated person in the nation. Statutes and regulation are conceptually imposed uniformly across entire industries and all communities, even when they are ineffective. By contrast, common-law courts enjoy the luxury of seeking effective solutions and holding the offending party's feet to fire until a solution is applied.

Anderson v. American Smelting & Refining Co. (265 F. 928 D.Utah, [1919]) demonstrates how this worked in an early air pollution case involving Anderson, a farmer, and American Smelting, which at the time was one of the nation's largest mining and smeltering firms. To add a bit more color, American Smelting was located in Utah, a state where politicians would likely have looked kindly on one of the state's major industries.

Anderson complained because the smelter spewed arsenic and sulphur oxides that injured his cattle and crops. He sought an injunction to stop the smelter from polluting. The smelter argued there was simply no technical fix for the problem and pointed out the relative magnitude of the smelting operation. Anderson was just one farmer, but the court found for him, even though noting the importance of the industry. The court stated: "[T]here can be no solution [to the] smelting smoke problem . . . unless SO_2 is removed entirely from the smoke stream . . . or so diffused . . . [that] the concentration . . . will be reduced to the a point imperceptible to the senses." Announcing the common-law rule, the court pointed out that no "industry, however important, can justly claim the right to live or operate which creates a nuisance in operation or trespasses upon the property or the inherent personal rights of others" (265 F. at 943).

But the court was caught on the horns of a dilemma. The farmer had rights, but there was no known technical solution to the emission problem. Recognizing this, the court ordered the smelter to come forward with a solution or at least an approach that would lead systematically to a solution. Failing that, the court promised to order the injunction. In other words, common law could be technology-forcing.

One of the canons of common law indicated here and in other cases relates to the use of scientific evidence. Common-law courts require a demonstration of harm that can hold up under scientific scrutiny. A 1953 case involving crop dusting illustrates how a lack of evidence led to a decision favoring the polluter. In *Gainey v. Folkman* (114 F. Supp. 231 [D. Az., 1953]), a cattle rancher sued an adjoining landowner for injunctive relief against further crop dusting of cotton, for damages to the plaintiff's cattle and for injuries to the plaintiff's employees, allegedly caused when chemicals from dusting drifted over the plaintiff's ranch. Chemicals included DDT, Ben-Hex, and Parathion. These were applied properly by the crop duster, but some blew across the road onto employees, cattle, and cattle feed. The plaintiff claimed an employee became ill and that the cattle lost weight, reducing their value.

Testimony from USDA and University of Arizona Extension Service experts supported the defendant's position that the chemicals were properly applied and that there was no scientific evidence that the level of exposure was harmful to humans or cattle. A toxicologist reported that there was no evidence that the levels of exposure were harmful and that the levels found in a cow that was autopsied were below harmful levels. The court noted that if the exposure had been shown to be harmful, the action would have been proper as a nuisance, but since evidence was to the contrary, judgment was for the defendant.

We find a similar judgment in *Bradley v. American Smelting and Refining Co.* (104 Wash.2d 677, 709 P.2d 782 [S.Ct., Wash., 1985]). The Bradleys lived on Vashon Island, Washington, four miles from a copper refinery run by American Smelting (ASARCO). The Bradleys sued ASARCO, a New Jersey corporation, in federal court in Washington for damages in trespass and nuisance from the deposit on their property of airborne particles of heavy metals from ASARCO's smelter. The smelter had operated since 1905; it was regulated by state and federal air pollution laws and was in compliance with all regulations. The gases that passed over and landed on the Bradley's land could not be seen or smelled by humans; they required microscopic detection.

The federal court, which would use Washington common law to determine the case, was uncertain as to what that law was since there were so few cases in the area. The court asked the Washington Supreme Court to tell it the status of Washington common law of nuisance and trespass as applied to air pollution.

The Washington high court held that ASARCO "had the intent requisite to commit intentional trespass." Even though no harm was intended, and even though ASARCO did not know the Bradleys, the company knew particles were being emitted from its facilities. Secondly, the court held that "An intentional deposit of microscopic particulates, undetectable by the human senses, gives rise to a cause of action for trespass as well as a claim of nuisance." Hence, the ASARCO emissions created a nuisance and a trespass. The court noted that for a cause of action for nuisance or trespass to be successful, there must be "proof of actual and substantial damages." Under the statute of limitations, the plaintiffs had three years to file the action once the injury became known. And the court held that the case was not prohibited by the Washington Clean Air Act, the state equivalent of the federal Clean Air Act. Upon return to federal court, the case was dismissed for lack of evidence of damage to plaintiffs or their property from the air pollution.

As noted earlier, common law supports voluntary contracting between a polluter and individuals who hold environmental rights. A firm that knows that it will pollute can arrange in advance to make satisfactory payments to the recipient, in effect buying or leasing the recipient's rights. The resulting gains from trade can lead to optimal environmental use. This was the approach taken in *Fairview Farms, Inc. v. Reynolds Metals Co.* (176 F. Supp. 178 [D. Ore., 1959]).

In this case, the Reynolds aluminum plant caused acidic gases (fluorides) to settle on the plaintiff's adjoining farm, rendering parts of the forage on the farm unusable for the dairy cattle, causing some injury to the herd, and making some milk useless. Reynolds knew of the problem, which constitutes an intentional tort of trespass, and had installed improved fume control equipment over the years. Starting in the 1940s, Reynolds made payments to Fairview for the damages and some years paid Fairview to keep no dairy cattle in the fields. Reynolds maintained communications with Fairview and indicated that it was constantly working to improve emission controls (emission levels did drop over the years) and that its scientists would take samples from Fairview property to constantly check for dangerous levels of contamination to the herd and its forage.

During the 1950s, Reynolds decided the emissions were no longer at a harmful level and ceased payments. Fairview sued in tort for damages and an injunction; the court, reviewing procedural claims, held that Fairview could go forward with a claim for trespass for damages. The court held that Reynolds must take measures "to minimize the escape of fluorides from its plants . . . [to] the maximum possible consistent with practical operating requirements," that is, it must use state-of-the-art equipment. Reynolds would continue to be liable to Fairview for any damages, but an injunction against any emissions from Reynolds was denied for as long as Reynolds could show it was meeting industry standards for emission controls. In other words, the two parties were returned to the market status quo, where the polluter paid for the environmental rights acquired from the farmer.

This standard applied by the court is seen again in *R. L. Renken et al. v. Harvey Aluminum, Inc.* (226 F. Supp. 169 [D. Ore., 1963]). In this case, landowners near an aluminum plant in The Dalles, Oregon, sued in trespass and nuisance for air pollution emitted by plant (fluoride and other toxic gases). The plant was the largest employer in the town (550 employees). In the 1950s the plant had installed various emission control devices, including scrubbing towers and sprayers, which stopped over 90 percent of the emissions; nevertheless, about 1,300 pounds of fluoride escaped during daily operations. The company asserted that nothing more could be done. Experts testified that emission controls could be tightened, but only at substantial cost.

The court ordered the company to pay surrounding orchards for damages to their crops caused by the trespass of the damaging gases. The company was also ordered to install the new emission control equipment within one year, or an injunction against any further emissions (i.e., plant shutdown) would be issued, as requested by the plaintiffs.

The pattern continued in 1964, in *Reynolds Metals Co. v. Martin* (337 F.2d 780 [9th Cir., 1964]). Here, the Martin family owned a 1,500 acre cattle ranch that suffered from pollution emitted from the Reynolds plant. They sued for $1.4 million for actual damages, $1 million for punitive damages, and asked for an injunction if Reynolds did not install better emission control equipment. Reynolds moved for dismissal, which was denied by district court, so Reynolds appealed.

The court denied the appeal, holding there was a trespass, which the Oregon high court has defined as "any intrusion which invades the possessor's protected interest in exclusive possession, whether that intrusion is by visible or invisible pieces of matter or by energy which can be measured only by the mathematical language of the physicist." There is also a nuisance here, but in Oregon the key action in such cases is trespass. Suit to proceed.

Lessons from Other Common Law-Jurisdictions

In a break with U.S. case law, we return to England and provide a vignette on a common-law case involving a British angling association and discussed by Brubaker (1995, 282-284), which sheds light on how common-law suits protected water quality for anglers. In *Pride of Derby and Derbyshire Angling v. British Celanese Ltd. and Others* ([1953] 1 Ch. 149), action was brought by a fishing club, Pride of Derby, and its association, Derbyshire Angling Association, against the Borough of Derby, British Celanese, and the British Electricity Authority. The three defendants discharged respectively untreated sewage, industrial waste, and heated effluent that polluted and raised the temperature of the River Derwent damaging the environmental rights of the anglers. Pride of Derby and Derbyshire Angling owned a fishery in the river. The suit by the fishing clubs requesting that the polluters be enjoined was joined by the Earl of Harrington, who owned land along the river, giving him riparian rights to undisturbed water quality.

The lower court issued an injunction restraining the three defendants from reducing the quality of the river's water, but then suspended the injunction for two years, which allowed time for the defendants to alter their operations. On appeal to the Chancery, the court upheld the injunction. The Chancery Court rejected the argument by the Borough of Derby that it had statutory authority to pollute provided by Parliament when the borough was authorized to build a sewage treatment works. The court noted that the statute did not authorize pollution and in fact prohibited discharge that "shall be a nuisance or injurious to the health or reasonable comfort of the inhabitants [in the region]" (Brubaker 1995, 283). The Borough also asked the court to substitute damages for injunction, since the community could not easily rebuild its sewage treatment plant. Rejecting the petition, the court noted, "In the present case, it is plain that damages would be a wholly inadequate remedy for [the angling club], who have not been incorporated in order to fish for monthly sums" (Brubaker 1995, 284). The common-law injunction required the borough to redesign its sewage system, Celanese to change its discharge practices, and British Electricity Authority to reduce its discharge of superheated water.

The Evolution and Interaction of Common Law

As discussed earlier, common-law remedies were pushed to the background during the late 1960s and early 1970s when state and federal statutes spawned regulation for the purpose of controlling environmental use. Common law's inferior position was the result of two factors. First, pollution cases involving more than one state, covered by what was called federal common law, became subject to federal statutes.[10] Judges deferred to federal administrative bodies, like the U.S. Environmental Protection Agency, and to statutory remedies. Actions that might be taken within the individual states for the most part were another matter. Unless barred by state law, common-law remedies were still available, but often more expensive for plaintiffs and less rewarding to their attorneys than those offered by administrative bodies, since many federal statutes require a polluter to pay plaintiffs' legal fees. Simply put, a property owner who felt damaged by a polluter would generally be advised to contact the state environmental regulators. Failing there, the next stop was the state legislature. The political process provided access and remedies that would be applied to all similarly situated parties.

The environmental statutes offered another attractive feature for environmentalists who could not make a valid claim of damages in a common-law court, but who nonetheless felt driven to correct perceived environmental harms. Under the statutes, any citizen could file an administrative complaint, which merely had to show an infraction of rules created by statute, and seek access to a federal court. Under federal statutes, infractions of federal rules automatically contain a federal question. The old common-law requirements of standing and demonstration of damages were not required. In effect, the statute law of the 1970s made every U.S. citizen an environmental deputy. Even so, common-law pleadings are often included in cases brought under statute and administrative law. As some lawyers put it, they include everything but the kitchen sink, hoping that something would stick.

Cases That Show the Transition

Two actions taken by courts during the transition period help to illustrate how the process worked. Preemption by state law is seen in *Commonwealth v. Glen Alden Corp.* (210.A.2d 256 [Penn. 1965]). This was a public nuisance case brought by the state; it dealt with noxious gases from a burning refuse pile, a common problem in Pennsylvania coal country. On hearing the evidence of harm and damages, the court determined that "the Legislature has provided a statutory method [the Air Pollution Control Act] for resolution of the alleged problem set forth in the Commonwealth's complaint, and therefore it must be strictly pursued." Notice here that the judge was referring to the state government, which had passed the noted statute. Going further, the court said, "The Commonwealth had failed to allege and we see no reason why it should be permitted to short-circuit the method provided by the Legislature for resolving the present controversy." State statutes tend to prevail over state common law. The case was dismissed.

Illinois v. Milwaukee (406 U.S. 91 [1972]), was the last major water pollution case decided before passage of the 1972 Clean Water Act. In that case, Illinois sued Milwaukee and other Wisconsin cities for discharging sewage in Lake Michigan, thereby contaminating Chicago's drinking water supply. In final appeal before the Supreme Court, the Court noted that federal common law looked to state common law for guidance and said, "While federal law governs, consideration of state standards may be relevant. Thus, a state with high water-quality standards may well ask that its strict standards be honored and that it not be compelled to lower itself to the more degrading standards of a neighbor" (at 107). The Court held that an injunction against Milwaukee's pollution could be issued by the federal district court.

Months after the Court's ruling, Congress passed the 1972 Clean Water Act, which gave control of water quality to the U.S. EPA. Milwaukee returned to the Court seeking relief. In 1981, *Milwaukee v. Illinois* (451 U.S. 304 [1981]), the Supreme Court held that federal common law could not be used to impose more stringent standards than those established by EPA under the Clean Water statute. Milwaukee won in the final round.[11]

Similar court decisions in cases involving air pollution, hazardous waste, and other pollution problems make it clear that federal common law has been displaced by federal statutes. State attorney generals who in a public nuisance case might be seeking an injunction or damages against party in another state must look to federal agencies for relief. Cases like *Georgia v. Tennessee Copper* are no longer feasible. At the same time, private parties who seek common-law remedies to protect environmental rights against a polluter in their own state may still have access to state common law. However, even these actions may be shuffled toward state administrative agencies charged with setting and enforcing water quality standards.

Where Common Law Survived and Property Rights Flourished

Common-law causes of action are still available for parties within a state, in spite of the rich overlay of state and federal statute law. Federal statutes do not provide for a plaintiff to recover damages. Common law does. Indeed, federal pollution control regulations call for permits that allow pollution that can be damaging. Common-law actions appended to a federal suit frequently involve the operation of federal statutes that leave room of damaging pollution. In the post-federal statute period, common-law remedies may become even more prominent, since they award damages to those who are harmed, whereas federal statutes do not. In examining a few cases, we see the interaction of common law with statute law and an important restatement of old common-law rules for protecting property rights. Consider first these land pollution cases, which came after Congress passed the Superfund law in 1980 to regulate the cleanup of toxic waste sites.

In *Village of Watsonville v. SCA Services* (426 N.E.2d 824 [S.Ct., Ill., 1981]), the Illinois EPA, backed by the U.S. EPA, supported the right of a chemical waste landfill, which was alleged to be causing damage to a nearby village, to remain in operation. However, in spite of the support given by the federal regulator, the Illinois Supreme Court found that the landfill was causing groundwater contamination and that the current disposal technique could create a chemical explosion. The court held the landfill was a public and a private nuisance; the village residents had been there first.

The landfill had been built with state and federal approval, which encouraged the landfill owner to ignore consequences to its neighbors. The court noted that toxic landfills were legitimate, but held that they had to be constructed so as not to impose costs on surrounding landowners who had not agreed to the intrusion. The court issued a permanent injunction against the landfill and ordered that the toxic wastes be dug up and moved, and the land restored.

In *New York v. Schenectady Chemicals, Inc.* (459 N.Y.S.2d 971 [1983]), the court dismissed a claim for damages based on a state environmental statute and turned instead to common law for the appropriate remedy. Importantly, the court announced a rule of strict liability, which enforced the property rights of people who might be damaged by pollution.

Schenectady Chemicals (SC) had hired an incompetent firm to dispose of its toxic wastes during the 1950s and early 1960s. Across the two decades, the hauler dumped 46,300 tons of chemical wastes in a swampy thirteen-acre site that drained into an aquifer serving thousands of people. It became clear that some damage was being done to some wells served by the affected aquifer. Of the waste, 82.2 percent came from two other firms, who had already agreed to pay up; SC contributed 17.8 percent. The state sued for SC to pay its share of the remediation costs, and asked for assorted penalties under New York's Environmental Conservation Law (ECL).

The court held that the ECL did not apply; the dumping occurred before the permit system was established, so no penalties from that ECL were relevant. Turning to the common law, the court called for public nuisance as the appropriate cause of action. The court explained:

> A public, or as sometimes termed a common, nuisance is an offense against the State and is subject to abatement or prosecution on application of the proper governmental agency. . . . One who creates a nuisance through an inherently dangerous activity or use of an unreasonably dangerous product is absolutely liable for resulting damages, regardless of fault, and despite adhering to the highest standard of care.

SC was liable for its nuisance and was ordered to pay its pro-rata share of the cleanup expense. The fact that the ECL does not apply to this action does not preclude common-law liability. In *New York v. Monarch Chemicals et al.* (456 N.Y.S.2d 867 [App. Div., 1982]), the appellate court upheld liability based on nuisance for a landlord who leased land to Monarch Chemicals, which allowed chemicals to seep into groundwater while occupying the premises: "The legal concepts governing a landlord's liability for its tenant's activities have been expanded to the point that a landlord may now be held responsible for negligence in the selection of a tenant and also for the wrongdoing of the tenant when the landlord continues to exercise control over the premises." The landlord knew the tenant was using the property for toxic chemicals, was informed by an engineer that there were seepage problems, but ignored the situation. The court held the landlord to be responsible, like Monarch Chemicals, for some of the cost of the cleanup. The fact that the state's environmental statute did not apply did not absolve the landlord of liability. Common-law protection of environmental rights applied.

In *Wood v. Picillo* (433 A.2d 1244 [S.Ct., R.I., 1982]), neighbors sued a farmer who maintained a hazardous waste dump on his property. The plaintiffs claimed the dump emitted noxious fumes and polluted ground and surface waters. Here we see an application of improved technology for monitoring and demonstrating damages.

Holding for plaintiffs, the Rhode Island Supreme Court overturned a 1934 decision that would have held for defendant because groundwaters were "indefinite and obscure." The 1934 court had held that plaintiffs in pollution cases had to show that defendants should have "foreseen" the consequences of their action, that is, were negligent. The 1982 court held that since 1934, the science of groundwater hydrology as well as societal concern for environmental protection has developed dramatically. As a matter of scientific fact the course of subterranean waters are no longer obscure and mysterious. . . . We now hold that negligence is not a necessary element of a nuisance case involving contamination of public or private waters by pollutants percolating through the soil and traveling underground routes.

The court noted that a rule of strict liability is imposed on polluters who cause damage to ground and surface waters, indicating that the standard was consistent with old common-law tort rules imposing strict liability in case of hazardous materials.[12] Improved technology brought improved protection of environmental property rights.

The matter of strict liability was further refined in the 1983 case of *New Jersey Dept. of Environmental Protection v. Ventron Corp.* (468 A.2d 150 [S.Ct., N.J.]), in which New Jersey sued various parties for mercury pollution of a waterway. The state's supreme court stated,

We believe it is time to recognize expressly that the law of liability has evolved so that a landowner is strictly liable to others for harm caused by toxic wastes that are stored on his property and flow onto the property of others. Therefore, we overrule *Marshall v. Welwood* (N.J. S.Ct. 1876) and adopt the principle of liability originally declared in Rylands v. Fletcher [England, 1868]. The net result is that those who use, or permit others to use, land for the conduct of abnormally dangerous activities are strictly liable for resultant damages.

With the strict protection of environmental rights reemerging in common law, it is little wonder that polluters would seek any shield available when charged with damaging the environmental property of others. The 1985 case of *New York v. Shore Realty Corp.* (759 F.2d 1032 [2nd Cir., 1985]) illustrates a failed attempt by the defendant to use statute law as a shield from common-law liability. In the matter before the court, several acres had been used for chemical storage and about 700,000 gallons of chemical waste in assorted tanks, some of which leaked, had been placed on the land. Shore agreed to buy the land for real estate development, knowing that there would have to be cleanup, which one company estimated would cost about $1 million (the company reported that there was groundwater contamination). Using the cleanup company's report, Shore asked the New York State Dept. of Environmental Conservation (DEC) for a waiver of liability if the cleanup where performed; the waiver was denied, but Shore bought the property anyway and evicted the tenants (chemical dump operators). After the purchase, Shore took limited steps to clear away the waste, but the chemicals sat there, with some leakage still occurring. A New York regulatory agency operating under the state's mini-Superfund law sued to recover its emergency cleanup costs. Under this law (and the federal Superfund statute), Shore was liable along with all other parties involved for state-mandated cleanup even though Shore did not operate the dump.

Shore argued that since EPA did not put the site on the Superfund's National Priority List of sites to be cleaned, Shore could not be liable. The court held that that was irrelevant to state action. The court of appeals upheld the district court finding of liability based on public nuisance: "Shore, as a landowner, is subject to liability for either a public or private nuisance on its property upon learning of the nuisance and having a reasonable opportunity to abate it." Going further, the court said,

> It is immaterial . . . that other parties placed the chemicals on this site; Shore purchased it with knowledge of its condition—indeed of the approximate cost of cleaning it up—and with an opportunity to clean up the site. . . . Shore is liable for maintenance of a public nuisance irrespective of negligence or fault. Nor is there any requirement that the state prove actual, as opposed to threatened, harm from the nuisance in order to obtain abatement. Such liability is irrespective of state superfund liability; it exists under common law.

Finally, a recent water pollution cases illustrate how common-law protection of property rights has continued to operate, even though federal statutes might authorize a facility to pollute. In the 1986 South Carolina case of *Stoddard v. Western Carolina Sewer Authority* (784 F.2d 1200 [4th Cir. 1986]), three lakeshore property owners in South Carolina sued a public sewer authority for dumping untreated industrial and human waste into the lake, reducing the value of the owners' property. The landowners asked that the sewer authority be fined for violating the Clean Water Act and that they be compensated for damages and a taking of their property. The sewer authority claimed sovereign immunity.

Citing South Carolina law, the court rejected the sewer authority's immunity claim, and awarded $100,000 each to the aggrieved property owners. On appeal, the circuit court upheld the lower-court decision and ordered that the sewer authority be fined for federal statute violations. Common-law property rights were recognized.

Final Thoughts on Evolving Common-Law Rights

With the arrival of the third millenium, people in the United States will continue to hold environmental property rights protected by state common law. In the areas of earliest English settlement, the record of protection on this continent reaches back more than 300 years. We can add another 400 years or more when the history of English common law is added to that of the American colonies and states. Surely, much of our environmental patrimony is owed to the protection of environmental resources afforded by common law.

The durability of common law is illustrated by the first case and the last one discussed in this chapter. In both *William Aldred's Case* (1611) and *Stoddard v. Western Carolina Sewer Authority* (1986), the courts inquired about damages to the holder of common-law rights, made a determination of facts, and awarded damages and/or an injunction against the polluter. After more than 350 years, judges are still enforcing the common-law environmental rights held by ordinary people, even when in doing so, as in *Stoddard*, the decision goes against the position of the state and federal government.

The cases discussed in this chapter do more than illustrate how common law works in particular controversies. They also show how common law has evolved to deal with more complex technical matters and to use advanced methods for measuring and monitoring harm. We also see how common law interacts with statute law, where common law survived, and how communities lost their common-law rights for actions involving political units in more than one state when federal statutes preempted common law.

Common law, which is based on and supports property rights held by ordinary people, is part of the process approach for dealing with the commons problem. When cast in terms of Pigou versus Coase, the common law is clearly part of the Coase solution.

When told that common-law protection of environmental rights should be reinforced and perhaps relied on more fully for protecting the environment, some people respond with three criticisms. The first relates to the use of suits for protecting the environment: "I don't think we should rely on lawsuits to discipline polluters." The misconception here has to do with the notion that polluters would always take advantage of rightholders if no one sued them. It is no more likely that this would happen than that all individuals passing a home would drive across the yard to save a little time. Common law protects all environmental assets, including our front yards. The risk of suit and expected value of penalties figure into decisions made by firms and other organizations. We have seen that common-law judges can be tough on polluters. Those who deliberately trample the rights of others would not be treated kindly.

A second criticism relates to poor people who might not have the funds to bring suit against a polluter who has damaged their property. There is no doubt about it; common-law suits are expensive. Two responses may address the concern, neither of which is perfect. First, contingency fee lawyers regularly provide the means for bringing suit. With strong protection of common-law rights, lawyers are better able to estimate outcomes. Where the facts appear persuasive, a lawyer takes a relatively small risk in bringing a case against an industrial polluter with deep pockets. The next idea is more speculative. If common law were relied on as the principle means for protecting environmental rights, the provision of public defenders might not be a bad idea. Communities at large have an interest in environmental quality. Provision of some litigation support with public funds would address part of the problem faced by poor people who seek redress.

A final criticism frequently heard has to do with large numbers situations like automobile emissions, where there are a host of polluters and even more recipients of pollution. None of the recipients is usually harmed enough on a daily basis to have the incentive to track down a host of auto owners and bring suit. Obviously, common-law remedies cannot address every environmental problem. Other regulatory schemes will be used along with common law. However, even the regulatory schemes can learn from common law. Common-law actions are based on real damage to real people. The actions are based on scientific fact, not mere speculation, and the remedies are tailored to meet the conditions of the specific situation. When applied to the problem of auto emissions, these principles suggest that communities that face more severe auto pollution problems will impose stricter rules than those communities with very different human exposure and atmospheric conditions. Under common law, it is difficult to picture a situation in which a court would impose one solution on a community as vast and as diverse as the U.S. economy.

Notes

1. I call attention to riparian rights that are a part of the bundle held by owners of land adjacent to rivers, streams, and lakes. The holder of riparian rights has the right to reasonable use of water of undiminished quality that passes his land. Undiminished quality is qualified to read "unreasonably diminished in quality." Generally, invasions of riparian rights do not involve trespass, so in practice, discussion can focus on nuisance.

2. A chemical plant's emissions are enjoinable as public nuisance and also constitute a private nuisance allowing damages for diminution in property values (*Capurro* 1972).

3. See also *Ballenger* 1955; *State of N.Y.* 1985 (owners of waste disposal site must cleanup); *National Sea Clammers Assn.* 1981 (Plaintiffs brought action against government officials alleging they had permitted discharge of sewage which resulted in damage to their industry); *Philadelphia Elec. Co.* 1985; *U.S. v. Solvents* 1980 (Property owner sued corporation alleging contamination of groundwater and river as a result of operation of chemical plant. U.S. government brought action seeking injunctive relief against two corporations for allegedly polluting groundwater).

4. Specifically, the court in *Ballenger* noted the city's allegations as follows: "Appellant was a wholesale dealer in chickens; that in the pursuit of his business he erected a chicken house within a residential section of the City, the house being a temporary structure consisting of 'a big pen covered by a huge roof,'

this house or pen being adjacent to Green Street; that in the operation of his chicken house appellant loads and unloads chickens at all hours of the night, permits refuse, offal and feathers to accumulate therein and allows dead chickens to lie around the premises to such extent as to become a breeding place for flies; that the noises and foul odors emanating from the chicken house are such as to disturb the residents of the entire neighborhood, the noises keeping them awake at night and the foul odors making it impossible for them to sit in comfort on their porches or to eat their food without closing the doors and windows of their homes; 'that the dead chickens, the refuse from the chickens, the offal, and the decayed eggs together with the flies create a hazard which endangers the health of all the residents of this area.'"

5. See *People v. New Pennsylvania Mines, Inc.*, 212 Cal. App. 2d 667 (1963) (holding that the attorney general's power to sue for public nuisance was preempted by establishment of administrative apparatus to deal with water pollution).

6. A series of Pennsylvania cases illustrates this transformation. See *Sanderson v. Pennsylvania Coal Co.*, 86 Pa. 401(1878); *Pennsylvania Coal Co. v. Sanderson*, 94 Pennsylvania, 302 (1880); *Sanderson v. Pennsylvania Coal Co.*, 370 (1883), and *Pennsylvania Coal Co. v. Sanderson*, 113 Pennsylvania, 126 6 A. 453 (1886). In the first trial of the case, which involves water pollution from a railroad operation, the court stood by strict liability, turning down the railroad's public benefit argument. At the end of the appeal process, the court came down on the side of reasonable use of property, due care, and the utility provided by the railroad operation. Where these public policy standards are met, there may be harm, but there is no injury or nuisance.

7. Legalese is avoided as much as possible, but that is not difficult since judges used to write in clear English, unlike many judges and their clerks today who seem compelled to demonstrate their scholarly ability by writing difficult terms in large quantities.

8. 208 N.Y. 1 at 5.

9. Ibid., quoting *Weston Paper Co. v. Pope,* 155 Ind. 394, 57 N.E. 719.

10. The concept of federal common law controlling water pollution was considered by the Supreme Court as early as 1906 and then extended to air and other forms of pollution. See *Missouri,* 1906 and for air pollution, *Georgia,* 1907.

11. Similar decisions were reached for air pollution. (See *United States v. Kin-Buc, Inc.,* 532 F. Supp. 699 [D.N.J. 1982] and *National Audubon Society v. Los Angeles Department of Water*, 858 F.2d 1409 [9th Cir. 1988]). Where federal courts have allowed cases involving a federal question to be brought, the litigants are required to apply the law of the polluter's jurisdiction. (See *International Paper Co. v. Ouellette,* 479 U.S. 481 [1987]).

12. *Rylands v. Fletcher,* L.R. 3 H.L. 330 (1868), is a principal case for the proposition, "So use your own property as not to injure your neighbor's property." This principle comes from Roman law. See 5 *Water and Water Rights* Sec. 49.03(b) n. 43.

References

Bigelow, Melville M. 1875. *Leading Cases on the Law of Torts as Determined by the Courts of America and England.* Boston: Little, Brown & Co.

Brubaker, Elizabeth. 1995. *Property Rights in Defence of Nature.* London: Earthscan.

Ballenger v. City of Grand Saline. 1955. 276 S.W.2d 874 (Tex. Civ. App.—Waco, no writ)

Capurro v. Galaxy Chem. Co. 1972. 2 ELR 20386 (Md. Cir. Ct.).

Coyle, Dennis. 1993. Takings Jurisprudence and the Political Cultures of American Politics. *Catholic University Law Review* 42: 817-862.

Davis, Peter N. 1971. Theories of Water Pollution Litigation. *Wisconsin Law Review.*

Dicey, A.V. 1982. *The Law of the Constitution.* Indianapolis: Liberty Fund, Inc.

Enchave v. City of Grand Junction. 1948. 193 P.2d 277, 118 Colo. 165.

Georgia v. Tennessee Copper Co., 206 U.S. 230 (1907).

Groundwater Protection. 1987. Washington, D.C.: The Conservation Foundation, 36.

Hederman v. Cunningham, 283 S.W.2d 108 (Tex. Civ. App.—Beaumont 1955, no writ).

Holmes, Oliver Wendall. 1881. *The Common Law.* Boston: Little, Brown & Company.

Meiners, Roger E. 1995. Elements of Property Rights: The Common Law Alternative. In *Land Rights: The 1990s Property Rights Rebellion,* edited by Bruce Yandle. Lanham: Rowman & Littlefield Publishers.

Meiners, Roger E., and Bruce Yandle. 1993. Clean Water Legislation: Reauthorize or Repeal? In *Taking the Environment Seriously,* edited by Roger E. Meiners and Bruce Yandle. Lanham: Rowman & Littlefield Publishers.

Missouri v. Illinois, 200 U.S. 496 (1906).

National Sea Clammers Assn. v. City of N.Y., 616 F.2d 1222; judgment vacated 453 U.S. 1, 101 S.Ct. 2615 (1981).

Pennsylvania Coal Co. v. Sanderson, 94 Pa. 302 (1880).

Pennsylvania Coal Co. v. Sanderson, 113 Pa. 126 6 A. 453 (1886).

People v. New Penn Mines, Inc., 212 Cal. App. 2d 667 (1963).

Philadelphia Elec. Co. v. Hercules, Inc., 762 F.2d 303, 315, cert. denied 474 U.S. 980, 106 S.Ct. 384, 388 (1985).

Ryan v. City of Emmetsburg, 4 N.W.2d 435, 232 Iowa 600.

Sanderson v. Pennsylvania Coal Co., 370 (1883).

Sanderson v. Pennsylvania Coal Co., 86 Pa. 401 (1878).

Siegan, Bernard. 1971. *Economic Liberties and the Constitution.* Chicago: University of Chicago Press.

State of New York v. Shore Realty Corp. 759 F.2d 1032 (2d Cir. 1985) (owners of waste disposal site must clean up).

Stoughton v. Ft. Worth. 1955. 277 S.W.2d 150 (Tex. Ct. App.—Ft. Worth, no writ).

Towaliga Falls Power Co. v. Sims, 6 Ga. App. 749, 65 S.E. 844 (1909).

United States v. Solvents Recovery Serv. Etc., 496 F. Supp. 1127, 1142 (D. Conn. 1980).

U.S. Smelting Co. v. Sisam, 191 F. 293 (8th Cir. 1911).

Vann v. Bowie Sewerage Co., 127 Tex. 97, 90 S.W.2d 561 (1936).

Village of Euclid v. Ambler Realty. 1926. 272 U.S. 365, 388.

Yandle, Bruce. 1991. Organic Constitutions and Common Law. *Constitutional Political Economy* 2: 225-241.

Yandle, Bruce. 1993. Sir Edward Coke and the Struggle for a New Constitutional Order. *Constitutional Political Economy* 4: 263-285.

Chapter 5

Automobile Emissions: Avoiding A Hummingbird Economy

As indicated at the end of the previous chapter, emissions from mobile sources, such as automobiles, pose a real common-access resource challenge. Here we find the most serious case of many polluters and many receivers, and therefore high transaction costs. Add to this the fact that the emitters and sometimes the receivers are transient, and the environmental challenge is even more daunting. At first blush, it seems impossible to imagine a viable solution based on transactions among polluters and pollution recipients. Transactions at the immediate point of the problem—between auto drivers and pedestrians, for example—are just too costly. But does this imply that command-and-control applied at the level of the nation is the logical next step, or is there some intermediate scale of control that makes better sense?

In 1996, Andy Barnett, an economics professor at Auburn University, Mark Brandly, an Auburn doctoral student, and I began a research project that focused on emerging environmental policy for controlling automobile emissions (Barnett et al. 1996). Assessing new technologies, such as automobiles that use electricity, natural gas, and other nonpetroleum-based fuels, was a focal point of the research, but the project, as we defined it, required much more. We had to examine the evolving legal institutions that surround the control of auto emissions and to recommend a new set of institutions that might better protect environmental property rights.

The problem we faced was somewhat like the situation encountered by people along North Carolina's Tar River and by the Alaskan fishermen. A common-access resource was experiencing heavy use from competing demanders. Somehow the resource had to be rationed and less environmentally intensive use encouraged. But this time the problem had to do with airsheds instead of watersheds. Once again, the issue is how to reduce the cost of avoiding a hummingbird economy. Our research led to an examination of data on the problem along with the statutes and regulations that addressed it. Throughout our work, we sought to discover the evolving rules for managing auto emissions. We learned that efforts to deal with the urban air pollution problem have produced a thick overlay of rules, regulations, and mandates, an extreme example of the systems approach. Even so, the problem continues to plague a number of major U.S. cities. Is there a productive way out of the thicket, one that delivers better protection to the environment and environmental property rights? Can common-law thinking, even if not common law itself, help us?

This chapter addresses these questions. The next section gives details on the air pollution problem challenging major cities and regions and describes the major statutes that address the problem; it then explains the institutional framework that affects the market for all vehicles and especially those using alternative fuels. The next section examines the problem confronted when there is no market for cleaner air and provides details on federal and state legislation that address the issue. Finally, institutional issues are discussed, and the newly emerging decentralized approach to the clean air problem is emphasized. Drawing on the theme of decentralization and common-law thinking, the concluding section provides a policy proposal for alternative fuel vehicles and any other technologies that might improve air quality.

The Urban Air Quality Challenge

A growing number of U.S. cities face a severe regulatory challenge. The EPA has announced plans to tighten air quality standards that relate to the production of ozone (Krupnick and Anderson 1996, 6-9). The problem of achieving the standards already legislated was severe enough. Based on the 1990 Clean Air Act guidelines, twenty-two U.S. cities, twelve northeastern states, and California were already in trouble. By statute, if not by desire, these cities and states must achieve significant reductions in the formation of ozone and certain specified pollutants that come from automobiles, other mobile sources, and industry. Maintaining urban air quality is an age-old challenge. Urban air pollution, whether from chimneys, smokestacks, or automobiles, is documented as far back as commentary can be found. First addressed by common law, later by city and state regulation, the pollution challenge became the object of federal control in 1970 with passage of the Clean Air Act (Schuchman 1950, 489-506). Statute law, a systems approach, was chosen to address the problem. Since then, significant progress has been made in cleaning the air, but never enough to meet the national standards nationwide. In heavily populated regions, pollution from individual vehicles and other sources has been reduced, but the number of sources has increased. Indeed, vehicle travel has doubled since 1970.[1]

But change is in the air. The emphasis on particular cities and regions represents a fundamental change in the way the nation has attempted to achieve clean air goals. A process approach seems to be entering the system-dominated way we have developed to clean the air. The 1990 Clean Air Act (CAA) recognized that the one-suit-fits-all approach specified by earlier federal statutes would not get the job done. Air pollution is a regional phenomenon; its solution requires a decentralized approach.

Following the blueprint of previous clean air statutes, the CAA set tighter national standards and even tighter strictures for the more troubled regions, indeed, some suggest, tighter than science can justify.[2] To address the urban air pollution problem, federal regulators have mandated rules calling for tighter controls for mobile and stationary sources and have ordered cities and states facing the more difficult pollution problems to set up prescribed systems for inspecting and maintaining automobile emission controls. Of course, stationary sources and conventional vehicles can only do so much. Rising incremental costs soon make it practically impossible to achieve significant gains in pollution reduction from autos or any other primary sources.

In the face of the ever-tightening constraints, communities, states, and regions have searched for new ways to address the problem. A few have established a credit trading program that allows polluters who bring their emissions below mandated levels to sell credits to others who face higher costs.[3] Some have pushed for the use of cleaner-burning fuels. Others have experimented with ways to induce greater use of mass transit systems and clean-fuel vehicles, and California has pushed to remove older and dirtier cars from the highway by allowing industrial polluters to gain credits when they purchase the old junkers.

Added to these state and local programs are national legislative mandates and presidential executive orders calling for the development of alternative fuel vehicles (AFVs). These are cleaner and also play a part in meeting another statute-based challenge, reducing U.S. dependence on petroleum imports. If cleaner automobiles emerge in the market, then part of the emission control battle might be won. But few would place a large bet on the sudden emergence of nonpolluting vehicles.[4] On the other hand, getting the right market- and property-right incentives in place may accelerate the process.

The Smog Problem

Auto and other emissions can have a number of adverse effects when the emission levels are high enough. Chief among these is the production of smog, heavy clouds that form and remain over cities, carrying with them substances such as ozone, with potential adverse effects for human health. What is ozone and why should it be regulated (*Ozone* 1995, 57)? To understand the problem we must first understand ozone. There are two categories of ozone. In the upper atmosphere, beneficial ozone protects us from intense rays from the sun that cause skin cancer. Lower atmospheric or terrestrial ozone is produced by a complex reaction of nitrogen oxide (NOx) and volatile organic compounds (VOCs), such as hydrocarbons, in the presence of sunlight. NOx and VOCs, along with carbon monoxide, a source of another pollution problem, are common emissions from automobiles. Lower atmospheric ozone yields smog;

smog causes respiratory and other health problems and damage to agricultural crops (Chilton and Boemer 1996, 12).

Ozone is produced each day, increasing with the amount of sunlight and falling to low levels at night. There is little if any accumulation from one day to the next, though ozone can travel as far as 100 miles from its source. Since heat and light are necessary for ozone reaction, the levels produced follow seasonal patterns, with the worst periods occurring in the spring and summer.

Dealing with the Problem by Statute

Beginning with the 1970 Clean Air Act, Congress directed the EPA to establish a set of national ambient air quality standards (NAAQS) to be achieved at every geographic point in the nation. Then, command-and-control, technology-based standards were developed and the resulting rules were imposed on stationary and mobile emission sources. Evolving standards for automobiles focused on reducing tailpipe emissions, leading to the development and requirement of catalytic converters and other emission control equipment for all new vehicles sold in the United States.

Once announced, the NAAQS left an imprint on the map. Some areas were in attainment for all the specified pollutants; others were in attainment for some. Others were a long way from attaining any of the standards. A number of major cities, particularly Los Angeles were nonattainment areas that then struggled to achieve the national goals. Later clean air legislation tightened standards yet always allowed more time for nonattainment areas to come into compliance. By the time 1990 rolled around, a number of major metropolitan areas still failed to meet EPA's air quality tests, even after having met the command-and-control requirements for automobiles and for most stationary emission sources, such as refineries and power plants.

The nonattainment problem plaguing U.S. cities and addressed specifically by the 1990 CAA was based on 1988-1990 emissions data. Unfortunately, the 1988-1990 data was biased by a heavy drought that had affected much of the nation. The absence of moisture aggravated the ozone readings, causing some ninety-six cities to fall into the category of facing moderate to extreme ozone attainment problems (U.S. Department of Energy 1994). When those facing a moderate attainment problem are removed, there are twenty-two cities that face the difficult challenge of meeting the NAAQS ozone requirement. Another thirteen metropolitan areas exceeded NAAQS for carbon monoxide, again using 1988-1990 data.

To address the nonattainment and other vehicle emissions problems, the CAA set tighter emission standards for the national auto fleet to be fully achieved by the 1996 model year (U.S. Environmental Protection Agency 1994). The standard for exhaust emissions of hydrocarbons was cut from the 1990 standard of 0.41 grams per mile (gpm) to 0.25 gpm. The standard for nitrogen oxides was changed from 1.0 gpm to 0.4 gpm. Emission limits for carbon monoxide remained at 3.4 gpm. A comparison of these standards with the 1970 standards shows how far gasoline-fueled vehicles have come in reducing emissions. The 1970 standard called for a maximum of 3.9 gpm for hydrocarbons, 33.3 gpm for carbon monoxide, and no control of nitrogen oxides (Hahn 1993). It is worth emphasizing that the standard for hydrocarbon emissions has been cut from 3.9 gpm to 0.25 gpm for most of the nation. Obviously, the incremental cost of achieving the last marginal reduction has risen substantially.

Breaking with the national scheme, the statute set stricter hydrocarbon emission standards for a California pilot program (0.125 gpm), effectively establishing two standards to be met by auto producers.[5] The 1990 CAA took yet one more step toward decentralized control by establishing a northeastern state ozone control region that had to reach beyond the national baseline standards. In addition, the 1990 law ordered auto firms to provide cleaner if not zero emission automobiles, and mandated the sale of reformulated, cleaner-burning gasoline. Reaching even further, the CAA required EPA to focus on emissions from boats, farm equipment, lawn mowers, and construction machinery.

The statute also focused on alternative (nonpetroleum-based) fuels, but did not require their use. Following a strict systems approach to the problem, the 1990 CAA ordered cleaner-burning gasoline to be marketed in cities that failed to meet NAAQS for carbon monoxide (CO) and ozone.[6] Starting in 1992, thirty-nine CO nonattainment areas were required to use oxygenated fuels during part of the year, which blends oxygenated compounds with gasoline thereby reducing hydrocarbon and CO emissions.[7]

Under the CAA, ozone nonattainment areas are to develop state implementation plans (SIPs) to bring 15 percent ozone reductions in areas classified as moderate, serious, severe, and extreme ozone nonattainment areas. The statute requires a Clean Fuel Fleet program for operators of ten or more centrally refueled vehicles in these areas. However, the law does not mandate the use of any particular fuel but simply requires that California emission standards be met (Sperling 1993, 74-37 to 74-39). Beginning in 1996, the nonattainment areas are to show an additional 3 percent reduction each year until the attainment goal is achieved. Failure to accomplish these goals can lead to losses of federal transportation funds and stiff offset requirements from existing polluters before new pollution sources are approved.

The Ozone Transport Region

Obviously, air pollution is not a national problem in the sense of having some well-specified set of pollutants that can uniformly affect every citizen in the country. Air pollution is a decidedly local and regional problem, which the CAA begins to recognize. By way of summary, the statute sets national baseline standards, which must be achieved throughout the nation, sets standards for California cars, establishes tighter controls for twenty-two urban areas, and establishes an Ozone Transport Region, which is defined as twelve northeastern states, reaching from northern Virginia, including the District of Columbia, and extending to Maine.[8]

The CAA effectively establishes an environmental cartel for the twelve-state region this is managed by the Ozone Transport Commission. The commission consists of state governors, the EPA administrator, EPA regional administrators, and state air pollution control officers.

Like all cartels, there are problems in gaining agreement across diverse groups. The commission is charged with the difficult task of determining a *uniform* strategy for dealing with ozone pollution in the region. By statute, the commission may select California standards and California vehicles or some clean fuel strategy, but the commission may not settle on a technology that requires the auto industry to produce a third vehicle for the U.S. market.[9]

The auto industry persuaded the commission to adopt a cleaner-fuel approach and committed itself to provide a national low emission vehicle that would satisfy the ozone reduction requirements of the Northeast Ozone Transport Region.[10] The new cleaner vehicles, which would reduce ozone-related emissions by 50 percent relative to the standard set for the national fleet, will be introduced in the northeastern and mid-Atlantic states beginning in 1996. They will be introduced nationally in 2001. The successful salvo by the auto industry advanced the prospects for some alternative fuel vehicles in the large northeastern market, but practically eliminated the prospects there for electric cars.

The Energy Policy Act of 1992

Energy security, a motivating force for the Energy Policy Act of 1992 (EPACT), is a second force pushing for alternative fuel vehicles. The EPACT was passed in the wake of the Persian Gulf War and is a prime example of crisis-born legislation. The Gulf region provides about 50 percent of U.S. consumed crude oil, a share that is predicted to rise to 60 percent over the next ten years (National Defense Council Foundation 1995, i; U.S. Department of Energy 1996, 4).

Since 1951 there have been thirteen encounters that disrupted petroleum supply lines from the Gulf, with the largest supply shortfall occurring during the Iraqi invasion of Kuwait in August-October 1990.[11] In each case, the U.S. economy was seriously affected, and in each case, after declaring an energy crisis at hand, the Congress responded by passing legislation that sought to buffer the economy from future oil shocks.

As described by the U.S. Department of Energy, EPACT "was enacted to stimulate the research, development, and accelerated introduction of technologies that can potentially shift the focus of national energy demand away from imported oil and toward renewable or domestically produced energy sources" (U.S. Department of Energy 1995, 3). EPACT requires the DOE to promote alternative fuels that reduce consumption of gasoline and diesel fuel and to determine the feasibility of meeting EPACT requirements of replacing 10 percent of all petroleum-based motor fuels by the year 2000 and 30 percent by 2010.

The definition of alternative fuels turns on the effort to reduce reliance on imported petroleum products. Alternative fuels include methanol, ethanol, mixtures containing 85 percent or more by volume of alcohols with gasoline, compressed natural gas (CNG), liquefied petroleum gas (LPG), hydrogen, coal-derived fuels, electricity, and anything else that is clearly not petroleum. Reformulated gasoline and innovative fuels such as mixtures of water and benzene that may be cleaner than the fuels just mentioned will not receive EPACT's blessing.

Of course, EPACT was not born an orphan. Its legislative parents were the Alternative Motor Fuel Act of 1988 and the Clean Air Act Amendments of 1990. These were then strengthened by executive orders issued in 1991 by President Bush and in 1993 by President Clinton. Both executive orders accelerated the purchase of alternative fuel vehicles for the federal fleet. President Clinton's order called for 1993-95 purchases of 7,500, 11,250, and 15,000 vehicles respectively.

The Infrastructure Problem

The alternative fuel effort recognized immediately that any significant move to other fuels requires a distribution system for technologies that are generally limited. DOE's program, like that in the CAA, first focuses on fleet operators where centralized refueling and maintenance is cheaper. The program combines education, voluntary commitments from alternative fuel suppliers to build distribution infrastructure, and requirements for alternative fuel providers and other federal and state fleet operators to expand the number of AFVs. The Department of Energy's March 27, 1996, announcement of purchase requirements to be met by alternative fuel providers like producers and distributors of natural gas will add major stimulus to the number of AFVs (U.S. Department of Energy 1996).

Referring to EPACT, the rules mandate purchase of AFVs by state and local governments, fuel providers, and related petroleum and chemical companies. Some 10 percent of newly purchased light-duty vehicles for the affected fleets must be AFVs for model year 1997. The share rises in subsequent years, reaching 75 percent for model year 2001 and thereafter. To encourage accelerated progress toward the ultimate goal, the rules include a system of tradeable credits that arise when a purchaser goes beyond the minimum number required in a given model year. These credits can be applied in subsequent years to fill out a purchase shortfall or they can be sold to another fleet owner who fails to meet requirements. The DOE initiatives include a program called Clean Cities that promotes greater use of clean-fuel buses and fleets, a push for tax incentives, and state grants and strategic efforts to locate the placement of mandated Federal AFVs.[12] In January 1995, about thirty-four cities had joined the Clean Cities effort. DOE's overall goal is to expand the nation's AFV fleet from fewer than 1000 vehicles in 1995 to almost 2.5 million by 2010. Funding for the DOE effort has expanded from $7 million in fiscal year 1993 to $30 million in FY 1995. But funding for future budgets is in serious doubt.

Of the alternative fuels, compressed natural gas and electricity are the most common. The two energy sources are supplied to homes, businesses, and industries throughout the country. The electricity available at a home or business is ready to be used for charging an automobile battery. However, the gas that enters a home or business is not compressed. A significant investment in a compressor and related equipment is required for a filling station to become a natural gas dispenser. A home user can purchase a $500 compressor that gives overnight filling capacity for vehicles equipped to burn natural gas.

LPG is also widely available, but does not compare with the wide distribution of CNG. Ethanol, which is typically produced from corn, can be produced anywhere and distributed across large regions. However, ethanol production to fuel fleets dispersed across the United States does not currently exist.

According to the DOE, there were 1,398 AFV refueling stations in the nation's metropolitan areas in 1992. Compressed natural gas (313) and propane fuels (782) accounted for 1,095 of these; in 1995, the number nationwide had risen to 4,587 (U.S. Department of Energy 1993, Sec. 1). In a country with more than 200,000 filling stations, the number looks rather pale, but every state now has at least some refueling capability and some major cities have a score.[13]

When assessing availability, it is important to keep the fleets that are being targeted in mind. In the early stages of entry, AFVs will surely be concentrated in locations with infrastructure capability. In some cases, those will be for fleets of trucks and light vehicles that operate exclusively in particular metropolitan areas or regions. In other cases, the fleets will be a city bus system or vehicles that support a major airport operation. As fleets grow, and with growth as demand increases, supply points will follow. However, in the early stages of market development the chicken egg puzzle will always plague the supporting industry. Just how large is the U.S. alternative fleet and what are its future prospects? At the time of a DOE 1996 survey, there were some 421,000 AFVs in the U.S. fleet, with most of them operating in private fleets (U.S. Department of Energy 1996, 10).

State Regulatory Hurdles

The progress made thus far by the entry of AFV technology has been in spite of old-style public utility regulation that affects primarily the distribution of natural gas. The identical problem would face electricity providers if electric cars became a significant competing technology. The central issue relates to the regulation of prices charged by local distribution companies, which are set by state public utility commissions. Viewed as a monopolist, the natural gas distributor has an exclusive area franchise in which it operates. There is no direct competition from other natural providers in the sale of the product to typical residential and commercial customers, while large users may contract with gas producers and have their gas shipped from distant points.

Public utility commissions engage in rate-of-return regulation when setting prices. Using a standard, but complicated, approach, the regulatory body identifies an appropriate rate base, determines what is to be included, and approves a pricing scheme that yields some predicted rate of return to the gas provider. Providers and regulators engage in periodic struggles when prices are to be altered.

The AFV market is different in significant ways from the market for residential, commercial, and industrial gas in that CNG will compete head-to-head with gasoline at the pump. Of course, natural gas competes with electricity in its traditional market, but that market exists only so long as the potential customer is determining which technology to use. Once a boiler or furnace is selected, the competition over fuel ends.

Competition at the filling station is continuous, particularly for dual-fueled vehicles, and the market turnover of automobiles occurs more frequently than the turnover of home furnaces and industrial machinery. At the same time, the natural gas provider is still a monopolist, at least for that single fuel. The central problem here relates to incentives for natural gas providers to assume a new market risk. With traditional rate regulation, there is no risk premium paid for the development of a new market.

A conceptual solution to the problem lies in separating the assets that serve the AFV market and allowing gas providers complete freedom in setting price. Alternately, gas providers can be allowed to establish separate firms dedicated to the AFV market. These firms would buy natural gas from pipelines or producers, paying the market price. Then, they would sell the gas to the AFV market at prices determined by market competition. Old-fashioned economic regulation applied traditionally to natural gas providers will not work in the AFV market. For the new technology to enter, regulatory reform will be necessary.

The Inherently Local Nature of the Problem

As indicated earlier and recognized explicitly by the CAA, the ozone creation problem is inherently local, and there are wide differences across cities. Chilton and Boemer point out that

> Ozone's real-world chemistry is even more dynamic than this, however—VOC-NOx ratios can change throughout a single day. Ratios also vary by metropolitan area and can differ within portions of an individual city. Further, the relative amounts of VOCs and NOx in the air are linked to the location and size of their sources and the movement of air masses. VOCs originate mostly from vehicle emissions, chemical and petroleum refining companies, industrial solvents and natural vegetation (1996, 18).

Continuing with their discussion, Chilton and Boemer indicate that trees and other vegetation are significant sources of background VOCs and of course, urban vegetation varies significantly across metropolitan areas. Indeed, the National Research Council of the National Academy of Science (NRC) estimates that background levels of ozone, are of "comparable magnitude" to manmade VOC emissions and that complete elimination of manmade sources could leave enough VOC sources to produce smog.[14] Finally, the NRC indicates that solutions to local ozone problems that are not custom-tailored to local conditions will not succeed.[15]

The variation in ozone levels and conditions across cities can be seen in yet another way. Since passage of the CAA, ozone levels have changed dramatically in a number of cities. Jones and Adler indicate that it "is difficult to identify a significant air pollution problem outside California" (Jones and Adler 1995, 7). Across 1992-1994, the reduction in exceedances for rest of the nation fell by 57 percent, for California, the reduction was 27 percent. In 1988-90, the years reflected in the CAA mandate, the nonattainment regions totaled eighty-five, with forty marginal. In 1992-94, total was eighteen with twelve marginal.[16] Even so, the 1988-90 data define the problem, and the various control regions, even those that are cleaner, must follow the CAA prescription.

Now, consider this: There are distinct regional differences in the ozone problem and differences in how people in various regions are addressing the problem. There significant differences in the availability of AFV fuels across regions as well as the likely concentration of AFVs that could ultimately form viable markets.[17] Given the differences in the air quality gap to be closed and the regional options for closing it, logic suggests that the instruments of control should be decentralized, encouraging cities and states to reactivate the programs that were cleaning the air prior to the passage of the initial federal air pollution control statutes. The success of CAA and EPACT rely on actions to be taken by cities, states, and regions. With NAAQs as a baseline, California standards tougher than the baseline, and with promises of cleaner fuel autos, logic further suggests that city, state, and regional control groups should be given complete flexibility in determining incentive-based rules for inducing technological change.

How can regions that seek cleaner air make their desires known in the market place? After all, markets for air quality are few and far between. Should communities and regions consider modifying fuel taxes to make cleaner-burning fuels more attractive? Should subsidies be provided to investors who build clean fuel filling stations? Or should consumers be given incentives to purchase cleaner cars and fuels? How would these incentives be calculated? And where might the zone of control be located?

Economic Incentives for the Production of Cleaner Air

Finding reliable incentives that encourage people to treat air quality with owner-like concern is the crux of the environmental challenge. In the absence of transactions costs, the problem seems simple. We could follow a process or market approach. Property rights to defined elements of the atmosphere could be placed in the hands of owners, be they environmental organizations or private entrepreneurs, and the owner would predictably manage the valuable asset to maximize its value. Lovers of cleaner air and people who wish to produce goods and services would compete for use of the valuable rights. In theory, the market process would yield an effective and efficient outcome.

Taking another approach, we could look to Professor Pigou. Wise politicians seeking to serve the public interest could calculate taxes and fees to be imposed on individuals who use the scarce atmosphere. Campers who build fires and drivers of automobiles would receive bills that reflect the cost they impose when consuming the environment. Again, we assume that information is free, enforcement is costless, and transactions costs are negligible. Were it not for transactions costs, we could rely on common-law rules that endow environmental rights to all property owners and offer protection when those rights are violated against the owners' will. But while common law works well for pollutants that have a known source that is readily controlled, the rule of law faces severe challenges when the problem has to do with millions of small emission sources that collectively produce unwanted clouds called smog.

Taking a leaf from the Tar-Pamlico watershed story, we can imagine a community that sets a baseline for air quality that is monitored continuously. The community could reward activities that improve baseline conditions and penalize those whose actions tend to undermine it. The community could provide a scheme of subsidies and taxes that affect the decisions of ordinary people, whether they be environmentalists or not. Going further, the community could organize a market for emission rights where those who find ways to reduce emissions below the baseline could sell the rights to others who face higher control costs. All along, air quality would improve, and a primitive but important set of property rights would emerge.

The U.S. struggle to improve air quality has reached a point where the gains from employing economic incentives, like a permit market or emission fees and subsidies, are large enough to cover some meaningful transactions costs. Emission permit markets are now in place nationally for sulfur dioxide emission allowance. Southern California has an emissions market, and the city of Chicago has a burgeoning market underway. A plethora of special taxes, subsidies, and other incentive programs are in place across the states, and the federal government has modulated fuel taxes to favor or penalize certain fuels.

The rich variety of state, local, and regional programs illustrates the range of experiments that can take place in America's national laboratory of the states. Recognizing that air pollution problems are almost always local and regional, the approaches we observe at least offer the prospects for discovering lower-cost ways to produce and guard cleaner air. In effect, states and cities compete for population and economic activities, which are highly mobile. Those public units that impose burdensome rules will be punished when people vote with their feet; those that find lower-cost ways to achieve air quality goals will be rewarded. The resulting ferment leads to adjustments in taxes, subsidies, and permit markets that make it possible for an efficient mix of control instruments to emerge.

The Systems Experiments

Actions take by the federal government to improve air quality and affect the expansion of the AFV fleet are just as pervasive as those found at the state and local level. There are taxes, subsidies, permit markets, and a heavy dose of mandates. When considered together, the federal programs seem to reveal a crude effort to encourage the use of cleaner fuels and cleaner fuel vehicles. But unlike the local and state government, the federal government cannot very well fit its schemes to the air quality goal sought by most people. Conditions vary markedly across cities and states, but federal programs can only offer a uniform approach.

An examination of federal and state incentive programs illustrates some of the points and indicates the richer variation of state programs. We also find that some fuel types are penalized heavily relative to others, and that one searching for programs based primarily on the goal of providing cleaner air is apt to be disappointed by the evidence to be presented.

Federal Incentive Programs

At the federal level, tax credits and deductions are offered for the purchase AFVs and certain fuels. Federal tax law also provides subsidies in the form of differential fuel excise taxes for those who purchase alternative fuels. Federal income tax deductions are provided under the EPACT for the incremental costs of engine modification, fuel storage and delivery systems, and emission control systems (retrofit). Deductions are also allowed for refueling facility expenditures. The following limits are placed on these deductions:

1. Up to $2,000 for vehicles that weigh less than 10,000 pounds;
2. $10,000 for vehicles that weigh between 10,000 and 26,000 pounds;
3. $50,000 for trucks and vans over 26,000 pounds and for buses with seating capacity of twenty or more adults;
4. $100,000 for AFV refueling facilities; and
5. For flexible-fuel vehicles, only the incremental costs of qualified items can be deducted.

The EPACT also provides for a 10 percent credit for purchases of electric vehicles, up to a maximum of $4,000, a credit scheduled to fall by 25 percent in 2002, by one-half in 2003, and by 75 percent in 2004 (U.S. Department of Energy 1994, 128-30).

Alcohol receives unusually favorable treatment. For example, section 40 of the federal tax code provides a federal income tax credit of sixty cents per gallon for alcohol content in fuel when used as either a mixture (at least 10 percent alcohol) or as a straight fuel. Ethanol producers are provided a tax credit of ten cents for each gallon of fuel, up to 15 million gallons per year, that is sold to buyers who use it in fuel mixtures or to retail purchasers. These credits do not apply to alcohol produced from petroleum, natural gas, or coal (i.e., methanol). Under current law, these credits are to expire on 1 January 2001. The federal tax code also provides a tax credit of three dollars per barrel-of-oil equivalent for domestic production of oil, gas, and synthetic fuels derived from nonconventional sources.[18]

Federal highway motor fuel taxes differ for all major conventional and alternative fuels. The current rate on gasoline is 18.4¢ per gallon. The rate for diesel fuel is 24.4¢ per gallon. All but 6.9¢ of these taxes is allocated to the highway trust fund, with the balance earmarked for deficit reduction and cleanup of underground storage tanks. Liquified petroleum gas, liquified natural gas, methanol (from natural gas), and 10 percent ethanol fuels are taxed at 18.3¢ 18.4¢, 11.4¢, and 13¢, respectively. Compressed natural gas is taxed as the equivalent of 5.6¢ per gallon of gasoline, which is 48.54¢ per million Btu.

By making some major assumptions, we can gain some insight into the consequences of the net tax or subsidy, relative to gasoline, provided by the federal government for the purchase of AFVs and use of alternative fuels. Assume that the income tax credit for the purchase of alcohol fuels amounts to six cents per gallon for 10 percent ethanol blends. Using a 28 percent marginal tax rate, when calculations are made that account for the various subsidy programs, we find that the net value of the tax reductions is largest for electric vehicles. Ethanol is some distance away in second place. And compressed natural gas comes in third. The value of the tax reductions for the other fuels is probably too small to make much difference in consumer behavior. Even with the large tax subsidies, electric vehicles have not been able to emerge as a competing technology, nor has ethanol production been stimulated in recent years. With a price tax for electric vehicles exceeding $30,000 and with battery replacement costs running close to half that amount, the lack of market penetration of electric is surely understandable. As to ethanol, the high demand for corn has driven up its price, making alcohol production a less attractive proposition.

What about the Pigovian tax principle? Do federal fuel taxes in any way reflect the environmental damages associated with the various fuels? The principle here suggests that cleaner-burning fuels should be taxed less than dirtier ones. Pigou would be greatly disappointed. Federal taxes penalize compressed natural gas, which is the cleanest-burning nonelectric fuel. Ethanol blends, a petroleum-based fuel, enjoy lower taxes. And electric vehicles, which get the largest incentives of all, do not penetrate the market. Apparently, federal taxes are more about special interest politics than efficient protection of the environment.

State Alternative Fuel Regulations, Laws, and Incentives

What about the states? Has the systems approach yielded environmental protection? Interest among the states in alternative fuel vehicles appears to be universal. As of November 1994, all fifty states and the District of Columbia had either enacted statutes or regulations, or had executive orders that in some way facilitate the use of alternative fuels in motor vehicles. These measures range from very minor and relatively passive measures to complicated and detailed mandates, tax credits, tax deductions, grants, and other measures supporting the acquisition of AFVs and stimulation of AFV technologies (U.S. Department of Energy 1995).

California, for example, has a comprehensive set of subsidies and mandates contained in at least fifteen statutes related to the use of vehicles that produce lower emissions than conventional gasoline-powered vehicles. One such statute requires the state to purchase 25 percent AFVs as it replaces the state fleet. Another statute allows a 55 percent tax credit, up to $1,000 per passenger vehicle and up to $3,500 for heavier vehicles, for those who purchase low emission vehicles or retrofit conventional vehicles. California also sets an excise tax on fuels with 85 percent ethanol or methanol that is one-half the rate charged on gasoline. For operators of flexible-fuel vehicles in the air quality district, the Sacramento Metropolitan Air Quality Management District annually offers $500 to consumers for the purchase of 85 percent methanol fuels.

At the other extreme, Indiana provides no state funds or mandates for AFVs, but the state government offers assistance to private firms and localities in attracting federal grants for AFV activities. Like Indiana, Kentucky has no incentives or mandates, but has several small demonstration projects and has received DOE funding for four retail CNG refueling stations.

As noted earlier, federal motor fuel excise taxes favor alternative fuels over gasoline and diesel fuel, but place a relative penalty on some of the cleaner fuels. State taxes paint an entirely different picture. When each fuel is examined separately, we find that on average compressed natural gas enjoys the lowest tax, methanol next, and then propane. Ethanol blends face a higher tax that is almost equal to that of gasoline. Unlike the federal taxing authorities, those in the states seem to be better equipped to tax on the basis of environmental cost. Why might this be the case? Apparently, federal politicians face larger incentives that cause them to favor special interest groups. The fact that the federal government is a taxing monopolist that cannot easily be escaped strengthens its hand. To avoid federal taxes, one must leave the country. In contrast, state taxing authorities worry about the fees charged in the adjoining state. People can move and avoid a particular state's taxing power at a much lower cost.

Urban Air Pollution and Environmental Zones

Remember that urban air pollution is a regional, not a national, problem. The biological envelope that matters is generally local. Different atmospheric conditions, population densities, and other characteristics deny the prospects for defining a detailed national solution for smog reduction. As the history of the CAA demonstrates, uniform command-and-control simply will not get the job done.

To address the urban air quality problem, consider the possibility of establishing the counterpart of a river basin association, perhaps called an environmental zone. Each zone would be organized by interest groups—people in a region who have incentives to do something about air pollution problems. The regions would be defined by characteristics of the environmental issue to be addressed. Since smog production is a local phenomenon that is tied directly to emissions from mobile and stationary sources of particular pollutants, the geographic concentration of sources and receivers of smog would set the limits of control. The 1990 Clean Air Act gives a crude recognition of environmental zones by defining metropolitan areas and the Ozone Transport Region as the controlling units. Some pieces of a decentralized approach appear to be falling into place.

Each environmental zone could be granted open-ended flexibility in achieving baseline air quality goals determined by the community. An overall performance standard based on air quality monitoring could replace technology-based command-and-control regulation. That is, zones would be free to devise their own solutions to address their pollution problems, so long as they progressed to meeting air quality standards based on goals related to public health. Of course under existing statutes, relaxation of EPA and other mandates would require approval by federal authorities; a given metropolitan area or control region would apply for the zone designation and exemption from current command-and-control. Those applying would specify how they plan to achieve smog-reduction goals, giving details on actions to be taken and how the region will monitor outcomes and enforce actions. The plan would be outcome-, not input-based.

The environmental zone application could describe a combination of policy instruments. The region might base its fuel taxes on emission characteristics. These could include

· Differential fuel taxes that reflect different emission characteristics;
· Provision of tax credits or deductions for the purchase of AFVs and construction of refueling facilities;
· Specification of AFVs to be used in particular locations;
· Purchase of clean fuel vehicles by public and private entities;
· Inspection and maintenance programs that provide low cost, effective means for ensuring emission reductions;
· Congesting pricing that reduces the use of private automobiles, and
· Development of emissions trading schemes that provide incentives for the use of cleaner fuels and technologies.

Since each zone would have unique features, each package would likely focus on different elements. In some cases, control of NOx is more important than obtaining reductions in VOCs. In other cases, stationary controls are more crucial than obtaining additional emissions reductions from mobile sources. But each request would have one common element: The proposals would be outcome-based. Inputs alone, that is, meeting some federal definition of the kind of control equipment a polluter was using, would not count.

Competition for zone designation would set in motion a discovery process that is likely to lead to fresh approaches for improving environmental quality. Metropolitan areas, states, and regions are in a competitive market for high quality economic growth. Environmental quality is an important consideration for people and firms when making location decisions. But the means chosen for maintaining and improving environmental quality matter as well. If one region can provide cleaner air at a lower cost than another, then more wealth will be produced in the low-cost region. The resulting competition would likely reduce inflexible federal command-and-control regulations, eliminate strict rules requiring centralized inspection of vehicles, and remove high taxes on emissions and burdensome transportation plans. These could be replaced with more flexible market-based approaches that are generated by persons, firms, groups, and governments at the local and regional levels who will live with and pay for the outcomes.

If the current statutory framework remains in place, the national government would play an important role in the process. By statute, there are goals to be achieved. Those seeking to establish environmental zones would first be challenged to achieve the national goal, but they are obviously free to go beyond it. Given rising incomes and strong preferences for improved air quality, it is likely that the process would inspire a (less costly and more efficient) race to the top. Allowing flexibility to achieve outcomes means air quality monitoring is much more important. The EPA would be challenged to provide better, more complete data on emission levels, and to give regular progress reports for each operating zone.

The federal government also plays a key role in leveling the playing field for competing fuels and AFVs. As indicated in the section on taxes and incentives, federal tax policy currently favors electric vehicles and penalizes the use of propane. All fuels and AFVs should be treated equally by federal taxing authorities. Vehicle taxes should be set on the basis of gasoline equivalence, relying fundamentally on the notion of taxes as a highway user fee.

But why not take a fresh approach to the whole problem? Why not admit that today's world no longer fits statutes that began their evolutionary journey in 1970 when little was known about the sources and effects of air pollution? A fresh approach would allow states and multistate regions formed by compact to set their own air quality standards and then find the means to achieve them. If a national baseline is still needed at all, it should be based on a public health rationale and applied when state and regional governments fail in their efforts to deal with air quality problems. The concept of environmental zones could then be applied within the boundaries of states and regions.

Environmental Zones As a General Concept

The outline of the zone concept has been developed in terms of clean air and national security goals. However, the concept is a general one that can be used to manage all forms of pollution. Few of the environmental challenges are truly national in scope; they are typically local or regional in nature. Indeed, the history of environmental law indicates that the entry of the federal government's entry into environmental regulation first related to efforts to coordinate state and local actions. Even after the formation of the federal blueprint in the 1970s, the federal government continued to rely on the states for operating federally approved programs and in the case of water quality, setting water quality goals for streams, rivers, and lakes. All attempts to impose uniform standards across the entire country have met with frustration, exemptions, delays, and variable enforcement. To some degree, the variation obtained reflects differences in the nature of the pollution problems encountered and the ability of communities to deal with the national goals.

We have seen the emergence of North Carolina's Tar-Pamlico River Basin Association and other community-based approaches for managing hummingbird economies. The relevant aspect of Tar-Pamlico relates to EPA's agreement to alter its command-and-control approach to point-source controls, which could not achieve the desired standard, and allow the association to meet a water quality performance standard. An embryonic community approach to managing urban air quality is seen in the Washington-Baltimore Endzone program (Krupnick and Anderson 1996, 6-9). Relying on the power of information and community cooperation, Endzone provides information on ozone levels and encourages citizens to cut back on driving on bad days. People are also encouraged to avoid refueling, using volatile paints and gasoline-powered lawn and garden equipment. EPA sanctions that might be imposed on regions like Washington-Baltimore provide an incentive for governments to cooperate, but unfortunately, EPA regulations and the Clean Air Act currently provides no encouragement for such community action. Managers of environmental zones could at least encourage this kind of cooperation and perhaps find ways to reward smaller communities and indivduals who are wiling to bear some cost in protecting environmental rights.

We have also seen visions of environmental zones in other countries. As explained earlier, all of the rivers in France are managed by autonomous and distinct regional authorities (Bower 1981). Each of the associations must obtain its own funding, and each is accountable for improving water quality. In the United States, EPA's bubble and offset policies for air pollution control represents steps in the direction of environmental zones (Hahn and Hester 1989, 361-406). These instruments decentralize control by allowing plant operators to meet overall standards, instead of meeting standards at each and every source, and to obtain pollution offsets from other plants. In other words, the rudimentary environmental zones are emerging (Maloney and Yandle 1983, 283-320).

Recognition of the evolutionary nature of institutions devised to protect environmental assets carries us back to chapter 1 and the first discussion of hummingbird economies. It was there that we saw the importance of economizing based on the specialized knowledge held by those who lived on the commons. They were not only the best informed about the peculiar aspects of the commons problem, they also had the largest incentive to minimize cost in managing the commons. Whether it be a fishery, a pasture, or the air mantle over a large city, the problem is generally the same. Effective and efficient solutions will come from the community that has the most at stake. In discussing property rights and how they evolve, Elinor Ostrom and Edella Schlager cogently summarize the general nature of the problem to be addressed:

> The complexity of natural settings is immense. The likelihood is small that any set of uniform rule for all natural resource systems within a large territory will produce optimal results. Instead of attempting to derive or identify the single best set of rules for governing natural resources, theoretical and empirical research is better used to help inform those who are close to particular natural resource systems, as well as those in larger, overarching agencies, about principles they can use to improve performance. (1996, 128-129)

If common-law logic is included in building a statutory framework, the chances for resolving urban smog and other environmental problems will be enhanced.

Notes

1. New car emissions of hydrocarbons have fallen 97 percent since 1970, and California standards call for the equivalent of a 99 percent reduction. Between 1982 and 1991, ozone forming emissions decreased 13 percent and CO levels, even with an increase in the number of vehicles owned and miles driven (U.S. Department of Energy 1994, 33).

2. The deepest criticism of the massive efforts to deal with the ozone problem relates to the 1988 data that forms the premise of the problem. The critics point out that 1988 was an outlier year for draught and temperature, which contribute to higher ozone readings. Examination of a longer time series, before and after 1988, reduces significantly the ozone readings for the designated ozone cities and regions. (On this see, Jones and Adler 1995; and Chilton and Boemer 1996.)

3. Passell points out that Chicago is establishing a market for Volatile Organic Chemicals (VOCs) (Passell 1995, C1). Major corporate polluters—Caterpillar, Abbott Labs, Amoco, Corn Products—are participating in the planning phase. The program involves six counties and hundreds of polluters. The 300 that emit more than ten tons annually will be obligated to participate. By 2007 total allowable emissions will be reduced 60 percent. The program will also facilitate the purchase and destruction of older, higher-emission cars. Holden describes the Regional Clean Air Incentive Market or RECLAIM and reports that the Pacific Stock Exchange has created an electronic trading system for Southern California pollution credits called the SMOG exchange (Holden 1995, B3). Just twenty-four companies listed credits.

4. When the CAA was passed, clean vehicles were far more than just a gleam in some inventor's eye. Propane-burning vehicles, which accounted for 10 percent of the vehicles in Holland in 1992, had been used in the United States for decades. Methanol- and ethanol-based fuels, used widely in Brazil, were available for conventional vehicles throughout most U.S. markets. Compressed natural gas vehicles had dominated a small part of the Italian market and were a clear contender for expanded use in the United States, and electric vehicles, long seen in airports and on golf courses in miniature form, were being developed and demonstrated for commuters in U.S. cities. In addition, reformulated gasoline was in the works, and the auto companies were heavily involved in improving the emission performance of their gasoline burning engines.

5. The California standards are far more complex than indicated here. The standards involve three auto tiers—transitional low emission vehicles (TLEVs), which are to meet the standard stated in the text, low emission vehicles (LEVs), which are to meet a stricter standard, and ultra low emission vehicles (ULEVs) that are to achieve a standard that is close to zero. Speaking in terms of a composite emission standard called non-methane organic gases, a precursor for smog, the California Air Resources Board estimates that *lifetime* emissions of the three vehicle types will be fifty-five pounds, thirty-three pounds, and eighteen pounds respectively. The Society of Automotive Engineers estimates that improved gasoline engine vehicles could reduce emissions to the level of the LEV vehicles. (For discussion, see Hahn 1993, 2-4.)

6. The nine cities are Los Angeles, Houston, New York, Baltimore, Chicago, San Diego, Philadelphia, Milwaukee, and Ventura, California (U.S. Department of Energy 1994, 35).

7. When the oxygen content is increased, hydrocarbon and CO emissions can be reduced by 7.0 and 9.3 percent respectively (Sperling 1993, 74-9). Requirements for reformulated (cleaner) gasoline, a distinct gasoline product, not to be confused with oxygenated gasoline, add yet one more dimension to the clean air arsenal. Mandated for the country's nine worst ozone areas starting in 1995, a two-phase program calls for a 15 percent reduction in volatile organic compounds, beginning in 1995, and a 25 percent reduction, beginning in 2000. According to DOE estimates, the total reformulated fuel requirements for these urban markets and others that may choose to require the same fuel will quickly reach 60 percent of all gasoline sold in the United States (U.S. Department of Energy 1994, 23-24).

8. The states include Connecticut, Delaware, Maine, Maryland, Massachusetts, New Hampshire, New Jersey, New York, Pennsylvania, Rhode Island, Vermont and the consolidated metropolitan statistical area of D.C., which includes part of Virginia. The CAA allows for creation of other such regions, when the EPA deems necessary (Trinkle 1995, 169-199).

9. In 1994, the Commission attempted to require California low emission vehicles (LEVs) as a major component of the ozone reduction scheme. The LEVs would have been electric vehicles. However, no agreement could be reached across the twelve states, and the U.S. auto industry filed suit in those states that had adopted the LEV rule, arguing that an LEV for the northeast would be a third car. In brief, the argument turned on the notion that because of differences in climate—colder starts and requirements for heaters—a northeastern LEV would be different from a California LEV. Virginia joined the auto industry suit (Trinkle 1995, 179).

10. NLEV tailpipe emissions would be limited to 0.2 grams per mile for nitrogen oxide and 0.075 grams per mile for hydrocarbons, the two pollutants that produce ozone. Those caps would be 50 percent and 70 percent below current limits, respectively (*Natural Gas Week* 1996, 6-7).

11. The 1990 Kuwait invasion, still fresh in the memories of most Americans, led to a daily curtailment of 7 percent. The Iranian revolution of 1978-79 and the Arab Embargo of 1973-74 had smaller daily impacts on the flow of oil but lasted far longer than the Kuwait disruptions. To put the disruptions in perspective, the daily reductions during the 1978 revolution was equal to roughly 5.5 percent of world daily consumption (U.S. Department of Energy 1996, 35).

12. In addition to these programs for stimulating demand for AFVs, EPACT specifically requires DOE to engage in research and development activities that focus on the development of improved technologies for using natural gas and other alternative fuels.

13. Compressed natural gas and LPG together account for more than 4,400 of these. In November 1995, *USA Today* reported that another four compressed natural gas stations were opening each week. As might be expected, concentration by state is associated with the relative abundance of the fuel type. California shows a relatively large number of compressed natural gas and liquified petroleum gas stations, as does Texas and other gas-producing states (U.S. Department of Energy, 1994, 35; Curley 1995, 3A).

14. In making this point, Chilton and Boemer quote from a National Research Council report, Chilton and Boemer state: "On days conducive to ozone formation, 'this VOC background should be able to generate ozone concentrations that exceed the NAAQS concentration of 0.12 ppm,' says the NRC. Computer-generated simulations have shown that reactions between prevailing levels of NOx and VOCs alone can generate ozone concentrations above 0.08 ppm in the Ohio River Valley and the entire Northeast corridor" (Chilton and Boemer 1996, 18).

15. Beard explains the situation this way: "Control of ozone is especially tricky because each city has its own air chemistry, to which is added unburned hydrocarbons (HC) and oxides of nitrogen (NOX) from cars (Beard 1995, 105-110). Because the ratio is critical, locations with excess HC—in Atlanta, for example, vegetation is a major source of HC—are particularly sensitive to addi-

tional NOX and insensitive to more HC. The reverse is true in area where coal-burning power plants produce NOX. Cars, however, are not tailored to locations, except for statewide regulations specific to California. With cars, the regulators' plan is simply to eliminate as much HC and NOx as possible and hope for the best" (1995, 107).

16. Similar findings are reported for the northeastern states where 1988 data shows thirty-nine nonattainment areas, with twenty-three marginal, six moderate, six serious and three severe. Based on 1992-94 data, the total is thirteen, with six marginal, and no serious or severe (Jones and Adler 1995, 7).

17. There is yet another complicating factor to consider. NOX emissions from mobile and stationary sources become nitrogen pollution in rivers, lakes, and streams, which leads to the eutrophication and fish kills. This in turn leads to a watershed management problem, which is again local or regional in character (Shields 1996, B1 and B5).

18. This credit was initiated when the average wellhead price of domestic oil reaches $23.50, and phase out is to occur when the price of domestic oil reaches $29.50. To qualify for the credit, production has to be in service before 1997.

References

Barnett, Andy H., Mark Brandly, and Bruce Yandle. 1996. *Clean Air and Emerging Alternative Fuel Vehicles: A Time for Environmental Innovation Areas*. Washington: Progress & Freedom Foundation (July).

Beard, Patrick. 1995. Still Smoggy after All These Years. *Car and Driver* (April).

Bower, Blair. 1981. *Incentives in Water Quality Management: France and the Ruhr Area*. Washington: Resources for the Future.

Chilton, Kenneth, and Christopher Boemer. 1996. *Smog in America: The High Cost of Hysteria*. St. Louis: Center for the Study of American Business (January).

Curley, Tim. 1995. Natural Gas Makes Inroads As Auto Fuel. *USA Today* (November 13).

Hahn, Robert H. 1993. *Choosing Among Fuels and Technologies for Cleaning Up the Air*. Washington: American Enterprise Institute (December).

Hahn, Robert W., and Gordon L. Hester. 1989. Marketable Permits: Lessons from Theory and Practice. *Ecology Law Quarterly* 16.

Holden, Benjamin A. 1995. Dirt in Hollywood? Californians Have Pollution-Rights Market Ready for It. *The Wall Street Journal* (April 12).

Jones, K. H., and Jonathan Adler. 1995. Time to Reopen the Clean Air Act: Clearing Away the Regulatory Smog. *Policy Analysis*. Washington: Cato Institute (July 11).

Krupnick, Alan J., and J. W. Anderson. 1996. Revising the Ozone Standard. *Resources* (Fall).

Maloney, Michael T., and Bruce Yandle. 1983. Building Markets for Tradable Pollution Permits. In *Water Rights,* edited by Terry Anderson. San Francisco: Pacific Institute for Public Policy Research.

National Defense Council Foundation. 1995. *Natural Gas Vehicles: Helping Ensure America's Energy Security.* Washington: (October).

Natural Gas Week. 1996. Cloudy Prospects for NGVs May Soon Find Clear Air (January).

Ostrom, Elinor, and Edella Schlager. 1966. The Formation of Property Rights. In *Rights to Nature,* edited by Susan S. Hanna, Carl Folke, and Karl-Goran Maler. Washington: Island Press.

Ozone. 1995. *Automotive Engineering* (April).

Passell, Peter. 1995. Illinois Is Looking to Market Forces to Help Reduce Its Smog. *New York Times* (March 30).

Schuchman, F. E. 1950. Pittsburgh—"Smokeless City." *National Municipal Review* (November).

Shields, Todd. 1996. Scientist Tracks Pollution Back to Stacks in the Midwest. *The Washington Post* (April 30).

Sperling, Gilbert. 1993. Alternative Fuel Vehicles. In *Energy Law & Transactions,* Release 5. Oakland: Matthew Bender & Co.: 74-9.

Trinkle, Daniel B. 1995. Cars, Congress, and Clean Air for the Northeast: A Separation of Powers Analysis of the Ozone Transport Commission. *Environmental Affairs* 23: 169-201

U.S. Department of Energy. 1993. *First Interim Report of the Federal Fleet Conversion Task Force.* Washington, D.C. (August).

U.S. Department of Energy. 1994. *Alternatives to Traditional Transportation Fuels: An Overview.* Washington, D.C. (August).

U.S. Department of Energy. 1994. *Comparative Alternative/Clean Fuels Provisions of the Clean Air Act Amendments of 1990 and the Energy Policy Act of 1992.* Washington, D.C. (August).

U.S. Department of Energy. 1995. *EPACT Initiatives for Alternative Fuel Vehicles.* Washington, D.C. (March).

U.S. Department of Energy. 1996. *Alternative Fueled Vehicles for State Government and Fuel Provider Fleets, A Guide.* Washington, D.C. (March).

U.S. Department of Energy. 1996. *U.S. Energy Outlook and Implications for Energy R&D.* Hearing of the Subcommittee on Energy and Environment, Committee on Science, U.S. House of Representatives (March 14).

U.S. Department of Energy. 1996. *Statement of Jay Hakes.* Administrator, Energy Information Administration, Department of Energy. Testimony before the Subcommittee on Energy and Environment of the Committee on Science, U.S. House of Representatives (March 14).

U.S. Department of Energy. 1996. *Statement of Joseph Romm*. As Acting Principal Deputy Assistant Secretary, Office of Energy Efficiency and Renewable Energy. Testimony before the Subcommittee on Energy and Environment of the Committee on Science, U.S. House of Representatives (March 14).

U.S. Environmental Protection Agency. 1994. *Motor Vehicles and the 1990 Clean Air Act*. EPA 400-F-92-013, Washington, D.C. (August).

Chapter 6

The Decline and Recovery of Common Law

Over the last five years, I have spent a few weeks each summer in Bozeman, Montana. In the midst of the amazing beauty of Yellowstone, the Rockies, and the Gallatin Valley, I work with colleagues at PERC (the Political Economy Research Center) teaching a short course for university students and helping guide the research of graduate fellows on environmental issues. In 1994, I worked with Marlow Green, a law student from Cornell Law School who took on the task of examining common-law environmental protection. Marlow and I discussed some of the topics included in the earlier chapters of this book and searched to discover why common-law actions were not being pursued more frequently. At the outset, we had an explanation for the attractiveness of statute-based command-and-control regulation. As pointed out in chapter 3, a one-suit-fits-all approach offers significant opportunities for special interest groups to gain at the expense of less-organized, highly diverse, citizens. We also understood that some problems such as mobile source emissions simply did not lend themselves to common-law case-by-case litigation. Yet we also recognized a host of other situations where polluters were small in number and damages readily identifiable. We wanted to know why the effective working of common law had somehow become lost in the nation's effort to manage environmental quality.

Upon returning to Clemson, I continued to work on the question, but being an empirical economist, I wanted to know more about the data on common-law cases. I realized that describing many cases, such as those in chapter 4, may illustrate key points and trends, but that more data are needed if one is to talk about overall tendencies. The search for more data led me to organize a student research team who were given the task of finding every reported state and federal case over the last fifty years that involved air and water pollution for a sample of eight western states where common-law pleadings were included. In other words, we looked for nuisance and trespass cases among the full data set. The combined work of Marlow Green and my Clemson students contributes to the first part of this chapter. In the chapter's next part I assess current environmental law discussions that are making a case for the resurgence of common law. The last major section puts forward some ideas on new institutions that assign a major role to common-law environmental protection.

Common and Statute Law Competition

Competition and Market Share

The world is a practical place. The institutions developed by communities for protecting environmental and other assets are part of an evolutionary process that can lead to a lower-cost world where the supply of environmental quality is expanded. Alternately, the institutions we observe may be more the result of interest-group struggles to obtain specialized benefits. On the one hand, we have an efficiency story that conserves resources while reaching for environmental goals. On the other, we find a redistribution story, where some groups gain and others lose, while the body politic seeks environmental improvement. Whether by the rules of common law or by the use of regulations derived from statutes, people will choose among available institutions when they attempt to solve environmental problems. Given all the rules and strictures that condition the legal world, common-law courts and administrative agencies compete to serve the interests of people who seek to resolve problems. The choice between legal arrangements, like other choices, involves consideration of cost and expected benefits as perceived by individuals operating in the political economy.

If common law offers the lower-cost route for resolving an environmental controversy as perceived by the litigants, people will take that option. If the administrative procedures of regulation form the low cost route, it will be chosen. By considering the record and comparing options, we may make fact-based judgments about the relative merits of system versus process for environmental management.

Competition between the Two Systems

The flurry of statutory activity for environmental protection that occurred in the 1970s, and the regulations that followed, created a vast assortment of administrative procedures that people could use when confronting an environmental problem. When faced with what appeared to be a problem, people could contact a state or federal administrator and file a statute-based complaint. No attorney was needed. All persons, no matter what their connection with the problem, if any at all, gained standing by statute. Unlike a common-law suit, no scientific evidence of harm had to be proffered. All that was necessary was demonstration of a technical violation of a statute. The statutes and regulations seemed to spell out what constituted a violation. The list included failing to install and operate stipulated pollution-control equipment, exceeding the amount of discharge allowed by a permit, failing to submit timely and appropriate reports, and, of course, damaging people and the environment through intentional, negligent, or accidental pollution. To make things even more attractive for the petitioner, instead of receiving a bill for lawyer services, the citizen could be paid for informing an administrator of a statute violation.

In addition to lowering out-of-pocket cost for potential plaintiffs, the statutes allowed for citizen suits, which could be organized by attorneys and, if successful, paid for by the polluter. Instead of being a costly endeavor for concerned citizens, the statutes made environmental activism a paying proposition, especially for better-organized groups. A person contemplating which way to go, common law or administrative law, is likely to choose the latter.

In 1972, the regulation of water quality in some states was already traveling the administrative route, so much so that EPA, operating under the Clean Water Act, quickly delegated authority to those states to operate the EPA permit and compliance programs. Other states never obtained EPA delegation. Today, we have state and federal regulatory agencies working in tandem to manage water quality and achieve federal goals. Citizens in any states have access to federal authorities, as well as to state agencies that operate under state and federal programs. As we have seen, the passage of federal statutes ended an era of federal common law as it applied to interstate pollution problems. But the statutes did not end the use of common law in controversies between parties within the boundaries of a state.

How has this competition worked out? Has common law maintained its share of the market in the post-1970 period? Or have statute-law remedies taken the field? To get at these questions, my research assistants and I counted all the reported cases for eight western states for air and water pollution in both state and federal courts for the years 1940 through 1994. I point out that federal court cases must involve a federal question. A federal question may relate to diversity—a situation where the plaintiff and defendant are in two states—or it may relate to a federal statute like the Clean Water Act.

We first counted the total number of cases for each court system—federal and state—and then summed the two numbers by year. We then calculated the share of all cases where common-law pleadings involving nuisance and trespass were included. Examination of total cases told us what had happened to total activity across more than fifty years. The share data spoke to market share and how common law had fared in competition with federal statute law.

Chart 6.1 presents the total case data, which change markedly in the post-1970 period. Federal court activity operated at a low and relatively stable level before 1970 and expanded after the passage of the federal statutes. It is obvious that the federal statutes spawned a large volume of suits in both court systems, with the largest level of activity occurring in federal courts. Litigants concerned about pollution had little difficulty finding a federal question in the post-1970 period.

Chart 6.2 shows the common-law share of cases based on nuisance and trespass pleadings. Nuisance and trespass as a share of all cases has fallen systematically since 1940. But why the earlier decline? Why did common-law activity fall before the 1970s? Peter Davis encountered this same question after investigating 445 common-law cases that reached from the nineteenth century through 1969 (Davis 1971, 738-781). He was struck by the sharp decline of common-law activity recorded in the 1960s. Part of the explanation must relate to the rise of state statutes and regulation. In the pre-1970 period, states were building bodies of administrative law that addressed pollution problems. Common law first competed with state statutes and later competed with state and federal statutes.

What about individual states? Is the pattern always the same? To address these questions, we examined data for eight western states, selecting states that represented distinct regions and geographic conditions. Included in the sample are Arizona, California, Idaho, Louisiana, New Mexico, Oregon, and Texas. We calculated the share of all air and water pollution cases where common-law pleadings were included. Charts 6.3 and 6.4 form two distinct groups. Chart 6.3, containing data for California, Oregon, and Texas, shows erratic but higher levels of common-law activity in the pre-1970 period. Chart 6.4, with data for Arizona, Idaho, Kansas, Louisiana, and New Mexico, shows just the reverse. Examination of the data suggests that the costs of bringing common-law actions became relatively lower over time, or access to administrative law became more difficult, for the states in Chart 6.4 compared with those in Chart 6.3. Differences in state statutes and other factors undoubtedly had a significant bearing on the outcomes. In addition, the closer cooperation of state and federal officials probably yielded lower out-of-pocket costs for obtaining administrative relief in the states with declining common-law activities. In any case, the data suggest competition between common law and statute law is real and effective across this sample of states.

What Can We Say about Efficient Outcomes?

The fact that citizens are subsidized for successfully bringing statute-based environmental cases is reason enough to think that common law would suffer. But how does this subsidy affect outcomes based on the idea that enforcement resources should be deployed where the net social benefits are largest? Think back to the EPA study of how its congressionally mandated use of resources matched the relative risks of national environmental problems. Then, think for a moment of how you would allocate environmental actions if you had command

Chart 6.1

Federal & State Common Law Cases
Weighted by GDP

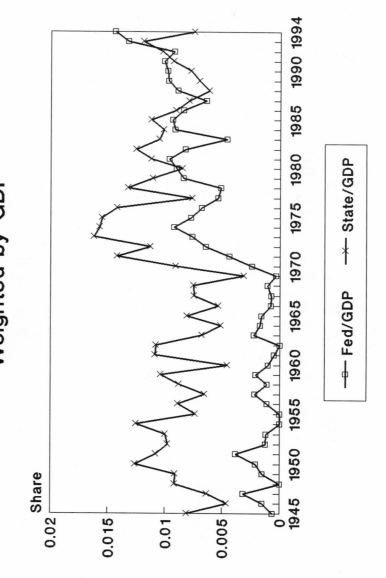

Chart 6.2
Common Law Share of Water & Air
Pollution Cases: 1945–1994

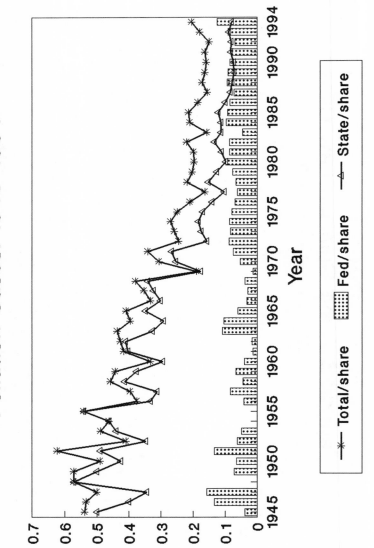

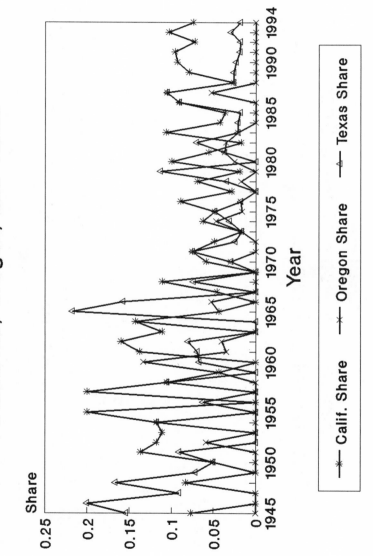

Chart 6.3
Common Law Activity: State Share
California, Oregon, and Texas

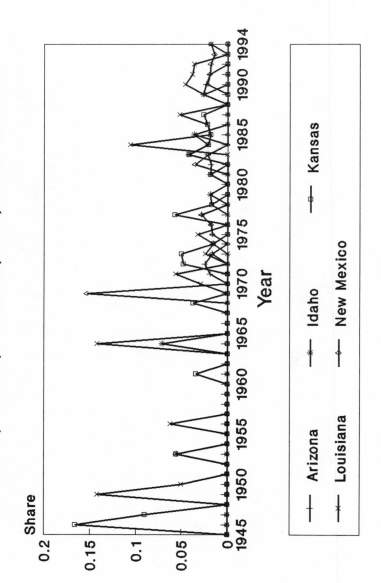

Chart 6.4
Common Law Activity: State Share
Arizona, Idaho, Kansas, LA., New Mexico

of a state's limited machinery for protecting environmental assets. In performing this mental experiment, some would assign higher value to features of nature than to the value of land along rivers or in cities. Some would assign higher value to human well-being than to endangered species. But everyone would be able to rank an array of problems and give them higher and lower priorities. The development of such a ranking would yield a downward-sloping curve like the one shown in Figure 6.1. Here we see environmental benefit on the vertical axis and a count of actions on the horizontal. The position of the curve indicates that just a few activities have a higher return, but as more and more actions are considered, the return falls. At the extreme, some actions would yield little benefit at all.

The upward-sloping line in the figure measures cost or difficulty in taking actions. Its shape and position reflect the common-sense notion that taking more actions in a fixed period of time will require more resources and give less success. The worst pollution cases will be taken on first by a rational decision maker. The two function together to form a simple supply and demand analysis of legal actions taken to protect environmental assets or rights. Their intersection indicates a point where the additional benefits of taking another protective action will just equal the additional costs of doing so. Beyond that point, the cost in terms of resources used to take an action is less than the gain. Going beyond the intersection would generate wasted effort.

Now if environmental action were generated by the private expenditure of funds, as with private nuisance at common law, those seeking redress would tend to stop at the intersection point in the figure. However, if taking action imposes no cost on the litigants, as with some statute-based actions, then the litigants tend to proceed beyond the intersection in an effort to solve more environmental problems, however they define them. When the actual costs of obtaining relief are hidden from us, we tend to consume more of the apparently cheap item.

Consider what happens if actions are subsidized. Instead of paying or not paying, we get paid. A subsidy affects the cost of taking action, the supply curve in Figure 6.1. If the subsidy is large enough, the supply curve will no longer be relevant to individuals or groups seeking improved environmental quality. Indeed, the subsidy can be so attractive that individuals will begin to search for actions to take. The list of problems to be solved will grow. Some environmental public interest law firms earn good revenues by filing citizen suits for CWA violation. Even trivial violations can pay well. Even the most trivial environmental problem will deserve regulatory attention. By contrast, common law procedures impose cost and force litigants to ration their efforts. Rationing brings focus. For example, instead of considering all hazardous waste sites to be equal, since they contain some amount of hazardous waste, the sites will tend to be ranked on the basis of potential damage to people and the environment.

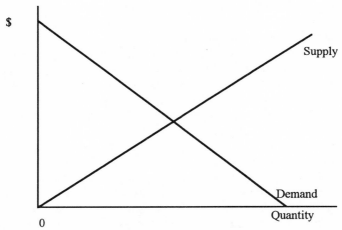

Figure 6.1 Allocating Environmental Protection

Those that pose the greatest risk will be addressed first. Those that pose trivial threats may not be addressed at all.

While this mental experiment tells us nothing about the actual efficiency of the two competing systems of law, it does suggest an inescapable logic for law enforcement. Whether by common law or statute law, actions taken to protect environmental assets and rights should be filtered on some logical basis. The common law asks for scientific evidence of actual or potential harm. Access to the court is provided only to those who are actual parties to a controversy—those who demonstrate that they or their property have been damaged—and the remedies can provide payment for damages and injunctions that stop the harmful activity.

By comparison, statute law and regulation require demonstration that rules have been violated; they do not require evidence of damages. Any person can file a complaint, whether damages can be shown or not. The remedies that result provide no payment to those whose land values may have suffered or whose enjoyment of life has been compromised. Instead, the remedies give payment to those who brought an action (the lawyer) and impose penalties on those who violated the rules that may not be remotely related to the value of the damage done. In short, the two approaches contain different rationing systems and different reward outcomes. It is no wonder that the balance between common-law and statute-law activities changed dramatically in the post-1970 period.

Lawyers and the Common-Law Decision

When Marlow Green and I were working in Montana, trying to understand where common law stood as a protector of environmental rights, we decided to pose some questions to lawyers. After all, when someone is troubled by pollution and decides to take legal action, the potential plaintiff eventually must work with an officer of the court, a lawyer. After listening to the facts of the situation, the lawyer will advise the client as to action. Will the advice lean toward statute or common law? And if it leans one way or the other, why?

Marlow and I developed a set of questions to be posed based on a hypothetical situation. The situation and questions are as follows:

A factory that owns and operates its own water treatment works is discharging into a stream. Cattle of a downstream water rights holder (either riparian or appropriative) are getting sick because of the plant's discharge.

1. Assuming that the discharger is violating its EPA discharge permit and is unwilling to answer your correspondence and phone messages (i.e., settlement is not an option), what legal course of action will you take, if representing the plaintiff, or what legal actions would you expect to face when representing the plaintiff?

Supplemental questions asked:
a. In what court will you sue?
b. What claims do you consider most viable and thus will actively pursue?
c. Are there any claims that you would consider fluff, but would include in your complaint just to cover yourself?

2. Now assume the discharger is in compliance with its permit. What legal course of action will you take?

3. What is your sense of the viability of common-law remedies in your environmental law practice?

Marlow identified thirty-eight major law firms located in major cities and called to talk with attorneys who practiced environmental law. He had useful conversations with seventeen attorneys.[1]

While not a scientific sample or poll, the results of Marlow's calls tell us something about the role of the policeman at the intersection, the lawyer who directs "traffic" to particular locations. On the first question, thirteen of the seventeen attorneys contacted immediately mentioned the use of citizens suits under the Clean Water Act, which meant going to federal court. To them, the statute route seemed simpler and more direct than the common-law route. Two of the remaining four recommended a common-law action in state court, and the remaining two offered no opinion. Statute law clearly won round one of the survey.

In his 1971 report on water pollution litigation, law professor Peter Davis reports on the work of DeBraal, who examined court records in seven Wisconsin counties for evidence of common-law water pollution suits between 1947 and 1967 (Davis 1971, 776). The counties surveyed were the locations of much of Wisconsin's pulp and paper industry. DeBraal found only six common-law cases for the twenty-year period. DeBraal speculated that citizens were content to let state regulators deal with pollution problems. Wisconsin had strongly enforced pollution-control statutes during the time of the study. Apparently, Wisconsin attorneys were advising their clients to contact state agencies when troubled by pollution. Davis also tells how he conducted an informal survey of Wassau, Wisconsin, attorneys to determine their preferences for common-law versus administrative-law actions (Davis 1971, at 780). At the time of the survey, there was no major federal water pollution control program, but his results were more extreme than ours. He could find no attorney in the Wassau, Wisconsin, area who had even been consulted. He concluded that private landowners had either (1) chosen to live with the relatively constant level of pollution found in rivers at the time, (2) lacked awareness of common-law remedies, or (3) had been discouraged by past actions that seemed to favor industrial firms. But the research reported by Davis also gave considerable detail about steps taken by Wisconsin polluters to purchase environmental rights from downstream owners if not the riparian land itself. In other words, there may have been few suits because there was little damage done to property owners by pollution.

Marlow Green's survey had a second question: What if a polluter is operating within the limits of its permit, but damage is still imposed on the farmer? Twelve of the attorneys called for common-law action. One recommended that no action be taken, and one called for a Clean Water Act citizen's suit. Of those recommending a common-law nuisance of trespass action, four indicated that winning would be tough. While being in compliance was not necessarily a shield, the permit and good data on discharge was often persuasive and hard to defeat. One attorney recommending suing EPA if the permit was not violated and cows were still injured.

With respect to the last question on our survey regarding common law, nine of the seventeen attorneys gave an unqualified yes to common-law viability. Seven others discussed its usefulness but qualified their answer by indicating that most problems had statute-based solutions. In those situations, common-law pleadings are often added to the complaint for the sake of covering all possible bases. Only one of the seventeen attorneys contacted said that common law was a thing of the past. Our survey suggests that statute-law and common-law pleadings will be combined.

To see how common law can interact with statute law, consider *Concerned Area Residents for the Environment (CARE) v. Southview Farms* (34 F.3d 114, 1995). This case illustrates how a citizens suit brought under the Clean Water Act was augmented with common-law pleadings (Copeland 1995, 237-288). But instead of a factory imposing cost on a downstream farmer, *CARE* involved a dairy operation that allegedly violated the Clean Water Act and imposed cost on neighboring farms and other property owners. The dairy farm included 1,100 acres of land and 2,200 farm animals that were confined in barns and stalls except at milking time. Large amounts of manure had to be disposed of, and the dairy operator did that in a number of logical ways, including filtration of solids that were then spread by tractors for farming purposes and spraying liquefied waste on fields.

Until the *CARE* decision, farming practices like those of Southview Farms were exempt from the pollution discharge permitting requirements of the Clean Water Act. The exemption applied to agricultural operations that were not concentrated animal feeding operations. Since Southview combined a large amount of cattle with a farming operation that provided space for distributing manure, it seemed to qualify for the exemption. If Southview was a polluter, it was a nonpoint source.

A combination of manure spreading and rainfall triggered the complaint. During periods of heavy rainfall, when the fields were saturated, some of Southview's manure-laden effluent washed into creeks and made its way into a nearby river. The neighbors complained that the dairy had violated part of the Clean Water Act, that the dairy should have been required to have EPA permits for its operation, and that the tractors that spread the manure were really point sources of pollution, not nonpoint sources. The complaints were filed with the EPA and state regulators who declined to take action because of a lack of evidence that Southview was a significant source of pollution. Failing there, the plaintiffs filed a citizen's lawsuit under the authority of the Clean Water Act. Along with the alleged violations, the plaintiffs also sued under common law for damages under the law of trespass. The court granted a jury trial.

The first hurdle to leap would be interpretation of the statute so as to place the dairy in violation of the statute, proving that Southview was a concentrated animal-feeding operation, not a farm. After successfully leaping that hurdle, the plaintiffs would have to demonstrate damages in order to secure the common-law remedy. After a series of trials and on appeal to the federal court, the plaintiff won. Tractors spreading manure were defined as point sources of pollution, which meant that tractor operators would have to have EPA permits. In addition, the dairy was judged to be a concentrated animal-feeding operation, like a feedlot where cattle are fattened for market, and therefore another EPA permit was needed. The dairy was penalized for violating the statute and was required to pay damages of $4,101 for trespass. The decision led to requirements for EPA permits for manure spreaders as well as other disposal machinery used by dairies with a specified number of cattle. In addition, the *CARE* decision defined a depression in the ground that held manure-concentrated rainfall as a point source.

What about the environment? Did the *CARE* outcome provide improved protection? Defining dairy operations as subject to the permitting requirements of the Clean Water Act has triggered significant changes in dairy operations. First, dairy and other animal-intensive operations of a given size must install settlement lagoons and avoid the distribution of manure on farmland. After all, distribution requires that every tractor have an EPA permit. Lagoon operations concentrate pollutants that generally pose a higher environmental risk than when manure is spread over farmland. In addition, requiring costly lagoons and other technology places a differential burden on dairies, depending on their size. Otherwise small, land-intensive animal operations will be uneconomic if required to install the *CARE*-specified technology (Copeland 1995, 238). Consolidation means that larger, more animal-intensive operations will be the norm. In short, it is impossible to know if the *CARE* decision provides better or worse protection for water quality.

The technical provisions of the Clean Water Act made it easier for the plaintiffs to bring a citizen's suit. Success on that part of the case paved the way for success with the common-law pleadings, which were added to provide a remedy for the damaged party; the statute makes no allowances for recovery of harm.

Without the Clean Water Act, the same plaintiffs would have had to demonstrate that they, as property owners, were damaged by having a dairy with 2,200 animals in the vicinity. Proof of damages would require demonstration that effluent from the dairy infringed on property rights, the environment, or a healthful existence for the plaintiffs. If the plaintiffs had moved to the area after the dairy was in operation, their complaint could have been deflected by the "coming to the nuisance" doctrine. The fact that a tractor might be called a point source or nonpoint source would have no bearing at common law. Harm or the potential of harm would matter.

If, in the common-law situation, a few close neighbors had felt harmed but failed to bring suit, it is possible that the community as a whole could request that a public nuisance action be brought by the public defender. Again, there would have to be proof of harm or its potential, and property owners, not interested passersby, would have to seek action.

The relative simplicity of statute-based action helps to explain why statute-law actions tend to drive out common-law actions. But in driving out common law, it is possible that the realism of common law is lost. Under statute law, the anchors of property rights are no longer secure. Proof of harm is not necessary. Risk is not a necessary consideration. Statute violation is. It is possible that low-risk polluters will be pursued at great cost, while higher-risk polluters are overlooked.

Modeling the Uncertainties

Our investigation of guidance given by lawyers to clients suggests a process conditioned by probabilities. Think of it this way: Given an environmental episode like the one we posed in our survey, what is the probability that the episode itself can be addressed by common law? With a value less than or equal to one, but greater than zero, call this probability P(CL). Then, given P(CL), what is the probability that a qualified attorney will advise a client to pursue a common-law remedy. Call this P(CR). Since the last event depends on the first outcome, we find the conditional probability of recommending common-law action by multiplying the two, which is P(CL)P(CR).

In the situation we posed, there was a probability of 1.00 that the farmer could bring a common-law action. The Clean Water Act did not preclude suits within a state. But thirteen of the seventeen attorneys stated that they would recommend action based on the Clean Water Act (not common law), meaning a probability of 0.24 for common-law action. The joint probability is therefore 0.24. At the extreme, if the damage had involved a mill in one state and a farmer in another, then the probability of bringing a common-law suit would be reduced to zero. This means that the probability of an attorney advising such action would be zero.

When the attorneys considered the situation in which the polluter was operating within the limits of its permit but still damaging the farmer, thirteen of seventeen recommended action under common law, a probability of 0.76. Given the fact that plaintiffs were not barred from bringing such actions, we have P(CL)P(CR) equal to 1(0.76) or a joint probability of 0.76. It is easy to see how changes in the relative complexity of suing and other features of federal statutes could change these probabilities and thus affect the share of common-law suits brought in a given state.

If we consider the fact that under the Clean Water Act plaintiffs are subsidized when successfully bringing a suit against a discharger that has violated a statute, then the outcome becomes even more tilted to favor statute law. What about the interest of the attorney who hears a problem like the one posed by Marlow Green in his survey? The attorney will logically consider the estimated present value of bringing and winning the suit. The conditional probabilities just discussed will affect part of his thinking. But the chances of winning, P(W), and then being paid, P(P), and how much he will be paid, W, also enters the calculations. These two new probabilities will affect the decision. With the defendant required to pay trial costs and to reward the plaintiff for bringing the suit, the prospects look better under statute law than common law.

Now, the entire procedure has become complicated. To estimate the payoff, the attorney must conceptually solve this equation:

$$\text{PAYOFF} = \{P(CL)P(CR)P(W)P(P)\}[W].$$

Each of the four probabilities has a value equal to or less than one, with no negative values. The results of the compound multiplication of each probability by the next is then multiplied by W, the value of the award. To illustrate, suppose each of the four probabilities has the same value, 0.50, and the value for W is one million dollars. Then, 0.50 raised to the fourth power is 0.0625, which multiplied by $1 million is $62,500.

To put the decision in final form, consider a situation involving a discharger who appears to have imposed unwanted costs on downstream property owners. Notice the uncertainty in the statement. It is not clear that the named discharger is the culprit, nor is it clear that damages have befallen the plaintiff. All of this will have to be proved in court. An attorney contacted by the plaintiff responds that the matter can be litigated under either a common-law or statute-law theory. The probabilities of going either way are equal to one. Then, the attorney considers the probability of winning, and, if so, the probability of being paid. For the average case, the stronger probability of being paid under a statute-based suit can offset the weaker probability of winning. The lawyer will logically steer the client toward a statute-based complaint. Common-law market share suffers.

Other Limitations on Common-Law Actions

Limitations other than federal statutes and estimates of success made by attorneys affect the probability of bringing a common-law suit for protecting environmental rights. For example, a large number of states by statute shield certain interest groups from nuisance and other common-law actions. Protection of farmers from nuisance suits involving odors and other potentially damaging environmental actions are the most common. In a 1983 survey of these shield statutes, Margaret Grossman and Thomas Fischer found that thirty-five states had enacted "right to farm" statutes that generally provided some kind of protection from nuisance suits (Grossman 1983, 95-165). Other states including Iowa, Kansas, Nebraska, Oklahoma, and Wisconsin have feedlot statutes that specifically shield the livestock industry in those states. The protection afforded to neighbors of such operations by common law is practically eliminated by such statutes.

But while removing the threat of common-law actions, these statutes frequently impose regulatory standards that must be satisfied. For example, a farm operator in North Carolina may not need to worry about common-law suits such as *William Aldred's Case* (1611) where odors from a piggery imposed damages on a downwind homeowner. However, the North Carolina farmer must meet the regulatory standards of his state that the odors or pollution from his farm do not threaten the health and life and the community. If these conditions are satisfied, the farmer can operate even though neighboring property owners are disgruntled and their property damaged.

Is Common Law Resurging?

In spite of the attractiveness of statute-based remedies for pollution and the presence of shields against common-law suits, there is evidence that common-law environmental protection is resurging. How could this be? And is the common law now making its way through statute-law cracks and crevices really the same as the old common law?

The evidence for resurgence is seen in actions involving hazardous waste cleanup under the Superfund program (Vickery and Baratta 1996, C1 and C3; Nelson and Fransen 1988/1989, 493-519; and Kuhnle 1996, 187-229). Oddly enough, one commentary heralding the recovery of common law begins with this criticism of statute law remedies: "Federal statutory causes of action, the cost recovery tools of the 1980s, have become burdensome and costly," critical words previously reserved for common law (Vickery and Baratta 1996, C3).

The problems addressed more effectively by common law first relate to recovery of damages, a recourse not available under statute law where all penalties are paid to the government or to court-designated environmental programs. In other words, environmental rights protected for ordinary people at common law are not recognized in statute law. A field of leaking drums may do serious damage to the property of adjacent landowners, but the affected landowners cannot recover. The damages problem can be far more complex than this. After all, Superfund cleanup efforts take more than ten years for the typical site. Once a parcel of land is identified as a Superfund site, an entire subdivision or community can suffer a stigma. Land values fall throughout the area; real estate goes on sale at distress prices. In some cases, decay sets in that can lead to permanent destruction of a community.[2] None of these consequential losses are recoverable under statute law.[3]

The next problem relates to exemptions. As a result of special interest struggles, damages from petroleum spills are exempted by Superfund. A water supply contaminated by leaking gasoline tanks, one of the most common environmental problems encountered by landowners, may eventually be cleaned by Superfund action, but the individuals who bore the cost of finding another source of drinking water, or moving to secure the same, cannot recover the related damages. Nuisance and trespass suits at common law provide an avenue for relief.

A recent example involving the Atlanta Gas Light Company and a community of property owners illustrates how common law can resolve problems that are not addressed or even attempted to be addressed by statute law (Seabrook 1996, D1). The suit was brought as a class action against the gas utility by more than

200 property owners in Augusta, Georgia, and involved a coal gasification plant that had previously operated for more than 100 years. With the passage of time, pollutants from the operation contaminated the soil in the surrounding area and then affected the community groundwater. According to news reports, state pollution control authorities did nothing to remedy the matter. In a court-administered settlement, the gas company agreed to purchase at market prices a church and forty homes located closest to the gas plant and pay relocation expenses for the owner occupants. Owners of more distant property are to receive damages to be determined by a special arbitrator. It is not possible to pass judgment on the facts of the case, but the logic used by the court follows the traditional common-law theme: Owners of land have the right not to be damaged or threatened by pollution. While statute law may force beneficial cleanup actions, common law protects environmental rights, compensates the losers, and punishes those who violate those rights.

But how has common law suddenly overcome the alleged handicaps that made it so unworkable that statute law had to come to the rescue? After all, critics said that common law was ineffective in dealing with environmental harms involving multiple culprits. Clear evidence of harm is required by common-law rule. And what about the problem of many receivers of harm, not all of whom are damaged sufficiently to have an incentive to bring an action?

Advances in science address the first problem. Computer modeling and the development of schemes for matching waste with its source make it feasible to identify pollution sources. And greater expectations that public prosecutors will pursue public nuisance cases bring a more effective response from attorneys general when a few citizens complain. For these and the previously mentioned reasons, members of the environmental bar now recommend that common-law pleadings be combined with complaints of statute-law violations when citizens bring suit against a hazardous waste polluter.

Common Law Recovery As Seen in Supreme Court Decisions

There is more fundamental evidence of common-law recovery than what might be termed the technical use of common-law pleadings by attorneys seeking to recover damages for pollution-harmed clients. In a series of recent Supreme Court decisions, the Court relied on common-law thinking and logic in requiring that the private rights of individuals matter. The mere assertion that lofty environmental goals hang in the balance is no longer enough to persuade the courts to circumvent the private rights of individuals who might otherwise bear the burden of providing somewhat speculative benefits to the broad public.

Michael Greve, head of the Center for Individual Rights in Washington, D.C., has recently examined actions by the Court and identifed a trend that seems to represent a return to common law (Greve, 1996). Greve's review of *Nollan v. California Coastal Council* (483 U.S. 825, [1987]), *Dolan v. City of*

Tigard (512 U.S. 374, [1994]), and *Lucas v. South Carolina Coastal Council* (505 U.S. 1003, [1992]) focuses more on the logic applied by the Court in reaching decisions favoring owners of private property rights than on the outcomes themselves. His sifting of information in the Court's opinions reveals a significant change in how the Court sees environmental controversies. In *Nollan* the issue had to do with the state's requirement that a private property owner provide, at his expense, access to a public beach in order to obtain a permit to build a structure on privately owned beachfront property. The Court held for the private property owner, arguing in effect that private property owners were not obligated to provide roads on private property for public use. In *Dolan*, the Court ruled in favor of the owner of a hardware store who had been ordered to provide bike paths and other facilities on her property for the public when she expanded her hardware store. The Court found no connection between operating a hardware store and increased use of bicycles and parks. In these cases, Greve calls attention to Court's recognition of private spheres of action that cannot be invaded unjustifiably by the state. He also notes the importance attached by the Court to identifying clearly the linkages between actions taken by a private landowner and external costs that might be imposed on others.

Lucas, which involved a state agency's efforts to impose set-back require-ments for the construction of a home on beachfront property, receives special attention in Greve's analysis. In *Lucas*, the state had argued that environmental concerns required new restrictions on development that for Lucas meant complete denial of the right to build a home. But the state was unable to provide hard evidence of environmental harm. Relying on the common law of nuisance, the Court remanded the case to the South Carolina Supreme Court requiring the state to justify its restrictions on the basis of South Carolina common law. The South Carolina court was unable to provide the justification. Lucas recovered the value of the property rights that had been taken by regulation.

After reviewing these and a large number of other recent court decisions, Greve's makes his case for the ascendancy of common law. But he defines carefully what he means by common law:

> By *common law* I do not mean the *historical* common law as it existed at the time of Blackstone or at the end of the nineteenth century. Rather, I have in mind the basic logic of a legal system whose principal purpose lies in protecting private orderings. Such a system guarantees robust individual rights to exclude others (property); provides avenues for voluntary exchange (contracts); and protects against aggression by outsiders (torts). (Greve 1996, 115)

Greve does not develop a vision of what might emerge as common-law logic and displaces special interest politics in the development of future environmental statutes. But he does build a strong case for what might be termed common-law environmentalism, a system of law that focuses on real environmental problems when they are actually confronted by real people. But while common-law logic may be coming to the fore, we should recognize that its progress will be constrained, if not accommodated, by statute law.

A crude example of this is seen in a recent Ninth Circuit Appeals Court decision involving a citizens suit seeking to enforce a higher quality standard on the city of Portland, Oregon. (*Northwest Environmental Advocates v. City of Portland* (74 F.3d 945 [1996]). The controversy before the court involved whether or not a citizens' group, funded with tax money under the Clean Water Act, could contest a water quality standard that was unrelated to an EPA permit. The city of Portland obtained a permit for the construction and operation of a new facility, but instead of contesting the details of the permit, the plaintiff chose to argue for higher water quality in the affected waters. The court ruled for the plaintiff, noting that this was the first such decision in the federal court system. Prior to this decision, courts had routinely ruled in favor of permit holders in such matters. The decision opens the door for citizens to seek environmental protection of the sort offered by common law. However, instead of requiring the plaintiff to organize their cases at their own expense, the Clean Water Act provides public funding. Now the scales may be tilting toward aggrieved citizens, with a subsidy provided by U.S. taxpayers.

Viewing Statute and Common Law in a Dialectic Process

The ongoing struggle between common law (process) and statute law (systems) approaches for protecting environmental rights forms an interesting dialectic, a process that begins with competing ideas or activities. In the dialectic process, the dominant system, in this case statute law, is referred to as the thesis. The reemerging competitor, common law, is the antithesis. Interaction of the two generates a synthesis, which becomes the new thesis. After this, the dialectic continues.

To examine the dialectic interplay of the two legal processes, let us consider them in highly stylized forms. Statute law emerges from a political struggle and tends to deal with expediencies—specialized situations—in highly technical ways. By constitutional rule, statutes dominate common law. By contract, common law emerges from a social process that produces general rules that condition human behavior. Few people know the details of statute law and the associated regulation. Many people understand the common sense of common law.

Turning to environmental matters, statute law embodies command-and-control regulation and specifies a host of technical violations that can trigger law enforcement actions. Any citizen can initiate an action, provided appropriate evidence of a violation is presented. There are no requirements for proof of damages or demonstration of being a party to a controversy. Statute-based remedies involve penalties imposed on law violators. There are no provisions for damages to affected property owners. Polluters and holders of environmental rights cannot engage in transactions that transfer rights to the polluter. Citizens cannot contract around the rule. All matters involving federal statutes and regulations are resolved in the federal court system.

As the antithesis, common-law remedies for environmental problems are based on the law of torts. To have standing to sue, a potential plaintiff must demonstrate that his or her property has been or will be unreasonably damaged. Hard evidence of harm is required, and the potential plaintiff must be connected to the source of harm. Remedies involve payment of damages to affected property owners and injunctions that stop pollution. Holders of common-law rights can transfer the rights to polluters. That is, individuals can contract around the rule. Common-law cases are tried in state common-law courts, unless common-law claims are appended to a federal suit brought under federal statute law. The attachment of common-law pleadings to statute-based complaints suggests a synthesis is forming. But what might be the final form taken by this new thesis? Put another way, what are the characteristics of the new legal framework for guarding environmental assets?

Public Choice and other economic theories of the political process enable us to do more than speculate about what the new dominant institution. As mentioned, the variety of common-law remedies that filter through statute law may strengthen the role of informal, community-based law in the final synthesis. Seen in this light, the statute provides a framework; the common law provides remedies based on common sense.

In its purest private property rights form, the new synthesis would eliminate exemptions and shields that now preclude common-law actions. But these shields and other special interest features of statutes explain why we have statutes in the first place. Attempts to purge statutes of special interest benefits in the name of protecting environmental rights would meet powerful resistance. Any attempt to modify statutes requires new legislation and provides other opportunities for special interest groups to obtain political favors. A first dialectic forecast suggests that new statutes will emerge that allow for expanded common-law pleadings, but which contain new forms of special interest protection.

How might we assess this amalgamated law? On the one hand, the statute may impose high-cost restrictions that have little to do with environmental quality but much to do with protecting special interest groups. Bootleggers and Baptists come to the fore. Yet on the other, the common-law content would again recognize environmental rights held by ordinary people. Any pollution that causes damages after statutes are enforced could be a basis for bringing suit. A crude system could emerge that mixes centrally managed public property with private rights recognized in courts of common law. Holding common-law effects constant, we can just as readily argue that special interest legislation detracts from efficiency and reduces incentives for people at the source of problems to find the lowest-cost solutions. However, holding constant the effects of statutes and regulation, we can argue that common-law remedies would add an element of efficiency to the resulting system.

Another synthesis forecast looks to the emergence of environmental zones, fashioned after river basin associations like Tar-Pamlico. State, regions, and communities could be given flexibility in developing the means for accomplishing statutory goals. For example, an area with hazardous waste sites to be cleaned could be seen as a zone that allows the community a major voice in how to deal with associated damages. Looking beyond the current Superfund program, which is generally considered flawed and failing, a troubled community could consider common-law remedies if a viable defendant is present, or move to make the site a public works project. Similar approaches might be used in zones for managing air quality and other pollution now subject to command-and-control regulation. One vital aspect of the spirit of common law would be preserved by taking a community-based approach to these problems. The scale of the solution would be tailored to the scale of the problem. The values and norms of the community would be called on, and common sense would tend to prevail.

A more radical synthesis sees centralized command-and-control declining in the face of low-cost information, improved monitoring, and wide recognition by environmental and other groups that centralized command-and-control accomplishes little and costs a lot. Detailed federal statutes would be allowed to expire. In their place, the federal government would call on the states to assume responsibility for protecting natural resources and environmental quality. Different approaches would emerge across the states, but each state's body of common law would again be seen as one major vehicle for protecting environmental rights.

In a recent article on the transition now occurring in environmental management, David Schoenbrod, a law professor at New York University and former senior attorney for the Natural Resources Defense Fund, described the federal government's frustrated efforts to manage the environment effectively and built a strong case for returning environmental protection to the states (1996, 18-25). He recommends that the EPA "be stripped of its power with four exceptions":

> The agency should (1) gather and publicize information on the environment and its consequences; (2) provide Congress with guidance for the control of interstate pollution not adequately protected by state action or which involves a special asset like the Grand Canyon; (3) provide Congressional guidance for mobile products such as autos that produce pollution and could be subject to differential state standards that limit competition; and (4) draft model state legislation and conduct studies of the various policy options considered or adopted by states. (Schoenbrod 1996, 24)

Schoenbrod recommends that states have the option of accepting or rejecting any federal standards. The four-part proposal is surely radical when compared with the antique regulatory framework it would displace. But devolution is already occurring. The EPA is yielding more authority to states, and state governments are calling for more. When environmental federalism comes, it will still involve statute law and local ordinances. But the zone for private action and common-law, market-based activity will be expanded. Competition among the states will hasten the evolutionary process that yields improved rules for protecting and creating wealth.

Final Thoughts

As we have seen, statute and common law are interacting to mold new forms of environmental law. While statute law plays the dominant role in this, common-law thinking continues to have a major influence, always pointing toward protection of private rights that are not ensured by statute law. The evolving legal system reminds us that private parties tend to apply common sense to environmental problems; they want to protect environmental rights that seem naturally theirs. Statute law may protect the environment, but it does not protect private citizens from losses of property rights. Common law seems best suited for protecting private rights but allegedly falls short in protecting the environment. The merger of the two seems to be the answer we seek. But, alas, there is still a problem, and that relates to the possibility of imposing overly strict rules by statute and then seeking additional private remedies at taxpayer expense.

By examining competition between the two legal processes as well as their interaction, we can see the need for a heavier dose of economic reality. When individuals, privately or collectively, seek to maintain and improve environmental quality, the implied rights they seek to protect or enhance must somehow be anchored. By specifying rules of property and liability in advance of actions, common law does just that. With the anchor in place, strict enforcement of environmental rights yields changes in behavior for all environmental users. First off, most users will respect the rights of others, just as most automobile users do not engage in auto theft. Maintaining reputations, expecting long-term relationships, and simply desiring to do the right thing combine to form powerful motivations for abiding by the law. With so much at risk, information on environmental quality becomes more valuable. Information providers will organize and compete to satisfy this demand. The cheaper the information, the more effective the environmental control. Then, in the spirit of statute law, public nuisance actions at common law must be accorded appropriate support. It is here that the federal court system offers some relief. Providing federal court jurisdiction for public nuisance and trespass actions could compensate for the tendency of local courts to balance benefits of employment against protection of environmental rights.

A final evolving form comes to mind. In antiquity, there were specialized courts that handled disputes involving forests, wildlife, and other matters. The law merchant handled business suits in parallel with common-law courts until the seventeenth century, when the two were merged by statute. A specialized system of state environmental courts could be the answer. A specialized court could make available technical expertise needed to determine the extent of harm imposed on holders of environmental rights. The court, relying on databases that provide continuous monitoring of environmental sites, could also supervise the implementation of remedies accorded to damaged parties. If common-law rules were applied by these environmental courts, the need for command-and-control regulation would diminish, and attention would then become focused on the environment, instead of on machinery, permits, and politics.

Notes

1. The cities in the final sample were Birmingham, Ala.; Bozeman, Mont.; Chicago, Ill.; Cleveland, Ohio; Dallas, Tex.; Washington, D.C.; Houston, Tex.; Kansas City, Mo.; Los Angeles, Calif.; Morristown, N.J.; Philadelphia, Pa.; Sacramento, Calif.; St. Louis, Mo.; Salt Lake City, Utah; San Francisco, Calif.; and Seattle, Wash.

2. In some recent research, Katherine A. Kiel estimated the effects of announced Superfund sites on a sample of 2,000 houses in the Boston metropolitan area using data for the period 1975-92. She estimated housing valuation effects prior to, at the time of, and following Superfund designation. Once the sites in question began to produce noxious odors, prices fell systematically as distance diminished between homes and sites. The Superfund announcement, which signalled efforts to clean the sites, brought a larger reduction in value. And once cleanup began, housing values fell again (Kiel 1995, 428-435).

3. There is often little or no environmental damage posed to neighbors by Superfund sites, but the name Superfund has such negative effects that property values fall for that reason. A less publicized and systematic cleanup would soften these nonrisk related effects.

References

Copeland, John D. 1995. The Criminalization of Environmental Law: Implications for Agriculture. *Oklahoma Law Review* 48.

Davis, Peter N. 1971. Theories of Water Pollution Litigation. *Wisconsin Law Review*.

Greve, Michael S. 1996. *The Demise of Environmentalism in American Law.* Washington: American Enterprise Institute Press.

Grossman, Margaret Rosso. 1983. Protecting the Right to Farm: Statutory Limits on Nuisance Actions against Farmers. *Wisconsin Law Review* 95.

Kiel, Katherine A. 1995. Measuring the Impact of the Discovery and Cleaning of Identified Hazardous Waste Sites on House Values. *Land Economics* 71 (November).

Kuhnle, Tom. 1996. The Rebirth of Common Law Actions for Addressing Hazardous Waste Contamination. *Stanford Environmental Law Journal* (January).

Nelson, Eric E., and Curt R. Fransen. 1988/1989. Playing with a Full Deck: State Use of Common Law Theories to Complement Relief Available Through CERCLA. *Idaho Law Review* 25.

Schoenbrod, David. 1996. Why States, Not EPA, Should Set Pollution Standards. *Regulation.*

Seabrook, Charles. 1996. Gas Utility to Buy Polluted Land. *The Atlanta Journal-Constitution* (December 14) D1.

Vickery, Randall G., and Robert M. Baratta Jr. 1996. Back to the Legal Future. *Environmental Law* (June 10).

Chapter 7

Some Final Thoughts on Hummingbird Economies

Looking for the Large Waves

When I was a youngster, my family moved from a small south Georgia town to Wilmington, N.C., where my father was employed by the city's daily newspaper. This was in 1936; Wilmington was a busy seaport and headquarters for the Atlantic Coastline Railroad. The old town, which predated the Revolutionary War, was a mecca for a small boy. Trolley cars provided transportation along major streets and, more importantly, connected the town to two beach communities where my family spent many Saturdays and Sunday afternoons. One of the beaches, Wrightsville, became my favorite.

Like most youngsters, I was fascinated by the ocean, fishing, shell collecting, and watching the breakers that rolled into shore. As I became older, the breakers became my friends. Carefully studying the currents, I found that I could predict the arrival of the largest of waves, the ones I hoped to meet and ride to shore. By looking beyond the shore where swirling subcurrents rolled a mass of water to the surface, I could spot infant breakers. Some would form an early crest that grew ever larger as it moved in. My forecasts were never perfect. Sometimes what appeared to be a large breaker would somehow subside and dissappear from view.

Making forecasts about evolving social institutions is like predicting the arrival of a large wave by observing tides and eddy currents that seem to be announcing significant change. We can point to institutions that are forming in the backwaters, observe their growth, and speculate about the next wave.

The Book's Evolutionary Story

This book began with a common-access world where human beings struggled to define and protect wealth-producing territories—the world of hummingbird economies. The problem faced when seeking to manage environmental and natural resources was then couched in terms of a struggle to ration use. Property rights, a pure abstraction invented by people and sanctioned by the community, became the instrument for managing the commons. Armed with two theories—Pigou and Coase—we considered two means for developing property rights instruments. One involves the systems approach, where public authorities actually claim ownership of the resource in question and then dictate precisely how the resource will be used. The other approach is decentralized. Termed process, it involves the use of private rights, calling on market forces to determine outcomes.

We saw how property rights take many forms—common, public, and private—and then discussed how legal structures grow with and around the rights. Statute law, which relies on political decision making, evolved with the systems approach. Common law, which is more evolutionary and decentralized, grew with markets. Statute law's focus is large scale; it controls vast regions and large numbers of people. Common law operates at the scale of two parties involved in a specific controversy and establishes rules of just conduct for communities.

Common-law rules for protecting environmental rights were shown to be in competition with statute laws and regulation, but the field of play always seems to favor statute writers. In the constitutional process, common law defers to written law. Yet the forces that form common law, like eddy currents in the sea, continue to swirl and try to form waves, in spite of sea walls that limit their growth.

Illustrations of costly environmental regulations were offered, and these were accompanied with explanations of how lower-cost options seem systematically rejected by interest groups who claim to seek increased supplies of environmental qualities. Why this is so led to a discussion of theories of regulation and stories about episodes where regulation is used strategically to limit competition and create otherwise unearned gains. In spite of the attractiveness of regulation, market-based, process approaches continue to emerge.

Two chapters of the book were devoted to rather in-depth discussions of the two competing approaches for managing environmental quality. Using a series of legal cases, detailed discussions were given of common law and how it works. As this treatment came to end, statute law and centralized decision making was seen to be rising in the sea. Then, a chapter was devoted to the systems approach, showing how urban air pollution has been addressed by statutes and regulation. The one-suit-fits-all approach taken initially in efforts to control urban smog was shown to be breaking down. Decentralization and common-law thinking were seen to be reemerging regulatory processes. Systems of property rights, markets, and contracts are entering the world of regulation.

The idea that regulation would crowd out common law and that common law would affect changes in regulation leaves us with a sense that new institutions are clearly evolving, and that the new institutions will have traits inherited from two evolutionary forebears, a topic that formed the focal point of the last chapter.

As illustrated there, common-law protection of private rights clearly declined in competition with statute law actions developed in the name of defining and ensuring public rights. At the same time, each statute and regulation written slows the evolutionary process and provides temporary protection to special interest groups. In this sense, environmental protection comes at the expense of burdensome rules that reduce income and therefore delay environmental improvement. But as the contest continued, we observed former critics of common law rallying on its behalf. As it turns out, public rights have not been protected so successfully, and private rights, in some cases, have been forgotten. Once again property rights form the bedrock for positions taken by ordinary people who find themselves harmed by legal pollution as well as by actions taken to abate environmental harms. The evolutionary story continues.

The Effects of Lower-Cost Information

It seems clear that market forces are propelling us as we make our way into the twenty-first century. It is equally clear that statutes define the world in which we live. Markets evolve constantly. But statutes change infrequently in a constantly changing world. Rules stated in 1972 might make little sense in 2002. For this reason, if not other, decentralizing market forces will dominate the fast-paced digital world of the twenty-first century. Widely available low-cost information will enable people in remote locations, those closest to problems and with the largest interest in outcomes, to engage in mutually beneficial exchanges. Markets embody information, encourage conservation of time and resources, and allow for less constrained use of mankind's creative energies. But statutes will form the container in which these expanding markets will thrive. The institutions for managing environmental quality in the future will be dominated by market forces, but wrapped in statutory language.

But think about the basic environmental problems to be addressed. In every case, people seek to make informed decisions, whether they are members of communities that share the environmental resources of an aquifer, river basin or airshed, or members of a legislative body that seeks to write statutes and rules. Imagine being able to search the World Wide Web for detailed environmental information on every major river, lake, and stream, to be informed about customs, rules, and regulations for every community, county, state, and country. It's not far away. What if decision makers could obtain low-cost records on environmental prices, fees, and taxes, on enforcement actions, and about court decisions.

With lower-cost environmental information, decision makers will be able to choose locations for life and work more intelligently, to know more about the effects of actions on scarce environmental assets, and to hold others and be held accountable for the use of property rights. Instantly available information and improved mobility will make it easier for people to vote with their feet, in effect punishing those locations that provide the wrong mix of environmental quality and other desirable features of life.

The possibilities for future environmental management may be seen in the burgeoning internet that connects millions of personal computer users in ways that eliminate distance and time from ordinary decision making. Think about environmental markets and consider Bill Gates's description of the computer-based, decision-making environment of the future:

> The interactive network will be the ultimate market. Markets from trading floors to malls are fundamental to human society, and I believe this new one will eventually be a central place where we social animals will buy, sell, trade, invest, haggle, pick stuff up, argue, meet new people, and hang out. . . . All manner of human activity will take place on the network, from billion-dollar deals to flirtations. Many transactions will involve money, tendered in digital form rather than currency. Digital information of all kinds, not just money, will be the medium of exchange in this market. (Gates 1995, 6)

Making the Transition to Information-Rich Markets

As we recall the stories, cases, and illustrations provided in the earlier chapters, let me summarize the evidence that points toward the dominance of information-laden markets and the inevitability of statutes. Recall the stories of fishing communities and the invention of marketable permits that limit the catch. Statutes form the framework. Markets and common law provide the vehicle. Information about limitations, fishery locations, and fishing activity form the basis of the control mechanism. Imagine what will happen in the emerging digital world where all participants in the managed fishery have constantly updated information on catches, prices, and movements of fish, all provided by the manager of the partly privatized community property.

Consider Tar-Pamlico and other river basin associations that operate elsewhere in the world. Low-cost information based on computer simulations of the effects of dischargers and users on water quality will provide the necessary management ingredients. Operators of sewage treatment works will know about the availability of unused discharge rights held by farmers. Buyers and sellers will conduct transactions by e-mail and direct bank deposits. Enforcers of contracts will know immediately about each transaction and the effects on stream quality. Any unexpected disturbance that affects aquatic life will be registered in the information system. Adjustments will be made across all water quality users as the price of discharge rights rise and fall.

Think about resurgence of common law in providing remedies for parties damaged by hazardous waste. New computer-based methods for linking polluters to waste stored in locations and for estimating the damaging effects of pollutants pave the way for private actions. Common-law rules, which are based on market forces, are being applied within the context of statutory law. Recall urban air pollution problems and how statutory remedies are not solving the problem. Air quality markets are emerging where people buy and sell environmental rights that can only exist in a world where air quality is monitored and information is widely accessible.

A summary of evidence of market dominance in the formation of new institutions must include other examples of how market forces are delivering a cleaner and safer world. Remember the McDonald's story, Audubon-certified golf courses, Campbell Soup, and Home Depot. The emergence of international standards for environmental management. The relationship between rising incomes, brandname capital, and demand for environmental quality. All of these point toward greater reliance on informed markets for providing and protecting environmental quality.

Speculating about the future of rights-based environmental markets is easier than describing how the actual institutions could work. Crucial pieces of the story are missing. Who would gather and provide all this information on water, air, and land quality? How would the information be paid for? How will environmental rights, now assigned to public sector regulators, be returned to private parties? What are the incentives for building and operating these emerging environmental markets? Where will the resources for operating these markets come from?

The transition problem described by questions that focus on environmental rights is exactly the same as that faced in eastern European countries where socially owned capital is being privatized (Rapaczynski 1996, 87-103). As economist Andrzej Rapaczynski sees that process, the institutions that address transition will evolve on their own. Market forces will direct outcomes:

> The market determines the strength of the various interest groups that formulate their plans for government institutions, including the establishment of property rights, and that regulation in turn modifies the forces of the market and the relative strength of the interest groups. The development of the legal-regulatory system, much as the development of other economic institutions, is not an outcome of a fully rational choice of "optimal" solutions, but rather a gradual, incremental and evolutionary process. . . . This political economy of property rights is all too often neglected in the economic discussions of the problems of transition. (Rapaczynski 1996, 88)

The transition to market economies in eastern Europe has been plagued by a weak judicial system, a lack of mechanisms for enforcing contracts, and in some cases, a loss of custom and tradition based on individual liberty and ownership of assets. These problems cannot be solved overnight, and no one can describe in advance exactly how different European communities will address and solve these problems.

The transition taking place for U.S. environmental assets is much simpler. A long, uninterrupted tradition of ownership and liberty accomodates a return to community and private ownership of environmental rights. We have a strong judiciary and an accepted constitutional framework that recognizes private spheres of action and strengthens and encourages trade and enforcement of contracts. What we seem to lack is the environmental market maker, the person or firm that can gain by enlarging the scope for transactions. For the market maker to emerge and be economically viable, constraints must be set to define conditions of scarcity. Tar-Pamlico comes to mind, along with river basins in France and Germany. Once environmental scarcity is sanctioned by a community or region, people closest to the problem will see opportunities to build institutions based on privately held environmental rights. The institutions may be privately owned, like real estate firms that constantly monitor the availability of land and match buyers to sellers. Real estate firms have an incentive to build national databases on the availability of homes and real property. They also develop and manage communities with characteristics that satisfy homeowners and businesses. Common law then protects the rights of the homeowners and businesses.

In the future, we should expect to see market makers emerge who will provide environmental information for users of air and water quality. If allowed, these market makers could buy Superfund sites and then manage or dispose of them in ways that satisfy both statutes and common law. Of course, none of this can happen in a world of command-and-control, where statutes provide uniform solutions for one and all across a vast country. Flexibility based on sanctioned scarcity must emerge before we see the day of the environmental market maker. But not just any sanctioned scarcity will do. When finally confronted, practically all real environmental problems are local or regional. The scale of the solution must match the scale of the problem.

But will the dominance of process approaches based on common-law logic end the evolutionary process? Hardly. The constant search for lower-cost and more effective ways to manage valuable resources does not end. As information becomes ever cheaper and smart technologies continue to emerge, linkages between action and effect will become clearer. Those who consume will pay. Property rights will become more vivid, and markets will expand.

Will markets, private rights, and informal law ultimately encompass the world of environmental use? Hardly. New hummingbird economies will emerge. New challenges will be encountered on commons yet to be discovered. Command-and-control will arise, and the evolutionary process will be repeated.

We live in a world that began as a commons—a thoroughgoing hummingbird economy. Huge amounts of wealth have been produced in this world, and human well-being has expanded far beyond the wildest dreams of early commentators. The wealth-creating process has been supported by evolving social institutions that have simultaneously protected rights and expanded human liberty. Today, large parts of this globe are still a commons. This means that even greater wealth can be created and human well-being enhanced as we expand the property rights boundaries of our world. With that wealth will be newfound liberty and greater human capacity for avoiding hummingbird economies. It will be a world of property rights and legal mechanisms based on common sense and rules of just conduct, such as those embodied in the common law that is the root of the American experience.

References

Gates, Bill. 1995. *The Road Ahead*. New York: Penguin Books.

Rapaczynski, Andrzej. 1996. The Roles of the State and the Market in Establishing Property Rights. *Journal of Economic Perspectives* 10 (Spring).

Index

Ackerman, Bruce A., 71
Adler, Jonathan, 71-72, 128
agency cost, 10-13
air pollution: Clean Air Act of 1970 and, 122; Clean Air Act of 1977 and, 71; Clean Air Act of 1990 and, 120-25; common law and, 101-7; environmental zones and, 133-37; federal impact on, 77-78; improvement in, 128-29, 137n1; market incentives and, 129-30. *See also* auto emissions
Alchian, Armen, 10
Aldred's Case, 88-89, 90, 93, 114, 158
Alternative Motor Fuel Act of 1988, 125
Anderson, J. W., 120, 136
Anderson, Terry, 17, 22
Anderson v. American Smelting & Refining Co., 104
appropriative rights, 31
Atlanta Gas Light Company, 159-60
auto emissons: alternative fuels and, 123-29, 131-35; Energy Policy Act of 1992 and, 124-25; federal incentive programs and, 131-32; national ambient air quality standards and, 122-23; ozone and, 121-22, 128, 137n2; state incentive programs and, 132-33

Ballenger v. City of Grand Saline, 92
Baltimore & Potomac Railroad Co. v. Fifth Baptist Church, 102
Baratta, Robert M., Jr., 159
Barnett, Andy, 119
Berkes, Fikret, 21
Boemer, Christopher, 122, 128
Boorstin, Daniel, 5-6
Bootleggers and Baptists theory, 68-75
Boudreaux, Don, xvii
Bower, Blair T., 25, 136
Bradley v. American Smelting & Refining, 105
brand name capital, 45
Brandly, Mark, 119
Brannlund, Rumar, 40
Brubaker, Elizabeth, 23, 107-8
Buchanan, James, 65
Burbee, Clark R., 71
Bush, George, 125

Calebresi, Guido, 31
Campbell Soup Company, 47
Carmichael v. City of Texarkana, 96-97
Center for Individual Rights, 160
Ceplo, Karol, 8-9, 11
Chilton, Kenneth, 122, 128
Clark, Mark, 78
Claude Lamb Charitable Foundation, xviii

About the Political Economy Forum and the Author

The Political Economy Research Center (PERC) is a nonprofit think tank in Bozeman, Montana. For over a decade, PERC has pioneered recognizing the value of the market, individual initiative, the importance of property rights, and voluntary activity in the management of natural resources. This approach is known as the New Resource Economics or free market environmentalism. PERC associates have applied this approach to a variety of issues, including resource development, water marketing, chemical risk, private provision of environmental amenities, global warming, ozone depletion, and endangered species protection.

In 1989, PERC first organized a forum aimed at applying the principles of political economy to important policy issues. The purpose of this forum is to bring together scholars in economics, law, political science, anthropology, history, and other disciplines to discuss and refine academic papers that explore new applications of political economy. It is increasingly evident that the interface between government and individuals in society is vital in determining the rate and direction of economic progress. Political economy examines this interface.

Common Sense and Common Law for the Environment, while not the product of a specific PERC meeting, follows the political economy theme of the other volumes in the series and draws on past forum discussions. We believe that books of this type can integrate cutting-edge academic work with crucial policy issues of the day. Future books in the series will provide stimulating ideas for other important policy issues.

Bruce Yandle is Alumni Distinguished Professor of Economics and Legal Studies at Clemson University and a senior associate of PERC. Director of Clemson's Center for Policy and Legal Studies, Yandle served as executive director of the Federal Trade Commission and as senior economist on the staff of the President's Council on Wage and Price Stability. He is the author of *The Political Limits of Environmental Regulation* and an author/editor of *Environmental Use and the Market, Benefit/Cost Analysis of Social Regulation, Regulatory Reform in the Reagan Era, Taking the Environment Seriously, The Economic Consequences of Liability Rules,* and *Land Rights: The 1990s' Property Rights Rebellion*, in addition to numerous articles in published journals. He received his A.B. degree from Mercer University and his M.B.A. and Ph.D. degrees from Georgia State University.